*This book is
dedicated to you*

Alan,

Here's to the future with
optimism, purpose and
a positive impact in the
world!

Kevin

For Ilan,

my son, who helps me see the world through the curiosity of a child; who challenges and teaches me every day; who reminds me to keep things simple and to follow my heart; and who is forever showing me the importance of a brighter future.

Published by: TheSumOf, in partnership with Brio Books
Editor: Kevin Finn
Copy Editor: Pru Engel
Proof Reader: Puddingburn
Publishing Agent: Julie Gibbs
Design & Illustration: Kevin Finn
Wood Print Texture: ShutterStock
Text Typeface: *Chronicle Display* by Hoefler & Co.
Chapter Numbers Typeface: *Cut* by MuirMcNeil
Printer: Reliance Printing
Paper Stock: Gold Sun 100 gsm uncoated wood free paper
Inks: Bantian Soy Ink

ISBN: 9781761282157
A catalogue for this book is available from the National Library
of Australia.

The opinions expressed in interviews, articles, reports and
videos appearing in this publication are those of the author(s)
and subject(s), and do not reflect the opinions of TheSumOf,
Brio Books, Booktopia or their editors.

Every effort has been made to trace copyright holders and
obtain permission to reproduce this material. The publishers
would be grateful if notified of any corrections that should be
incorporated in future reprints or editions of this publication.

Distribution:
Booktopia Publishing Services (Australia and New Zealand)
Amazon and Book Depository (International)

Brand Principles

How to be a 21st Century Brand

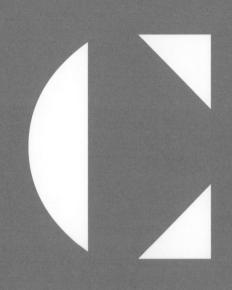

Contents

The Premise

Is your business a brand?

Think about it for a minute. This might sound like a simple question. You might even think it's a stupid one. But how would you answer it? You see, I've asked this question many times—to a variety of business leaders—and the response I get usually leaves me frustrated, because most of the time the immediate answer is an emphatic *"yes!"*

Let me explain.

In my design practice, I've encountered numerous businesses and start-ups who considered themselves brands—some of whom had yet to deliver a product or a service to the market. I've run branding sessions in start-up incubators and accelerators where, at the beginning of the session when I ask: "Is your business a brand?" most hands shoot up immediately. But by the end of the session—which covers the ideas in this book—few, if any, hands go up in response to the same question because they realise their claim is premature. They acknowledge their understanding has been based solely on a business idea they have yet to develop or mature and where the term 'brand' had perhaps offered a sense of immediate credibility. However, in most instances, they had equated their logo as being their brand. But this isn't limited to start-ups. Many established businesses also consider themselves as being a brand—regardless of whether or not they actually are. Why is this the case? What's going on? And, as we collectively face so many global challenges, why is being a brand even important? Well, let's start with some context.

While some brands have become almost universally recognised and valued, there are worrying indicators in the fields of design and business that suggest a deeper understanding of what it truly means to be a brand is required. The objective of this book is to provide practical guidance and advice to help businesses navigate some of these issues and to present a case for why it's important to address them.

To start, the word brand is often used to signify a 'type of thing' or a 'label for something'. For example: "I like that brand of coffee", which suggests a type of coffee. As opposed to, "I like that coffee brand", which identifies a distinct coffee-producing company, rather than a general type of coffee. Yet, when it comes to a commercial understanding of brands we enter into a very specific activity, one that is deliberately designed to differentiate a particular business and associate it with a set of clear Values, behaviours and value propositions. This is a much deeper, and a far more nuanced exercise. Or at least it should be.

Unfortunately, the commercial understanding of 'brand' has been steadily diluted, partly due to the fact it's regularly used as a substitute for the word 'business' (and any business will do). Compounding this, it's also becoming common practice to refer to logos as brands. (Here again, any logo will do.) And designers aren't helping things, either. Often, when visiting graphic design websites, it's not unusual to encounter a page featuring the heading 'Our Brands' sitting proudly above a selection of logos, identities, or work samples. However, this is a misrepresentation, because such a pronouncement openly assumes authority and ownership over someone else's business.

Obviously, designers can, and should, rightfully claim credit for developing the design, and much of the thinking involved with it. But this shouldn't translate into declaring ownership of an entire business or brand. Nor is the logo and its application a full reflection of them. At best, this assertion reduces the nuances of a brand down to a selection of communication items or, at worst, to a singular logo developed at a specific point in time. All this contributes to a superficial and misguided understanding of a brand—but also what it takes to develop and build one. This is problematic because it has the potential to mislead business owners (unintentionally, or not) and negatively influence their expectations and future impact as a result. It's bewildering why some designers propagate it so blatantly. But it goes even further.

My personal frustration increases when branding agencies, brand architects, brand consultants, brand designers, Design Thinkers, or any number of brand 'experts' suggest (with enthusiasm) that they can *create* or *build* a brand for you. Of course, I understand why a design firm would want to position themselves in this way, but their claim of "brand building" is not only disingenuous—it's dangerous. Now, you might think that sounds overly dramatic. You might be wondering: Is it really that dangerous?; Why does it matter?; Is it simply a case of semantics? You might even be a designer and have already labelled me a heretic, someone determined to chastise our industry for commercially strategic purposes. Regardless, the truth is, designers aren't in a position to build a brand on someone's behalf. Believing otherwise is the first step in misunderstanding how a brand is developed and what a brand actually is.

While there are exceptions, for the majority of instances a brand must come from the business itself—and it must be delivered, acted upon and lived up to every day. It's not an easy, quick or passive exercise. Nor is it something you can simply outsource. If you are serious about developing a brand, most of the long-term, heavy lifting and ongoing work required to build your brand must be done by you—and your entire staff—because it's your business. That's what makes it so powerful. Of course, your customers and society also play a critical role in building your brand, but more on this later.

Why can't external consultants build your brand?

Think about it. An external consultant simply can't develop or build your brand if they 'leave the building' once the marketing project has been completed. Once they've moved on to their next client engagement, they aren't focused on you anymore. They're not attending your regular business strategy meetings, or your product development sessions, where all the significant decisions are being made. And they're not regularly engaging with your customers, either. More to the point—as we'll discuss in Chapter 2—just because you have a business, this doesn't automatically mean you have a brand, least of all because an external consultant says you do as a result of a marketing exercise.

•

Think about it.
An external consultant
simply can't develop or
build your brand if they
'leave the building' once the
project has been completed.
Once they've moved on to
their next client engagement,
they aren't focused on
you anymore.

•

This is further complicated by the word 'branding' because of its association with the word 'brand'. In fact, it increases confusion and misrepresentation even more. So, to help clear things up, Chapter 1 presents some definitions to distinguish between *brand* and *branding*. But before that, let's acknowledge an important reality: an external consultant or firm has probably provided critical strategic advice on how to position your business, along with a suite of tools, frameworks, templates, logos, communication platforms, etc, to appropriately reflect your position in the market. If done well, all this is incredibly important—and immensely valuable— because it provides the building blocks and the focus to successfully articulate and communicate your business moving forward. This is where designers are useful and vital in co-creating a direction for the business with clarity and impact. But the designer isn't in a position to implement this every day. They don't have the resources, commitment or remuneration to adjust and/or leverage where needed, as business contexts change and shift over time. It's the business itself, and all its staff, that can react and respond, develop and evolve the business over the long-term. In fact, they're required to do so when building a brand—not the external designers or consultants.

A few exceptions

While branding designers and external consultants can't build your brand for you, there are three instances where designers actually are in a position to *help* build a brand:

1. *When they're long-term strategic partners*, actively involved with influencing strategy, planning, product development, processes and systems, HR and recruitment, Research & Development, customer service, and communications decisions in an ongoing manner, while regularly engaging with the Executive and Board. In some instances, the designer may also have equity in the business, which obviously increases their direct investment in the overall success of the venture.

2. *When they're the founder and/or owner,* working in the business on a daily basis, developing and helping to deliver the service or customer offer. Obviously—as a business owner who happens to be a designer—they can leverage their design skills, experience and understanding to further position the business with more efficiency. But it's a long-term, whole-of-organisation-effort, not a short-term external engagement.

3. *When they're working in-house* and in a position to contribute, challenge and shape the company as it grows and evolves. However, this often depends on the designer's seniority, whether they have influence in how the business operates, and how much the Executive and Board values design. While business leaders are increasingly seeing the tangible value designers can bring to the broader development of a business, unfortunately not all businesses are design-led and this often dilutes the designers' input, excluding them from critical decisions.

So, what's involved?

We often hear success stories of brands who appear to have emerged almost seamlessly. We observe the good fortune of familiar brands who seem to effortlessly capture the market and captivate customers. For a business owner working immensely hard to reach similar heights it can be difficult to see a pathway towards achieving this goal. However, for all those success stories, we rarely get a picture of the hurdles those brands had to overcome, or what effort and steps they had to undertake behind the scenes in order to achieve their eventual success. Perhaps we think they had a great marketing strategy, or a compelling advertising campaign. Maybe we think they were lucky and hit a particular vein with a product or service that resonated with the market. For everyone else trying to do this, it can be hard grind. And while luck might have played a role in the success of a business or brand, leveraging and maintaining what that luck provided still requires a lot of work.

Even the most successful brands have to work continuously at building and maintaining their brand. Seemingly successful brands can, and have, been deeply damaged almost overnight when their value proposition has missed the mark, or their customer experience hasn't lived up to their promise, or if the brand simply lied to the market and were exposed. (Think *Enron's* deceit, *BP's* Mexican Gulf oil spill crisis, *Facebook's Cambridge Analytica* scandal, *Starbucks'* racism debacle, *Volkswagen Group's* 'dieselgate' disaster, and various luxury brand's *Blackface* missteps, to name a few). As more brands emerge all over the world there is increasing competition to secure a share of the pie. The question is, how do you navigate this?

Unfortunately, we can never know all the backstories to all the successful brands that we're familiar with. And while there are numerous worthy books in circulation focusing on various aspects of brands and branding—many of which are great resources—a lot of them mainly focus on the outcomes rather than the process or principles behind them. Additionally, although case studies can be insightful on many levels, it's often difficult to apply those particular outcomes (which worked for a specific company in specific circumstances) to your own business, particularly if you're in a different category or segment—and operating at a different scale. In contrast, this book takes an alternative approach by focusing on the process and mindset involved in building a brand, based on 15 tried-and-tested principles, observed and developed over my nearly 30-year career in design and branding. It uses common language to encourage a mindset you can adopt in your own way, and which can be applied to any business, regardless of size or sector.

Let's begin...

1

Brand vs Branding

The term 'brand' is so overused (and increasingly misunderstood), its value and meaning is being eroded. It's now common to hear how companies have rebranded—particularly high-profile companies—but this is often misleading. Many of them have simply updated, revised, tweaked or changed their logo, while everything else remains the same and business-as-usual continues. In fact, most of them have simply engaged in what is referred to as an *identity refresh*.

If they were to truly *rebrand*, it would usually involve developing an alternative company name, a revised business strategy and a new core focus for the company, with an entirely new promise or offer to customers, which is a very serious undertaking. While an *identity refresh* can be an effective exercise on some levels, it's not a rebrand—even though it might currently be fashionable to refer to it as such. Regardless, there are many reasons for the confusion between *brand* and *branding* and it largely depends on who you talk to, their experiences with brands or branding and, of course, the context. With that in mind, it's vitally important to first clarify the definitions we'll be using for this book:

A *brand* is who you are, how you're perceived and how people *feel* about your business. It's the core value of your business offer, and a promise to your customers of the value they should expect. It is the sum of all the experiences someone has with your business. It's what you live and deliver every day. It cannot be manufactured, created or invented by an external consultant (because then you'll be required to live up to someone else's vision, rather than your own).

Branding is how you articulate and appropriately communicate your business—to your customers, and to the world—across a variety of channels. (This is where designers are useful.)

The distinction between *brand* and *branding* is important because outsourcing or handing over the process of 'building your brand' to an external party—who is *not* involved in your business every

•

Effective branding
makes you visible; it
makes you understood,
recognised and, in the
best-case scenario, it
can help *foster* trust.

•

day—makes it near impossible to achieve the desired outcome over the long haul and in a sustained manner. Essentially, you'll have relinquished accountability, placing the future perception of your business in the hands of someone external, based on their limited understanding of your business, ignoring their distance from any ongoing activity *in* the business, and solely reliant on a suite of marketing tools provided from *outside* the business. That said, when articulating and communicating your business, a designer's role is significant because they will question everything you assume about your company—or at least they should. They can help interrogate assumptions and uncover truths. In doing so, they can identify perceptions, internally and externally, which is incredibly important because—as we all know—perception is more powerful than truth. So, being aware of perceptions is essential in understanding how your business is *positioned in the minds of others.*

While all that work is vital in facilitating an independent and objective understanding of your business, the designers themselves don't live, breathe and champion it every day. They simply can't. It's difficult for them to have a long-term investment in your company beyond the terms of their engagement. Regardless, effective branding makes you visible; it makes you understood, recognised and, in the best-case scenario, it can help *foster* trust. All of this is essential in building a brand because, if it's done well, branding articulates your value proposition and attracts customers and staff who are willing to engage with your business. It provides clarity and focus—internally and externally.

Yet it also exposes you because you cannot hide from what you communicate to the world. Whether you like it or not, you will be expected to live up to your claims, one way or another. And there can be serious consequences for promising something that you don't—or can't—actually deliver on. If branding isn't done properly, and with due consideration, the result will most likely be arbitrary, purely aesthetic, and potentially superficial. Or worse: it will be disconnected from your business, or will simply be dishonest.

And this is how you will eventually be perceived. That's why it's critical to fully understand and distinguish between whether you're engaging in a *branding* exercise (which influences, communicates and reflects your entire organisation), or a *logo* design (which is essentially a badge for your business).

The designer's role

In a conversation with Ken Segall (ex-advertising Creative Director for *Apple*, and someone who worked closely with Steve Jobs for 12 years) I raised my concern about external consultants claiming to create or build brands on behalf of their clients. He sums up how advertising and design have *helped* position *Apple*:

"I do think that maybe I've been fortunate to have worked with brands that actually value their agency's input. Some more than others, of course. But I think we [advertising creatives] always considered ourselves as the steward of the brand because our advertising was the most visible thing they did. But, obviously, the brand is more than just the advertising. It's PR and all the things that the company does and which add up to what the brand is. But I think the agencies have a lot to say about that, and in the case of Apple maybe it was an unusual case because Steve Jobs loved marketing so much. He loved and understood the power of the brand. Many of our conversations were about that kind of stuff, whereas other companies might not treat their agency that way.

"We saw ourselves as being important and knew the advertising we put out really was going to shape the brand so it had to be consistent with the Values, the level of creativity—all of that. A good advertising/marketing person needs to be extremely aware of what they're doing to the brand work because you are a major contributor to what the brand is." [1]

---

1.   *The transformative power of simplicity,* Ken Segall in conversation with Kevin Finn for DESIGNerd, online article, March 2018.

The immense value of a business working collaboratively with external creatives—and focusing on how every element in the business contributes to building the brand—cannot be overstated. It also illustrates how visibility, consistency and communication, all of which design and advertising can facilitate, contributes towards positioning the brand in specific ways that both align with the brand but also help shape perceptions around it. But it's important to acknowledge that this was possible for Segall because he worked closely with Jobs and *Apple* over a 12-year period, and that Jobs both understood and valued design and brand. This proximity allowed Segall to align *Apple's* Values, approaches and philosophies across numerous communication touch-points in a consistent manner and in a way that reflected the evolution of the brand during that time. But, as Segall states, these activities alone do not build a brand. Nonetheless, their contribution is significant in helping to raise awareness, in making a business familiar and understood, and in shaping perceptions and expectations which, in *Apple's* case, could be delivered upon.

Of course, *Apple* is a massive corporation. However, the process involved in building and maintaining their brand can be applied to other businesses. That process requires close collaboration with design and marketing to communicate and convey—with consistency—every aspect of a business that's working hard to deliver value to customers, and which understands the importance of absolute clarity inside the organisation. But it's still only part of what is involved in building a brand. This takes time and rarely starts at the launch of a business, so let's investigate this further.

Business ≠ Brand
Brand = Business

It's vital to fully understand that a brand takes time to build. It takes context and awareness, and it takes constant evolution. It's not a *brand* at inception—it's a *business*; and that's an important distinction to acknowledge. Unfortunately, it seems to be routinely disregarded.

Just because a business has a logo, a website, perhaps a bricks-and-mortar presence and some customers, does not automatically make that business a *brand*. While it might be a *type of business*, it takes time and effort to build a brand: to earn trust; to become loved, familiar and accepted within a wide or niche community; to establish a tangible difference from competitors and to consistently deliver on the promise it makes to customers; and to build a culture that acts and behaves in a specific way. It takes time and effort to articulate and execute a value proposition in real terms. It takes context—and it takes influence—to command the term 'brand'. All of this is hard-earned. It requires investment and commitment to maintain and evolve. And it rarely happens at the inception of a business. Of course, it's no surprise that businesses want to equate themselves with being a 'brand' because of the status this label conveys. But simply adopting the term 'brand' for these reasons shows a deep lack of understanding for what it means—and for what it takes to achieve. In a frank conversation with Dutch-native Anne Miltenburg (founder of educational organisation *Brand The Change* and then Brand Lead at *Internet of Elephants*, an innovative conservation initiative based in Nairobi, Kenya) she confirmed this fact:

"I see a brands as people, movements, companies or causes that have achieved a certain amount of prominence in the minds of their audience. If I consider how much time we invested at Internet of Elephants to get to that place of prominence, we realised early on that without any serious marketing budget we were going to have to earn that place on our own steam. We decided to open up our product development process to the public, involving them at every stage over the course of two years. People joined in testing,

*ideation, hackathons, and crowdfunding. We invested a lot of
time in storytelling, talks at industry events, as well as videos; we
built relationships with journalists interested in innovation in the
environmental space and provided them with unique stories; we
wrote thought-leadership pieces for renowned media; we also
created partnerships with credible organisations in the conservation
space to show [that while] we are a tiny, young company, we have
an established audience base and press networks and should be
taken seriously. It's been a few years now and we're beginning to
harvest some results. We became one of Fast Company's 2018 most
innovative companies, we were awarded a National Geographic
Explorer Grant and we received some good press in Tech Crunch,
on CNN and BBC. When we encounter people in the conservation
space today, they often already know us and admire our work—which
is good evidence that there's some brand awareness; that the brand
is starting to do some of the heavy lifting for us. But that took three
years! It's not like: "Oh, we built something, we launch it, people will
love it, they will tell each other all about how great it is, and all this
will just spread based on its own merit."*

*"[Laughs] There's a myth that: If you build it, they will come. But it's
just not true for 99.9 percent of us. Instead, we're going to have to
build the brand one person at a time."* [1]

Wanting to become a brand is an understandable and justifiable
aspiration but, in many ways, it's actually customers and the
community who decide which businesses are brands, and which
are not, based on how they feel about the company, how relevant
it is in their lives, as well as the level, status and value it provides
to them. But the notions of *'brand'* and *'branding'* have been
conflated over recent decades. They've been used with abandon
in discussions and debates about business, and have become
interchangeable in the celebration and criticism of newly designed
'logos' (also referred to as 'identities'). Similarly, the terms 'brand'

1. *Branding for change (part 2)*, Anne Miltenburg in conversation with Kevin Finn for
    DESIGNerd, online article, April 2018. Slightly revised in 2022 by Anne Miltenburg.

and 'business' have also been conflated. Of course, there are many reasons for this. Part of the problem is due to the increased success and awareness of big brands in mainstream culture, but it's also due to the ambitions of business owners who aspire to achieve similar success. This has resulted in people adopting the term 'brand' as a replacement for the word 'business.' Why? The likelihood is that 'brand' simply conveys a sense of prestige and greater value. And brands are big business.

Awareness and recognition

There is yet another factor to consider. The reality is, we do associate *brands* with *logos*. Think of any brand and you're likely to summon a visual picture of that company—and it's usually their logo or symbol. Why? The logo is often the shorthand identifier for multiple associations we have with an organisation, allowing us to immediately distill these associations in unison through a recognisable 'mark'. That means we regularly associate everything we know and feel about a company with the logo that represents it, making it a vital element of branding. This symbol identifies the consistency, quality and status we've come to understand and expect from that particular company. And in an increasingly crowded market, it's a clear visual shorthand that cuts through the noise.

Consider when you're looking for something to eat in an unfamiliar country. You may scan the streetscape searching for a logo or symbol that denotes a restaurant, supermarket chain or eatery you recognise and are therefore comfortable with—perhaps *Starbucks, Panda Express, Matsuya, Subway or McDonald's*. The same could be said when you are shopping on an unfamiliar high-street, looking for logos that represent your favourite shops or stores. At a glance, people immediately recognise specific traits in branding, which they're familiar with because a logo or symbol has the ability to say so much, with so little—yet so quickly—*because of the associations built into it over time.* And that's an immensely valuable asset to any business.

•

The logo is the symbol of a brand; it's not the brand in isolation, because context matters. And in more commercial terms, the logo doesn't make the brand—*the brand gives the logo its value.*

•

At a more granular level, these logos, symbols and identities are elements that we are increasingly engaging with on a daily basis, particularly through our smartphones, where App buttons often feature an organisation's logo. We regularly search for—and recognise—what we're looking for in a quick, confident way. And we literally touch them. These logos have become familiar (digital) doorways to brands and businesses—with whom we seek specific products and services, and which we've come to recognise, understand, expect, and trust. Again, this takes time and effort to achieve. But that doesn't make it any less sought-after or less valuable. Quite the opposite. The more meaning embedded in a logo, the more valuable it becomes. Michael Bierut (New York Partner at the acclaimed international design firm *Pentagram*) has spent a successful career creating—and investigating—high-profile branding and shared his expert opinion with me:

"I've spent a lot of time trying to figure out how something like the Target logo, or the Nike 'swoosh' works. I've certainly encountered enough clients who seem to want the Nike swoosh logo and I've thought: "OK, what is it that they want?" You can say dismissively: "Oh, these poor fools want me to give them a logo that mysteriously already has millions of dollars invested in it, something as powerful as the Nike swoosh". Still, if you want something that will work that way, how do you do it? To me, a lot of it has to do with the way it appears at the moment of its inception. It isn't necessarily the way it's going to be fated to live in the world and how it plays out. And more frustratingly, you can't actually predict or control exactly how it's going to play out, right? You have to be able to accept that, particularly when it comes to identity design." [2]

He went on to say:

"The Target logo is the most boring thing in the world. And the Nike swoosh, it didn't even quite mean anything in the very beginning, you know? But, in both those cases and for decades, they provided a

2. *How to approach design,* Michael Bierut in conversation with Kevin Finn for Open Manifesto, Issue #8: Change, 2017, page 78.

canvas for creative ingenuity in the way that they were manipulated and their meaning was permitted to expand." [3]

In short, the logo is the symbol of a brand; it's not the brand in isolation, because context matters. And in more commercial terms, the logo doesn't make the brand—*the brand gives the logo its value.* Why are these important distinctions? Because, regardless of any initial design rationale, branding adopts meaning over time as it becomes understood as the shorthand interpretation of what that business stands for, what it believes in, how it behaves—and how it is *perceived in the minds of others.* Elements of this meaning might be present at inception—depending on media, marketing and any broader awareness—but this will inevitably mature and evolve over time as it becomes tangible in the minds of individuals (i.e. staff, customers, and society at large). This only becomes evident as people engage with the business and begin to rationalise their experiences into a series of specific associations. While businesses might have the ability to *influence* how they're perceived, the fact is, how people genuinely think about a business dictates how perception is shaped—and whether that perception actually translates into being a brand.

Logos as a canvas

As Bierut points out, logos provide a canvas for meaning over time. In some cases, they can be incredibly literal, for example the *Target* icon. In other cases, logos can be abstract or even downright weird. Obviously, there are numerous ways a logo or an identity design can be approached, and there are just as many reasons for why they look a certain way. However, for most logos and branding, whatever wider or deeper meaning we associate with a symbol will depend on our experiences, or our awareness, of the organisation in question— and this is constantly evolving. So, let's do a little experiment.

Do you recognise the symbol on the opposite page?

---

3. *How to approach design,* page 87.

Many readers will immediately know it as the symbol for *Chase Manhattan Bank*. But, do you know what the symbol means? Do you know what the symbol itself represents? Perhaps that's not as easy to answer. The origin of this particular symbol is interesting and it's a great example of how branding, identities and symbols have meaning embedded within them over time. In this case, it all began with a business merger. According to the designer, Tom Geismar, co-founder of one of America's most historic design firms *Chermayeff & Geismar*:

"When Chase National Bank merged with the Bank of the Manhattan Company to create Chase Manhattan Bank, the new company became the second largest in the United States. The new organisation needed a new graphic identity to represent it effectively... Banks at that time generally used trademarks that grew from their initials or an image of the bank's headquarters building. Chase Manhattan briefly used an awkward combination of a map of the United States, a representation of the globe, the name of the bank, and the phrase 'world-wide banking'. We became convinced that the bank would benefit from a simple symbol that could not only unite the two newly merged corporate cultures but also come to stand in for the company's long, unwieldy name in the public mind. However, there is no symbol that really means banking, and no symbol that represented Chase. We turned to the idea of using an abstract symbol, since we knew that Chase Manhattan had tremendous advertising resources that could quickly establish the symbol in the public mind." [4]

So, the icon meant very little at the beginning—at least nothing tangible. Instead, it was a deliberate open canvas allowing it to adopt meaning over time through customer experiences, extensive advertising and promotion, and numerous associations over decades that became embedded within the meaning of the symbol, and in the minds of the public. Of course, the specific design of the icon became a significant contributing factor in facilitating all of this to occur.

---

4. *From Mobil to Chase Bank, 6 Iconic Logos and How They Came to Be,* Steven Heller, The Atlantic, online article, 8 December 2011.

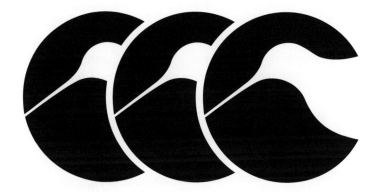

So, let's try another example, from a completely different industry sector. Do you recognise the logo on the previous page? Some readers might know it as *Canterbury*, a New Zealand clothing company established in 1904 in Canterbury, on New Zealand's South Island. In the early years of the company, it was called upon to make hard-wearing uniforms for the New Zealand and Australian armies during the First World War, and it then became synonymous with sportswear, particularly for producing official clothing for the *All Blacks*, New Zealand's national rugby powerhouse. But what about the logo? According to the *Canterbury* website:

"John Lane, Pringle Walker and Alfred Rudkin were English natives turned proud Kiwis [a term of reference for New Zealanders]. Such was their love for their adopted homeland, they named their company after the area in which they settled—Canterbury. From its very beginnings, this was a brand rooted in the New Zealand soil. Like the Kiwi landscape itself, it was rugged and uncompromising. When the time came to give the company a logo, the founders naturally chose three kiwis [a flightless bird native to New Zealand and a national emblem]."

There are lots of literal visual, historic and cultural references the founders could have adopted for the logo. However, they kept it simple, local and to the point—*the Kiwi bird*. The company was originally called *Canterbury Clothing Company* so the logo was developed from the silhouettes of three Kiwi birds creating the letters CCC, which also represented the three founders. However, little of this is evident from looking at the logo—other than the Kiwi bird silhouette, and of course that's not necessarily an internationally recognised bird. However, over time the *Canterbury* logo has become deeply associated with sports and their tagline— *Committed To The Game*—has cemented this association even further. Here again, the logo has become a canvas for meaning to be embedded over time, evolving the messaging and associations as contexts shift, as the business adapts, and as various perceptions are formed in the minds of others.

The business of brand

Now, I know it's easy to get caught up in the technical jargon and lingo involved in branding. In fact, I'm convinced this just adds to the confusion and/or dismissal of these terms. But there is a critical distinction between how a business might consider developing its logo versus how it might approach *building a brand*. The late and legendary branding guru Wally Olins (co-founder of the influential and seminal branding firm *Wolff Olins* and, later in his career, *Saffron*), once shared with me his insightful opinions around this topic:

"Brand identity and corporate identity and reputation—all of these words—stand for the same kinds of things. But there is no doubt, though, that the semantic difference between brand identity and corporate identity is profound. 'Corporate identity' is an academic, almost loose woolly term, whereas a 'Brand' is about money. So when you start talking about a brand you start talking about a subject that is very close to a corporation's real interests... When you talk to a commercial organisation about brand strategy they know that it is about money and is therefore worth talking about. The long-term implication is that it puts brand strategists and brand consultants right at the heart of the business world. Corporate identity does not do this." [5]

So, the difference between *corporate identity* and *brand* equates to the difference between what a business *looks like* (identity), and what a business *is* (in its entirety), including how it delivers value (what customers are willing to pay for). Those are all inextricably linked, since the symbols and logos facilitate another cultural aspect of brands and branding—*belonging*. Olins expands on the significance of this:

"Branding is at the heart of today's society simply because branding is about manifestations of identity. It's a demonstration of who and what

---

5. *Branding is the greatest gift that commerce has given to culture,* Wally Olins in conversation with Kevin Finn for Open Manifesto, Issue #5: Identity, 2009, page 25.

you belong to, and in a world that is increasingly competitive this is important, not just in commercial life but in every kind of activity you can think of including sport, the Nation, the city, the family. Inevitably then, what brand you choose to belong to, what brand you choose to associate yourself with is of profound significance." [6]

Apple, one of the most valuable companies in the world, is often cited as an example of a successful brand (and successful branding) fostering a tribe of loyal customers, bordering on what some might describe as religious. However, *Apple* is unique in many ways so it's disproportionate to compare it to most businesses. Yet, it's regularly referred to as the 'holy grail', because of its visibility and having become (for plenty of people) the pinnacle of commercial aspiration—and the envy of many business owners. Ken Segall reminds us how this was achieved:

"In my advertising consulting life—either through my own experiences or people I know who tell me—clients have said: 'We want to do something like what Apple would do.' Because, again, there is a perception that it looks simple, so people think it is. And this feeds the perception that Apple achieved it overnight. But it was over 20 years—doing it over and over and over again, building loyalty among people who appreciate a company that makes wonderful things simple." [7]

This alone is testament to the fact that it takes time and constant effort, not only to establish a brand, but to then build it and sustain it over the long-term. Simply willing your business to be a brand is not enough. And believing your business is a brand, due to a branding exercise or program, falls well short of the mark.

---

6. *Branding is the greatest gift that commerce has given to culture*, page 25.
7. *The transformative power of simplicity*, Ken Segall in conversation with Kevin Finn for DESIGNerd, online article, March 2018.

How can you tell if *your* business is a brand?

Perhaps you're already referring to your business as a brand. And perhaps that's warranted. But if you're unsure, it's worth assessing whether customers, the market and society (in general) consider your business as being truly a category leader—perhaps the one which most other competitors are measured against; that your Purpose and value propositions are clearly articulated and fully understood, both internally and externally; that you're known amongst customers for specific reasons (whether in a niche or a broad market); and that the majority of associations that people make about your business are consistent with your own views and aspirations. How can you do this? Simply by asking people—your staff, customers, suppliers, partners, investors, etc. However, the type of questions you ask are important; they need to be value-based, for example:

— *What genuinely sets us apart from others, and why?*
— *What specifically comes to mind when you think of our business, and why?*
— *What value do we provide in your life: how and why?*
— *How visible and understood are we in the market, and why?*
— *What's the top-of-mind brand in our category, and why?*
— *Would you classify us as a brand? If so, why?*

There are many other questions you could add, but rather than dispatch online surveys, it's more valuable to have honest, confidential conversations directly with people. In those instances it's easier to expand the discussion based on their responses, which often provides additional insights. You can also gauge things by tracking any media your business, products or services has generated. This will begin to highlight perceptions and the market position of your company. The stronger those perceptions are—and the greater the influence your business commands in the market—the more likely it is that your business is either a brand, or is becoming one in the minds of others. It's also worth checking whether customers recognise your logo or identity. As mentioned previously, recognition for your branding is vital, but don't get

A business becomes a
brand when enough
customers willingly align it
with their personal identity.
In return, the brand
continually adds tangible
value to customers' lives
through specific products,
services, status, experiences
and convenience, among
other things.

sidetracked by this alone. Remember: *the logo is the symbol of a brand; it's not the brand in isolation, because context matters. And in more commercial terms, the logo doesn't make the brand—the brand gives the logo its value.*

The most important point to remember is not to mistake your logo for the entirety of your business or brand. Instead, see branding and broader communications as a crucial visual and verbal representation of your business as it evolves. It's also important to acknowledge how long your business has been in operation and to consider the time it usually takes to generate a loyal customer following, a tribe of people willing to identify with your business and continuously appreciate the value propositions or status that you provide to them. Don't forget, *Apple* has spent decades building and reinforcing their brand as it has continuously evolved. At different stages this has been carried out in a consistent manner by associating it with a specific set of Values, beliefs and propositions that it has been able to constantly deliver on (for the most part) and which has resonated with legions of customers across various ages and demographics. So much so that, for a large swathe of customers, *Apple* has become part of their identity—a brand they're willing to associate with and a community they are happy to belong to. The same can be said—to varying degrees—of other familiar brands.

The value of branding
Still, some businesses view branding purely as a finite marketing exercise. They see it as being important—to a point—and often refer to their logo as their 'brand'. In doing so, they separate branding from being integral to the business—how the business runs, what the business stands for, and the reputation tied up in its actions, behaviours and value propositions, as well as the perceptions it fosters. They acknowledge the need for a recognisable 'badge' for the business, but that's about it. Yet, branding is a communication tool, making it vital in establishing your business with confidence and as a means for providing a platform to build your brand over time. It shouldn't be dismissed as a line item for the Marketing

Department, or a novel creative exercise that has some importance but is rarely thought of again—until the need to *'freshen up the logo'* at some future point. So, let's look at an example of how valuable branding can be.

In 1994, *Supreme* began as a small skateboarding store in Lower Manhattan, New York, but has since grown into one of the most sought-after fashion brands in the world. It's a remarkable and compelling 'rags to riches' story. Whether by luck, intuition or profound business savvy, *Supreme's* founder, British-American entrepreneur James Jebbia, successfully shepherded the business from a rebel upstart into a $1B brand, after private equity firm *The Carlyle Group* acquired a 50% stake for $500 million in 2017. Interestingly, *Supreme's* branding has played a particular role in helping position the business in the market—and in the minds of their loyal customers. In 2019, writing for *CNN* Style, Jacopo Prisco reported:

"Jebbia has rewritten the rules for streetwear brands in the process, building Supreme's fame through social media hype and scarcity. Its clothes can only be bought online or through a network of just 11 stores worldwide: one each in LA, Paris and London, two in New York and six in Japan. It was in Japan that Supreme perfected a sales tactic known as the 'drop'—releasing a limited quantity of new clothes on a weekly basis, rather than an entire new collection every season. The strategy, now widely replicated by traditional fashion brands, prompted long lines at Supreme's stores and fueled online resale marketplaces where prices skyrocketed.

'Over time, it really became a huge frenzy,' said David Fischer, founder of streetwear and lifestyle website Highsnobiety. 'It became a huge event, where Supreme fans from around the world would line up in front of Supreme stores to get a hold of the latest product... It's not only about standing in line to buy a new product. It's just as much about being there with a community that you're a part of. Supreme's most valuable asset is arguably its simple logo, a red rectangle

marked with the word "Supreme," which fashion platform Lyst crowned the industry's most powerful logo in 2018. It can turn almost anything into a collector's item.' [8]

With *Supreme,* Prisco illustrates how the business used an unconventional business model—based on a clear understanding of their customers—as a means to convert them into a community of avid fans who've adopted the brand as part of their personal identity. And all of this to the tune of $1B, which was built up over time and which leveraged the simplicity of its branding as a symbol of value. Yet, this value wasn't inherent in the logo at its inception. While the design co-opts artist Barbara Kruger's distinctive style—a celebrated American conceptual artist, whose work addresses topics of culture, power, identity, consumerism, and sexuality—it likely didn't initially have such deep meaning to a community of customers who eventually went on to embrace the logo and the brand as a means of personal expression. All of this was developed over time *by the business*—not by the branding designer. Of course, the branding designer made an enormously valuable *contribution* by providing clarity, distinction and a canvas for the business to build on. But it's the business and the community who actually built the brand over time.

All of this is further proof that a business becomes a brand when enough customers willingly align it with their personal identity. In return, the brand continually adds tangible value to customers' lives through specific products, services, status, experiences and convenience, among other things. All this is supported by the brand's actions and behaviours, which ultimately align with a customer's own aspirations and their view of the world. That's why brands constantly need to evolve and adapt as the world around us changes. However, while the brand adapts and changes, the *branding* can often remain the same.

---

8. *Battle of Supremes: How 'legal fakes' are challenging a $1B brand,* Jacopo Prisco, CNN Style, online article, 19 March 2019.

Design is deliberate

In one of my conversations with the late Dr. Edward de Bono he provided me with the best definition of design I have ever heard—one that I subscribe to and abide by to this day: *"Design is deliberate."*

It seems pretty simple, almost too simple. But whether you're involved in developing an identity, or an App, or a business model, or a city, or a system, or an experience, or a disruption in the market, you're taking deliberate steps and making deliberate decisions, towards a specific outcome. For businesses that have successfully become brands, they've done so deliberately by focusing on aligning their Purpose and value proposition with the needs and desires of their customers. And they've responded deliberately—and with intent—to feedback from the market. This means, any design process is underpinned by a motivation to achieve a specific goal. In many cases, that motivation is to improve upon—or to replace—what is currently in existence. The premise is the same for most endeavours: What do I seek to achieve and what must I do to achieve it? Even asking these questions is a deliberate action, designed to pursue a particular or specific outcome. In our conversation, Dr. de Bono expands on the value, importance and deliberate nature of design:

"I place a lot of importance on design, because design is putting together what you have to deliver, in terms of the values you want to provide. Most of our thinking at all levels—school, university, everything—is concerned with 'analysis'. Analysis is concerned with finding the 'truth'. Design, on the other hand, is producing something which isn't there, or wasn't there before...

So, how do we need to think to produce something that doesn't yet exist? Design is one particular aspect of that because it concerns itself with creating something that doesn't yet exist, as opposed to 'finding the truth', which is always there until we find it." [1]

---

1. *Thinking to create value,* Edward de Bono in conversation with Kevin Finn for Open Manifesto, Issue #7: Enlightened Self-interest, 2015, page 69.

Essentially, design is a partnership between creativity (which is being fearlessly inventive), strategy (which focuses on long-term objectives that can adapt as things develop) and tactics (which are the specific steps involved in implementing a strategy to achieve a particular goal). All are deliberate, conscious and considered. But the design process isn't linear. In entrepreneurial terms, pivoting and being agile are also deliberate decisions designed to move you closer to an outcome in real time. Similarly, bad design is also deliberate, and it can be enormously costly. Taking unnecessary short-cuts, disregarding expert advice or deciding not to seek the required information—these are deliberate decisions. Worse still, not caring or simply being lazy about your actions is also deliberate. These are choices which have been made. They didn't happen by accident.

Deliberate by design
Perhaps that all sounds a bit academic or theoretical. If so, how might this approach—this deliberate attitude and mindset—be applied to something specific; a more tangible or practical situation, as it were? Well, there's a wonderful example, which never ceases to inspire me. And it comes from the most unlikeliest of places. Founded in 1379, *New College* in England is—ironically—one of the oldest *University of Oxford* colleges, steeped in tradition and grandeur. Education institutions like *New College* trade off their academic achievements, but they also leverage their heritage and the status they can provide each generation of students stretching through their substantial alumni. Just think how the mere mention of *MIT* or *Harvard* in the United States, *Cambridge* in England, or Ireland's *Trinity College* in Dublin—to name a few— elicits immediate respect and admiration from many. Without even questioning an individual's qualifications, a university brand can provide insight into a person's achievements and their perceived expertise merely by mentioning the university's name. But let's get back to *New College*.

According to Gregory Bateson's version of the story (an English anthropologist, social scientist, linguist and cyberneticist, among other things), a century ago an entomologist realised the massive, beautiful oak beams that adorn the ceiling in the college's dining hall were being eaten away by beetles. This became an urgent issue for the college. Where would they quickly find mature oak trees to repair and replace the wood in this glorious ceiling? And what might it cost? After some investigation, it was discovered that, when the college was founded, a grove of oak trees was planted on the grounds—*for the specific purpose of replacing the dining room beams.* It was a ready-made solution, and one which the college owned; it was a long-term investment in the business—and ultimately in the brand—that was about to pay immediate dividends. Fortuitous as this might sound, it was only possible because the original architects and/or designers projected into the future, identified an inevitable scenario, and then deliberately designed a solution into their work to solve this very problem—centuries in advance.

This is a great example of a mindset that can analyse the context, synthesise all the details, forecast potential needs, operate within specific constraints and then design for efficiencies in (and for) the future. It's simplicity and deliberate design in action. Of course, to some readers this might sound like a quaint story. And you could be forgiven for thinking it has little to do with business—or *brand* for that matter. But when *New College* discovered the damaged oak beams, no doubt they would have been acutely aware of how repairing it with an inferior substitute would impact their name and reputation—their *brand*. Anything less than oak would decrease the perceived status they offer to students and it would disrespect the heritage the university leverages as a distinguished educational destination. How can we draw these conclusions? Because of the importance *New College* obviously places on how students experience their overall brand outside of academic achievement. Just consider how many students and visitors must use the dining hall. It's therefore not an assumption to conclude they obviously understand that every aspect of their college contributes to their *brand experience*. Many established universities trade off this kind of heritage, promoting their history and status, and protecting what differentiates them from their competitors. All of this adds to the value of their brand perception. In *New College's* case, the oak grove was also a deliberate business decision and a resources solution, ensuring future efficiencies, which may have perhaps felt unnecessary to the business at the time. But this is about having a conscious attention to detail. This is clear consideration of the *What if?* This is being deliberate by design.

Deliberately designed business

But what about a more holistic business case? How can this type of thinking be scaled up? That might sound daunting, but there are huge opportunities on multiple levels. So, let's get more specific about how deliberate design and creativity can be applied to an overall business. Let's talk about *cardboard*.

One of my long-time favourite examples has been well documented over the years. But it was Michael Pawlyn (a British architect noted for his work in the fields of biomimetic architecture and innovation) who most eloquently conveyed it as an example in his *TEDSalon* London talk in 2010. The project is widely referred to as the *Cardboard to Caviar* project, developed by Graham Wiles. As Pawlyn points out, within nature the waste from one organism becomes the nutrient for another organism and this became the basis for Wiles' *closed loop business model*. Its genesis was essentially a reaction to what Wiles observed in his local area: the amount of waste created by restaurants, which included lots of food, cardboard and plastic. In looking for a solution to this problem, Wiles started with cardboard. The best way to describe this closed loop business model is to outline the circular revenue streams that it generates.

Income Stream & Service #1

The closed loop begins with Wiles offering a service to remove the piles of cardboard boxes restaurants in the area produce as waste. The restaurants pay Wiles for this service.

Income Stream & Service #2

Wiles shreds the cardboard—a perfect material for horse bedding. He then sells this to equestrian centres and stables.

Income Stream & Service #3
When the horse bedding is soiled Wiles offers to remove it and the stables pay Wiles for this service.

Value Creation
The soiled bedding, which is a mix of the original cardboard, organic material and horse manure, is fed into a worm composting system, which generates a rich compost material, multiplying the worms in the process.

Income Stream & Service #4
The worms are then fed to Siberian sturgeon (fish), which produce caviar. This is packed in tins and cardboard boxes before being sold back to the restaurants, which paid Wiles to take away the cardboard boxes in the first place. He's then paid to take away new cardboard boxes, some of which are the ones into which he packed the latest caviar tins. This perpetuates the deliberately designed closed loop business model, based on deliberately converting waste into value.

As Pawlyn points out, this example clearly shows how we can move from a traditional linear process to a sustainable, revenue-rich closed loop model, creating more value. It also highlights the specific design decisions Wiles made to achieve this, not just in terms of his business model, but also in its impact model—on landfill, the environment and the various other businesses he's serving. Pawlyn describes this as turning waste streams into smart schemes that create value, and how deliberate design can turn a huge problem—waste—into a massive opportunity: increased revenue and a more environmentally conscious business. But this is the tip of the iceberg. With a deliberate design mindset, a more holistic approach, and a clear understanding of the contexts involved, along with a sprinkle of creativity, deliberately designed businesses can literally change the world.

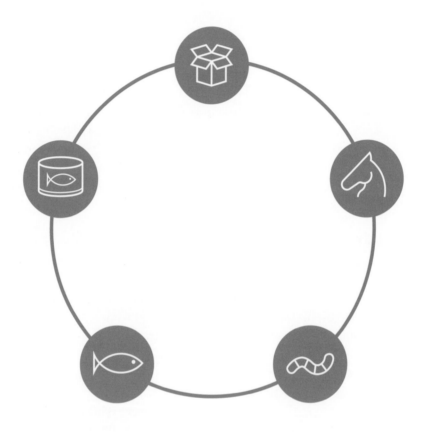

Depiction of Graham Wiles' 'Cardboard to Caviar' closed loop business model

Change by design

However, often we get caught up in the tools, in the delivery mechanisms and in the branding rather than the brand itself. We hear it in phrases like: *"It's the difference between working in the business versus working on the business."* But people and ideas are a powerful force, and when they use deliberate design to communicate or manifest those ideas the results can foster genuine impact and potentially significant change. So, while design absolutely is an *instrument* for delivering change, it is people who have a responsibility to use design in deliberate ways to deliver smart and valuable ideas that can change the world for the better. Ironically, that puts increased value and importance on design. In other words, as Bruce Mau, co-founder of *Massive Change Network*, once said:

"Now that we can do anything, what will we do? Massive change is not about the world of design; it's about the design of the world." [2]

When we look at things this way it becomes much easier to see how we might use design to change something for the better—whether that's a product, a business, a brand, a community, the world, or perhaps simply your own world. This mindset helps us appreciate how design is an incredibly effective tool, which can be applied specifically to deliver ideas that add value at scale. In some cases, that can even mean deliberately changing a country by design. How? Let's take a look at Japan.

Design by necessity

Over forty years ago, Japan was an economic superpower. This position was essentially a convergence of circumstances, ambition and approach. As American journalist Douglas McGray outlined in his 2009 *Foreign Policy* essay:

---

2. *Massive Change,* Bruce Mau and The Institute Without Borders, Phaidon Press, 21 October 2004, back cover.

"In the 1980s, Japan pioneered a new kind of superpower. Tokyo had no army to speak of, no puppet regimes to prop up, and no proxy wars to mind. Just an economy. What made Japan a superpower, more than just a wealthy country, was the way its great firms staked claim to a collective intellectual high ground that left competitors, even in the United States, scrambling to reverse-engineer Japanese successes. Seeking guidance on everything from 'quality circles' to 'just-in-time' inventory management, U.S. corporate executives bought stacks of books on Japanese management techniques. The key to Japan's economic ascendance was not ideology, at least not by Cold War standards; but it was a method, it drove the most dynamic economy of the era, and it was indisputably Japanese." [3]

But all of this collapsed. A decade-long recession, compounded by high unemployment, and a drop in GDP and the Yen—the national currency—meant Japan largely imploded. Even *Moody's Investors Service* at the time rated Japan as only slightly more creditworthy than Botswana. Staggering comparisons aside, it was an incredible and abrupt fall from grace. Japan had to acknowledge the fact it was in dire need of reinventing itself and McGray points out how they deliberately went about doing so: positioning the country through entertainment, arts and culture more broadly—and then supporting the businesses who were producing culture.

"Instead of collapsing beneath its political and economic misfortunes, Japan's global cultural influence has only grown. In fact, from pop music to consumer electronics, architecture to fashion, and food to art, Japan has far greater cultural influence now than it did in the 1980s, when it was an economic superpower.

Japan has made deep inroads into American culture, usually written off by the rest of the world as aggravatingly insular. Best-selling Sony Playstation and Nintendo home video games draw heavily on Japanese anime and manga for inspiration. So have Hollywood

---

3.   *Japan's Gross National Cool,* Douglas McGray, Foreign Policy, online article, 11 November 2009.

films, such as The Matrix, *and television series, including director James Cameron's* Dark Angel. *'Tokyo is the real international capital of fashion,' the style editor of the New York Times proposed [in the spring of 2009], spurning Paris, New York, and Milan as pretenders. Japanese anime-style cartoons currently fill the majority of time slots in the after-school and Saturday morning schedules on U.S. cable television. The cartoon and video game franchise Pokémon—broadcast in 65 countries and translated into more than 30 languages—even made the cover of* Time *magazine."* [4]

McGray describes this repositioning as Japan's 'Gross National Cool', a deliberate and considered campaign to bolster the domestic economy and export an updated national identity—Brand Japan—to the world. And it wasn't accidental.

"A cultural superpower needs a healthy economic base but not necessarily a healthy economy. Perversely, recession may have boosted Japan's national cool, discrediting Japan's rigid social hierarchy and empowering young entrepreneurs. It may also have loosened the grip a big-business career track had over so much of Japan's workforce, who now face fewer social stigmas for experimenting with art, music, or any number of similar, risky endeavors." [5]

The examples in this chapter underscore the mindset involved in deliberately designing solutions for various scenarios. And that particular mindset is essentially the convergence of two types of thinking, so let's explore it further in the next chapter.

---

4.   *Japan's Gross National Cool.*
5.   *Japan's Gross National Cool.*

Two types of thinking

It's not unusual for business owners to believe they aren't creative. But think about it. While most business owners aren't professional designers, the process they employ to shape their business is similar. It concerns itself with understanding a range of complex and interrelated components, making sense of them, and packaging the result as a series of value propositions to staff and customers in a way they can understand and appreciate. By its very nature, it is designed—and it *is* deliberate.

In the pursuit of achieving anything in life we are most often doing so deliberately—consciously or subconsciously. The steps we take, or the choices we avoid, are deliberate. The intention is to make the process more fruitful and the outcome more meaningful. Ultimately, being aware of how we make decisions is essential in deliberately designing a way forward. This has been reinforced over recent decades as the intersection between business and design has proliferated—and grown considerably in value. Some credit brands like *Apple* for this movement because they consciously embraced an holistic approach to design—internally and externally—through product design, hardware design, retail design, supply chains, organisational culture, communications, marketing, customer service, product development, and the design of its office spaces, among other aspects. So much so, this approach has been absorbed into their culture. It has become part of their DNA; and it has been recognised as a hallmark of their brand.

In other circles, some argue that business schools like *Stanford* identified how designers approach their professional practice and how this could be applied to business. Many refer to this approach as *Design Thinking* and it has been included in various business curricula, where it perhaps garnered more credibility than if it had emerged from design schools. Regardless, the objective for business became: *Disrupt, or be disrupted*— and Design Thinking seemed to offer a way to tackle this. Others cite consultancy firms like *IDEO* as significant influencers in the Design Thinking movement, due

•

Design Thinking has
been included in various
business curricula, where
it perhaps garnered
more credibility than
if it had emerged from
design schools.

•

to their focus on developing frameworks and processes to help businesses adopt and implement design principles in order to navigate our ever-changing and uncertain world.

Dr. Edward de Bono's work is perhaps the forerunner of what we now refer to as Design Thinking, given his pioneering career in fostering ground-breaking tools that support *creative thinking as a skill*. And as de Bono suggests, the value of design is based on creating something that wasn't there before, which can be a vital asset to a business in a highly competitive environment. But making a conscious switch to Design Thinking, or being a design-led business, can be difficult for many business leaders—partly due to traditional business training, partly due to the investment and uncertainty involved, and partly due to the fact that design is a creative pursuit and business owners might not be so comfortable with the messy, chaotic creative world. However, there may yet be another reason for business leaders to feel cautious about adopting a Design Thinking approach: it has often sounded more complicated and academic than it ought to.

Design Thinking versus Analytical Thinking

I've heard many explanations of Design Thinking and how it can be applied in business. But one that stands out for its simplicity was shared with me by Dean Poole (co-founder of influential design firm *Alt Group*, based in New Zealand). Poole outlines his view on the difference between how designers think versus traditional business leaders:

"Business thinking is defining what things are and trying to rationalise it through logic. Design Thinking is about imagining how things 'could be'. That's the fundamental difference. So, if you look at Roger Martin, from Rotman's School of Management, he explains the difference as being Analytical Thinking versus Design Thinking. Analytical Thinking is how people in business schools talk today and it's based on past data: try to rationalise it, figure out where the issues are then plot out a course of action based on what

we know and based on metrics, or whatever. But Design Thinking is about saying 'we could be this!' What and where this process works is when you put those two thinking processes together." [1]

This highlights some of the key challenges business leaders are faced with when adopting Design Thinking, because it often goes against their natural instincts. Essentially, it requires them to adopt a design mentality, to take a leap of faith, to jump into the unknown and—using specific frameworks— imagine a future that has yet to be designed. And that's just the first part. From there, this design mentality needs to be clearly articulated to others so they can understand the vision, become inspired by it, and be motivated about this new proposed future. In short, the business leaders need to *believe* in what they have designed and fully understand how it can materialise as a tangible outcome before encouraging others to commit to that uncertainty. They also need to be comfortable doing this without data, proof or modelling. As Poole explains, designers do this naturally:

"Designers are very good at taking little information, extrapolating out to some future point, imagining what that could be, contextualizing that and sharing it with others." [2]

To reassure business leaders about the process behind Design Thinking—while also minimising any doubts they may have about their perceived lack of 'creative abilities'—it's worth noting: where traditional design is often focused on artefacts and objects, Design Thinking is essentially about systems and contexts. Perhaps this fact alone offers some insight as to why Design Thinking has dovetailed so neatly with business.

---

1. *The art of design; a business strategy from Monopoly, the rise of Design Thinking; and guns for hire,* Dean Poole in conversation with Kevin Finn for Open Manifesto, Issue #6: Myth, 2012, page 81.
2. *The art of design; a business strategy from Monopoly, the rise of Design Thinking; and guns for hire,* page 80.

The process and the pitfalls

Even so, it might be easy to dismiss Design Thinking as a fanciful idea and a potentially costly exercise. For some business leaders, embracing the novel idea of *'what might be'* without a guaranteed return on investment is not reassuring. And, of course, there are dangers for traditional business leaders who adopt Design Thinking for the wrong reasons and without a full understanding of the process, or when their expectation is an immediate result. Helen Walters, Head of Curation at *TED*, who at the time of our conversation was the editor of innovation and design at *BusinessWeek*, offers some sobering insights:

"What does Design Thinking really mean, anyway? Ask even those who are in the business of promoting the discipline the most; all of them have slightly different definitions. Tim Brown [CEO] of IDEO talks of design applied to save the world. Roger Martin talks of the opposable mind and the tension between the creative and the analyst. Don Norman [author, professor and researcher] thinks it's a term that deserves to die, while Larry Keeley of Doblin calls for everyone to recognise the huge complexity of design and not to settle for superficial band-aid fixes, which won't last or satisfy in the long-term. Offering up Design Thinking as a design-based process that guarantees business success is disingenuous in the extreme, and perhaps designers, attuned to the mess and chaos of their own process, recognise this most clearly."

"The thing is, the truly successful marriage of design and business involves collaboration and insights shared throughout every department of an organisation. It's not good enough to create a prototype and hope it'll be somehow successful in the market. Designers and executives have to put down their suspicion and work together, each one reassuring the other that they're working towards the same goal. This happens all too rarely." [3]

---

3. *Design Thinking? Prove it!*, Helen Walters in conversation with Kevin Finn for Open Manifesto, Issue #6: Myth, 2012, page 85 and 88.

Unsurprisingly, there are similarities when it comes to brand building, which is also a whole-of-organisation effort, based on collaboration and genuine clarity about the objective, where instant results are never guaranteed and where commitment and investment over the long-term are essential. Hoping that a prototype—or some branding—will single-handedly deliver on expectations, while the company continues with 'business-as-usual', is flawed in the extreme. Obviously, businesses engage in design, branding and Design Thinking because they're looking to overcome specific challenges, or to avail themselves of particular opportunities, or to better leverage their position in the market. These are serious objectives, which impact the business in tangible ways. But they often first require transformation and change from within the business itself. There can't be an expectation that branding or Design Thinking alone will achieve the desired results, if the solution is seen as an external exercise and where the business doesn't take responsibility or accountability for how the outcomes are delivered on a daily basis. It simply doesn't work if the attitude is that 'business-as-usual' will continue as before. So how might you overcome this?

The creative myth

Whether intentional or not, there is a misplaced perception that the 'creative industries' have somehow successfully developed a monopoly on creativity—as though running a business doesn't require creativity. That being a teacher, or playing sport, or being a scientist, or even a parent doesn't call for any sort of creativity; or that engaging in 'regular' pursuits simply falls outside the realm of creative input. For example, Deb Knobelman is a neuroscientist by training. She has worked in the business side of science for most of her career and spent years on *Wall Street* before joining the C-suite of several biotech startups. Neither of these pursuits are traditionally understood to be creative, something Knobelman also believed. However, it took a particularly chaotic week in her life for her to acknowledge the folly of this myth:

•

"The truly successful marriage of design and business involves collaboration and insights shared throughout every department of an organisation."

•

"I haven't always considered myself a creative person. I love math and science, I worked on Wall Street. I am fascinated by the business side of any business. None of these things are traditionally considered creative endeavors. But in the midst of the chaos last week, I realised a few things. Creativity is important in all areas of life. Almost every area of life requires creativity to innovate and move forward. Of course creativity is important for artists. But startups need to approach their business from a unique perspective to carve out their own niche. On Wall Street, I needed a creative approach to analyzing biotech companies so I could find previously uncovered opportunities." [4]

The fact is, creativity has an incredibly wide application throughout society, although this is often overlooked. While de Bono has previously been criticised by some for not offering a definition for creativity, given that his work promotes creative thinking as a skill, in one of our conversations he offered this insight:

"Our general approach to creativity is a belief that it's not normal, that it's mysterious, that it's some strange talent that only certain people have, but most people don't have and there's nothing you can do about it except find people who are creative. That is so ridiculous. I look at creativity as an activity of the brain, an activity with patterned systems. Interestingly, the most important function of the brain, which amazingly philosophers have never mentioned and psychologists pay very little attention to, if any, is humour, because humour indicates the brain is working as a patterning system." [5]

Breaking this patterning system through humour is a powerful way of thinking because it works in a very specific manner. For example, consider this simple joke: "A guy is late for an important meeting, but he can't find a place to park. In desperation, he begins to pray: "Please Lord, if you help me find a parking spot *right now*, I promise

---

4. *The Best Way For Your Brain To Be More Creative Is More Routine,* Deb Knobelman, PhD, online blog article, 13 June 2019.
5. *Thinking to create value,* Edward de Bono in conversation with Kevin Finn for Open Manifesto, Issue #7: Enlightened Self-interest, 2015, page 71.

to go to church every Sunday and never drink vodka again!" A moment later, he sees an empty spot right next to the entrance and says: "Never mind. Found one!" De Bono describes how a joke like this works and what it has to do with creativity.

"[It] demonstrates a pattern, a perfectly logical pattern heading towards an end-point. But then a different end-point is introduced, which in hindsight is perfectly logical. If the brain can do that, then there's an absolute need for creativity because there are points in the brain, which you cannot get to with logic, but once you're there they are perfectly logical in hindsight. So without creativity you're never going to get to those points. Now, with regards to offering a definition of creativity, the problem with creativity in the English language is that it's so wide. It covers artistic creativity, intellectual creativity, etc. I would define creativity as developing an idea—or project, or product, or whatever it is—which in hindsight is valuable and logical but which you could not have gotten there by logical development. In hindsight, yes, but not with foresight. So, it's the asymmetry of patterns that defines creativity." [6]

Small creative moments

Creative acts present themselves in simple ways, every day. So much so, we often overlook them, partly because we don't recognise them as 'creativity', and partly because creativity only makes sense once it materialises—in hindsight, as de Bono points out. This is perhaps another example of why, as a society, we seem to be so fixated with outcomes, rather than the process involved. Another reason might be that we feel creativity needs to be the result of something big or significant. But this just isn't the case. For example, when I was Joint Creative Director of *Saatchi Design*, Sydney—part of the *Saatchi & Saatchi* global network—there was an internal email channel for staff, which was frequently used to make requests for research and project feedback, among other things. At one point, someone in the agency was conducting research along the lines of: *"When are you most creative?"*—perhaps

---

6. *Thinking to create value*, page 73.

not an unusual question for a creative company. This question was dispatched through the All-Staff email channel prompting numerous replies which, unsurprisingly, included various attempts by individuals at impressing their colleagues. Regardless, I remember thinking at the time that some responses were funny, some were insightful, some were unexpected, and some were shallow. However, I've now forgotten the content of each and every email reply—except for one. It went something like this:

"I'm not an Art Director or a Copywriter, I'm just a junior Account Manager. But I think the time I am most creative is in the morning, when I am standing in front of my wardrobe deciding what I'll wear for the day."

Given *Saatchi & Saatchi* has built a brand and a reputation around creativity, it was disheartening that she felt the need to state: *"I'm not an Art Director or a Copywriter, I'm just an Account Manager."* With that sentence, she immediately removed herself from the *creative class.* Yet, her response perfectly encapsulated the reality that being creative is an everyday occurence; that it happens everywhere, all the time—and to everyone! It's what makes human ingenuity so dynamic. In the junior Account Manager's case, every morning she was creatively assessing colour, texture, composition and—inherently—her personal identity, or her personal brand, through her choice of clothing. However, the fact she felt the most creative part of her day was *before* work is incredibly disconcerting.

How to approach creativity
For those of us who have been labelled 'creative' (because of our profession, our training or our hobbies) we must constantly remind ourselves—and others—that creativity is universal and incredibly varied. It doesn't belong to a specific segment of the community, nor does it fall into neat categories. To take the high ground and classify ourselves as something extraordinary is to fail to understand the true nature of creativity. Worse still: to make someone feel like they're not creative is reprehensible. The same

applies to business leaders who are dismissive of, or who look down upon, creativity (either from staff and/or professionals), seeing it as novel, vague, a luxury, or an activity with less value than other *tangible* business activities.

The fact is, most professional designers have years of training, experience and practice. This allows them to assess information and contexts, through empathy and observation, and intuitively join dots that are often overlooked or missed by others, among other traits. They naturally synthesise all this information, expressing it in ways that creates "something that wasn't there before." Of course this involves a high level of creativity but it's vital to view designers as professionals. I've heard so many anecdotes over the years about clients demanding that a logo is presented bigger (because they always feel 'bigger is better'). I've heard stories of clients coming into design meetings saying they want the colour to be *blue*, because their wife (and for some outdated reason, it always seems to be 'the wife') has just done some interior decorating, has used this particular shade of blue, and it looks good at home—so make it that blue! The point here is that designers are deliberate about their decisions. They're not being vague or woolly. Quite the opposite, in fact, because they employ another critical aspect to their decision-making: *editing*. Having ideas is one thing, but the true value is in knowing which ideas one should pursue. According to Dr. Mareike Wieth, a psychology professor at *Albion College* in Michigan:

"[A] very important part of creativity is being able to evaluate which ones of these [ideas] are worthwhile, which ones are meaningful, and which ones aren't really that original." [7]

This is oftentimes the most difficult and yet most valuable part of the process. Yet, designers are generally attuned to this because of their natural ability to understand a business' needs, as well as the contexts surrounding them, and being aware of societal shifts and technological advances. Equally, their willingness to embrace

---

7. *Science says this is the best time to brainstorm—and it's not when you think,* KC Ifeanyi, Fast Company, online article, 12 September 2019.

a *What if?* mindset allows them to make considered decisions in creative ways. Call it *informed intuition.* It's an activity that can often be intimidating for non-designers to explore or observe because it's both tangible (based on information) *and* creative (based on intuition). And while we're all creative, we need to defer to professionals on significant decisions, which may be something as seemingly simple as the size of a logo or the choice of colour. However, to think creativity is something that others have—but not you—is to view creativity through a narrow lens, one where creativity may have been educated out of you, or where you were somehow conditioned to exclude yourself from a natural ability that we all have. Being inherently creative gives everyone permission to contribute to a creative conversation and to suggest ideas. It's this collaborative and open approach where creativity thrives, which encourages vulnerability, and which helps everyone explore areas we may otherwise might not—and then to build on them. Remember Helen Walters' recommendation:

"Designers and executives have to put down their suspicion and work together, each one reassuring the other that they're working towards the same goal. This happens all too rarely."

While each individual involved in this collaboration has experience in specific areas of business and/or design, neither should act as though they have a monopoly on any aspect of the process. Think of it like this: where design can often be messy and chaotic, each decision is deliberately exploring new possibilities. It's the perfect environment to test and invent new things. In contrast, where business can often be conservative and linear, each decision is made deliberately in relation to the overall objectives of the business and the operational restraints it needs to juggle. It's the perfect environment to ground new ideas within the necessary context. Clearly, design and business overlap in how they both make deliberate decisions for specific outcomes. But it takes two types of thinking to harness the latent potential that sits within this vital partnership. As Simon Sinek succinctly puts it:

"Intelligence uses what is known to solve problems. Creativity uses what is unknown to discover possibilities." [8]

Remember, building a brand is a whole-of-organisation effort, based on a deliberately designed set of products, services or experiences, so it cannot be confined to the board room, or the C-Suite, or the Marketing Department, or the design studio. It has to be understood, believed-in and championed by everyone in the organisation. And this means analytical thinking and creative thinking have important roles in building the future of a business, whether it's a brand, or it's aspiring to become one.

---

8. *Science says this is the best time to brainstorm—and it's not when you think.*

Business, Brands and Innovation

In Chapter 3 we discussed design being deliberate. However, being deliberate in intention is only half the task. Our actions also need to be deliberate and that can often take courage to pursue. Ji Lee—a former Creative Director at *Facebook* for 10 years and an influential designer in his own right—sums this up beautifully when he says: *"Ideas are nothing, doing is everything."* [1] But now there are new pressures involved.

Increasingly, business and design are awash with the words *'innovation'* and *'disruption'*. It seems as if a business will be left behind or abandoned if they're not innovating (or at least talking about it, or thinking about it). We're told innovation and disruption hastens successful business, helping to establish a desirable and profitable brand. While there are cases where this is true, it's certainly not guaranteed. Regardless, investors flock to would-be 'innovators' and 'disruptors'—and for good reason. Many want to anticipate 'the next big thing' and perceptions around innovating are now so ingrained it's become an expectation for all serious businesses to pursue, even if in reality it can sometimes actually be a shallow tactic merely used to garner some extra attention. Still, the businesses and brands who are truly engaged in pushing the envelope—through technology, experience design, experimentation and business models, among other things—are a refreshing reminder of what can be achieved with new thinking, different approaches and deliberate action. The problem is, we usually only value the outcomes—because they are tangible and resolved; because they are easily understood and can therefore be consumed as being 'successful innovation'. But the messy, scary, exciting and uncertain process needed to get to the results receives less attention, even though it's equally important.

The trouble with hindsight
Traditional business is very measured, with metrics bound to KPIs, linear progress reporting and predictable results. It's a deliberate and familiar process. And while this is an acceptable

---

1. *Everything is connected,* Ji Lee in conversation with Kevin Finn for Open Manifesto, Issue #7: Enlightened Self-interest, 2015, page 41.

system for sustaining a business—underpinned by caution and consideration—design, innovation, disruption and transformational change are, by their very nature, the antithesis of this approach simply because, like creativity, they can only be measured (to a degree) with hindsight. Unfortunately, we can't foresee hindsight. Unsurprisingly, this can be a challenging approach for traditional business leaders to adopt, even in their rush to embrace design and innovation. It's far easier—and more certain—for people to focus on a successful outcome, one that is at the end of the process and has arrived ready-made to the market with an optimum solution. One that 'points the way'. However, even in those cases, business leaders still might hesitate in adopting a more innovative approach. For example, in my conversation with Ken Segall he recounted a discussion he once had with Steve Jobs:

"When the iMac was released Steve literally said: 'In about two or three months from now, you're gonna see a lot of these one-unit things out there: all-in-one, easy Internet, the whole bit.' That seemed obvious to us—but it didn't really happen. I remember a meeting with [Jobs] some time after the iMac launched and he said: 'I personally don't get it. We've showed them the playbook. And it's become the best-selling computer in the market. Yet people aren't copying it.' Not that it worried him..." [2]

Even though *Apple "showed them the playbook"*, even though the metrics, sales, media and impact were overwhelmingly positive, and even though *Apple* had presented a ready-made business case for this type of product, it's interesting that competitor's still didn't take the leap and follow, to iterate and/or innovate from there. What might be the reason for this?

Courage and conviction
It's one thing to want to copy something, but it's another thing entirely to understand how to deliver on it. That requires a very specific mindset. In a workshop that I once attended run by

---

2. *The transformative power of simplicity,* Ken Segall in conversation with Kevin Finn for DESIGNerd, online article, March 2018.

Blair Enns (founder of a sales training organisation for creative professionals and author of *Win Without Pitching* and *Pricing Creativity*) he referenced influential designer Yves Béhar, who routinely fields business Executives stating they want to be the *Apple* of their industry. Béhar responds with a very pointed question: *"Do you have the guts?"* [3] Because that's what it takes— courage, commitment and investment (of time, resources and finance). Because innovation is largely the result of process. And while it's an exciting process it's also filled with uncertainty, doubt—and potential failure. It's a hard grind because innovation comes from experimentation, from exploring new and often uncomfortable paths. And just like building a brand, it takes time, committed resolve and a lot of effort. But, in the scramble to be perceived as an innovator, many businesses naively talk as though they're innovating every other week. The truth is, innovation—real innovation and disruption—is a deliberate pursuit. Real innovation is a game-changer. That's not to say there aren't ways to move the needle in stages, to progress things quickly, or to create something that wasn't there before by minimising constraints. And it can be easier than we might imagine—but only if we remove the pressures and expectations to innovate. By doing so, we avoid the trap of thinking that 'innovation' has to be developed from scratch— because there is another way, a simpler way. It's called *hacking*.

At this point, it's wise to remove any images you might have of a young guy in a hoodie, sitting alone in a darkened basement barely illuminated by the soft glow of a laptop screen displaying encrypted coding, all set to take down the next corporate victim. In fact, hacking can be a positively creative act, one that's deliberately designed to build upon what is already in existence. Ji Lee explains:

"Hacking, or hijacking, is really the simplest way of taking what already exists and turning it into something new, making it your own, but in a very simple, ingenious, creative way." [4]

---

3. *All About Yves,* by Linda Tischler, FastCompany, online article, 10 October 2007.
4. *Everything is connected,* page 26.

The business end of hacking

So, how might hacking be applied, in practical terms, to a live business scenario? If we consider Lee's definition— *"taking what already exists and turning it into something new"*—we are in a better position to attune our mindset towards finding solutions that are already in use in one industry sector, re-appropriating them and then implementing the modified version into our specific situation. It sounds easy and difficult, right? So, let's explore an example. For most of 2014 I was a design associate at *Business Models Inc (BMI)*, a global business design consultancy headquartered in Amsterdam and specialising in strategy and innovation. (Incidentally, *BMI* is also the organisation that brought significant attention to the universal *Business Model Canvas* framework, among other business tools.) During a workshop I was co-facilitating, my then-colleague Michael Eales (*BMI* Partner Australia/New Zealand) presented a striking case study, which exemplifies business hacking in real terms.

The business in question is *citizenM*, a progressive hotel chain founded in 2005 with a clear mission: to become a contemporary luxury hotel for the cost-conscious traveller. Based on a modular architectural design, where rooms are manufactured off-site and then assembled in different configurations, there is a focus on high-end interior design and cutting edge connected technology within the rooms. Their mission was supported by a clear objective: to raise guest satisfaction front-of-house, while reducing costs back-of-house. I suspect that particular objective will most likely resonate with many business owners, but how *citizenM* tackled this was very smart, very creative and deliberately designed:

- **Eliminate:** *unnecessary services and products*
- **Reduce:** *labour intensiveness; GFA (gross floor area) per room ratio; influence third party distribution costs; construction time.*
- **Raise:** *luxury level in economy segment; quality of basic needs; level of standardisation.*
- **Create:** *lifestyle brand in economy segment; attractively priced hotels on A1 locations; personalisation.*

It's worth noting, they didn't assume they were a brand at inception, but instead set a clear objective to *create a lifestyle brand in the economy segment*. This is Chapter 2 in a nutshell. Unsurprisingly, much of the business and hotel design matched their initial objectives, but one strikingly simple hack stood out to me. Since convenience is a large part of *citizenM's* customer offer, but reducing labour and eliminating unnecessary services are also criteria, they re-thought their foyer and arrivals experience. Casting a 'hacker's eye' to other industry sectors, they considered airports —particularly the now ubiquitous self check-in booths.

Adopting this idea, and hacking it into their own hotel design, meant their foyers no longer needed permanent reception staff. Check-in could be done through an App, and self check-in booths reduced wait time on arrival for customers who might otherwise be queuing for available staff. However, if a customer needs assistance, the self-service cafeteria is deliberately located adjacent to the foyer, where staff (in their dual roles) are available. This illustrates how a business can creatively and deliberately design a 'hack' from a different sector and integrate it into its own business model. As a whole, *citizenM* certainly can be seen as an innovative business, considering its progressive manufacturing model and supply chain ecosystem, and with its specific focus on a targeted customer demographic, which they understood intimately as early as 2005. Either way, having a 'hacker's mindset' and channelling this into deliberately designing your business, offers tangible ways to maximise existing successful solutions from elsewhere in order to generate greater efficiencies in your business.

Types of innovation

Unsurprisingly, the pressure to innovate can often cause paralysis, complacency or confusion within an organisation—and questioning its intent, even at a basic level, can be overwhelming. When a task seems insurmountable, urgent, or simply a little ambiguous—as is the case when pursuing innovation—the challenge of 'where to start' can kill innovation before it begins. And, like other situations, it can be further compounded by specific words and language, which are increasingly being overused and misunderstood. But, it's worth remembering, innovation isn't isolated or compartmentalised: *all innovation has a lineage.* It's the aggregate of previous advances and various avenues of research, funding and experimentation. Unfortunately, this fact has been overshadowed by today's penchant for elevating individual entrepreneurs to exalted levels of 'genius'. In truth, innovation is an incredibly collective and collaborative process, which builds upon previous progress, experiments and advancements. In her thorough and influential book, *The Value of Everything: Making and taking in the global economy,* Mariana Mazzucato tackles this head-on and describes innovation as such:

"Innovation is collective: the interactions between different people in different roles and sectors (private, public, third sectors) are a critical part of the process. Those who might otherwise be seen as lone entrepreneurs in fact benefit from such collectivity; moreover, they stand on the shoulders of both previous entrepreneurs and taxpayers who [...] often contribute to the underlying infrastructure and technologies on which innovation builds." [5]

Mazzucato goes on to say:

"Both Bill Gates, CEO of Microsoft, and Eric Schmidt, Executive Chairman of Alphabet (the parent company of Google) have recently written about the immense benefits their companies gained from public investments: as well as the Internet and the html code behind the worldwide web written in CERN, a public lab in Europe, Google's very algorithm was funded by a National Science Foundation grant." [6]

Despite the rise of Open Source culture, the collective nature of innovation is often lost within the hyper-commercial and competitive landscape of our increasingly pressurised world.

---

5. *The Value of Everything: Making and taking in the global economy,* Mariana Mazzucato, Penguin Books, 2019, page 194.
6. *The Value Of Everything: Making and taking in the global economy,* page 194.

This environment has prompted businesses of all persuasions to promote any notion of perceived innovation in order to gain a competitive edge. I witnessed this firsthand many years ago when I was invited to attend an 'innovation' meeting with the partners of a major accountancy and consultancy firm. Their objective was to develop an Innovation Lab, but there was a lot of circular talk about what that meant. At one point in proceedings, one of the consultancy partners confidently stated how innovative they were and—more importantly—that clients expected them to be innovating. But when I quietly asked how he responded to clients who inquired about how they innovate he became immediately uncomfortable and struggled to find the words to reply.

In the end, he trailed off into commentary about their Mission and Vision. No case studies were provided; no examples, no evidence, no proof. I suggested they needed to focus less on developing an Innovation Lab and more on developing a culture of *innovative thinking* across the company. But I was met with blank stares. Perhaps the objective of the Innovation Lab was, instead, to provide the appearance of being innovative. Regardless, I believe the lab never got developed in the end. Sadly, this is often a grey area where businesses and brands can get caught up, and caught out, in a superficial pursuit of innovation—or at least the *idea* of it.

My view is that real innovation is a game-changer simply by default because it provides a leap into the unknown and offers a new solution or direction, which then influences and inspires a legion of followers. It was on this topic that I spoke with Ben Johnston (co-founder of *Josephmark*, an internationally accomplished Brisbane and L.A-based digital agency working at the intersection of design and digital entrepreneurship). We agreed that the language around innovation is tired and clichéd, but he also challenged my view about game-changing innovation by offering his understanding of *incremental innovation*:

"I find myself witnessing [people] talking about these concepts and almost being conscious not to use that clichéd language ['innovation' and 'disruption'], because it's thrown around so much—like it can be bought and picked up with your cornflakes in the morning. Yet, we're seeing more innovation than ever, although it's still very contained; it's still not affecting the riches of our society, or our corporate structures, or our government systems in the way that it fully could. But I think there is an opportunity in that.

However, there is also a word of caution because the language has almost become a constraint, as though it's more conceptual and theoretical than actual or tangible... I see innovation as both sides of the debate you've described. Game-changing innovation comes from experienced domain language and a creative mind that has the freedom, space, and confidence to assess a particular ecosystem in a specific landscape. This provides a level of assurance or confidence about suggesting a new concept or idea applied to a pre-existing format. To achieve this—to execute on those big ideas—is about balancing that Vision, yet trying to find the hidden valley in order to know where the Vision is going. It's a step-by-step process. An example of a familiar large innovative, disruptive company in the last decade is Uber. It's generally accepted that they're a fairly innovative company. But the steps to get there required a whole bunch of smaller innovations and an understanding of a customer journey before they could build trust in a whole new system and business model. So, it's neither one or the other. They are two levels of innovation together.

[Josephmark] associate innovation with making something better—that it's a progression, it's an evolution, and that ultimately innovation happens when the right foundations are in place, whether that's in a culture or in the mind-set of an individual. These foundations require a level of understanding and context—so it's not blind or accidental innovation. It also needs confidence and freedom. So I think that the framework for innovation starts with these foundations. Everybody needs to be comfortable and confident,

*because everyone involved is continually taking these small steps
into the unknown. To me that's innovation. And the only way that
you confidently do this is if you've got a clear Vision, which then
eventually becomes the big innovation."* [7]

Johnston raises some critical points, and follows Mazzucato's
observations around the collective nature of innovation, where
examples like *Uber* have relied on previous developments—
technological and societal. Of course, there have been numerous
steps involved, and continuous improvements in response
to feedback loops from customer experiences. All of this is
incremental, but it all largely involved improvements on the original,
game-changing Vision that was *Uber* in the first place—that big
initial idea around commercialising ride-sharing. Their insight
anticipated a growing cultural shift towards sharing versus sole
ownership and where those specific *incremental innovations* were
deliberate steps to help steadily shift societal behaviour and ensure
their innovative idea became widely accepted. Success came from
building on previous developments, applying them to a new concept,
in a new context—and from being the beneficiary of the 'right
timing'. Clearly, innovation is a precarious balancing act.

Designing disruption

A central tenet of innovation is a willingness to challenge and
question even the most accepted positions and principles. This
mindset is motivated by a restlessness to find better solutions *and*
from a frustration with the status quo. But its meaning can also be
co-opted for superficial and cosmetic purposes. In a conversation
with Daan Roosegaarde (founder of renowned and innovative
Rotterdam-based *Studio Roosegaarde* and a Young Leader at the
World Economic Forum) I discussed some of the impediments
around innovation. Though he himself is an internationally
recognised innovator, he was stark in his criticism about how
innovation is currently being interpreted:

---

7.   *The beauty, opportunity and challenge of exploring the future,* Ben Johnston in conversation
     with Kevin Finn for Open Manifesto, Issue #8: Change, 2017, pages 187 and 188.

"Every good idea has a consequence. Every good dream can be redefined. A lot of innovation is, indeed, focused on one component to do a new thing—but in the old way... These days, a lot of so-called innovation is defined as doing the same thing but less bad, five percent less worse. For me, this is not innovation. It's just damage control." [8]

Roosegaarde is not a lone voice. While the ideas of innovation and disruption have become ingrained in the business world, it's surprising how often they are misunderstood. Just like the words 'brand' and 'branding', 'innovation' and 'disruption' are often casually used to loosely describe whatever people want them to mean at any given time or situation. Even the late and legendary Clayton Christensen (who developed the theory of 'disruptive innovation') was concerned about how his theory was being misrepresented. So much so, that in 2015 he wrote an article for the *Harvard Business Review* with the sole intention of clarifying things. Writing with Michael E. Raynor and Rory McDonald, he said.

"The term 'disruptive innovation' is misleading when it is used to refer to a product or service at one fixed point, rather than to the evolution of that product or service over time. The first minicomputers were disruptive not merely because they were low-end upstarts when they appeared on the scene, nor because they were later heralded as superior to mainframes in many markets; they were disruptive by virtue of the path they followed from the fringe to the mainstream. Almost every innovation—disruptive or not—begins life as a small-scale experiment. Disrupters tend to focus on getting the business model, rather than merely the product, just right. When they succeed, their movement from the fringe (the low end of the market or a new market) to the mainstream erodes first the incumbents' market share and then their profitability. This process can take time, and incumbents can get quite creative in the defense of their established franchises." [9]

---

8. *Prototyping the future of cities*, Daan Roosegaarde in conversation with Kevin Finn for Open Manifesto, Issue #8: Change, 2017, page 26.
9. *What Is Disruptive Innovation?*, Clayton M. Christensen , Michael E. Raynor and Rory McDonald, Harvard Business Review, from the December 2015 Issue (reproduced online).

Into the unknown with Purpose

In our race to innovate, to disrupt before we are disrupted, we often overlook what this entails—a clear Vision and a deliberate design process, underpinned by a specific mindset and a genuine understanding of what it all means. At the very foundation of this exciting and increasingly necessary pursuit, we must ask some simple questions in order to assess whether we are willing and able to embrace a culture of innovation. *Are we ready? Are we brave enough?* Wading into the unknown requires courage and belief—because we are collectively designing in real time. And while hacking and incremental innovation are valuable approaches, game-changing innovation requires a bigger leap. This is all part of the design process—whether that's starting from scratch, or hacking an existing idea. Either way, it requires bringing the entire organisation on board with this process, ensuring staff are aware of the journey, and their role in it. This also adds to the brand—and the perceptions being shaped around it, particularly if pursuing innovation is a widely recognised pattern of behaviour in the business. With that in mind, it's vital to align everything you do with the Values, culture, impact and Purpose of the brand before communicating this clearly to staff and customers, packaged as a set of value propositions that are easily understood, and backed up with the potential for customer expectations to be met on a daily basis. Although this might sound daunting, Roosegaarde offers some encouraging words of advice:

"The true sense of innovation is redefining the Purpose. Who you are, what you want and how are we going to do it? And having the guts to question that." [10]

---

10. *Prototyping the future of cities,* page 26.

About Purpose

Over the past decade, or so, there's been an increased emphasis on the importance of *Purpose-driven* brands. This heightened interest has been framed in terms of a business' obligations to society, as much as being an opportunity for them to bolster their bottom line. However, the understanding of Purpose (with a capital *P*) seems to vary, from something deeply embedded in a company, through to shallow attempts at marketing spin as businesses jump on the 'buzzword' bandwagon. So, what's it all about? What defines a Purpose-driven brand?

When it comes to being Purpose-driven, we immediately think of social causes, charities, perhaps an alignment with the environment or a minority group. Historically, the business world has referred to this as *Corporate Social Responsibility* (CSR), but now it goes far deeper than this. Now it's about being guided by a clear and articulated social impact model that's central to the DNA of the business or brand, and one which staff and customers alike believe in and support. But it's important to first distinguish the difference between *'working with purpose'* versus a *'Purpose-driven business'*.

People 'working with purpose' are clear and determined about their roles. They know their KPIs, perhaps feel appreciated by management and have a good grasp of what they expect to get in return from their employer—whether that's monetary reward, improved status, or a career path, etc. This is different to being 'Purpose-driven', where support for a specific issue or cause underpins the business as a whole, and where every employee understands that their job is contributing to something bigger than themselves, and bigger than the company; their job is a place where they can contribute to an issue, a cause or a community which aligns with their personal Values—and which may even be part of their personal identity.

However, a business' Purpose is not always clear or evident. For example, during the research phase of my client engagements I always ask staff, customers and Executives: *What is the business' core Purpose, beyond making a profit?* Many are either unsure or unaware. Others adamantly respond with: *"Isn't a business' purpose to make money?"* This line of response is not surprising. In fact, many expand on it by adding that the Purpose is: *'to be a profitable business'*; *"to develop a sustainable business"*; *"to increase EBIT"* (Earnings Before Interest and Taxes); or, more broadly, *"to create shareholder value"*; etc. While these are all valid pursuits in the commercial world, it's important to clarify that making money is not a Purpose. It's a *function* of business. It's an *objective*; an *outcome*.

To be frank, 'making money' for the business is hardly a compelling Purpose for staff, who won't necessarily share in those riches. Or for customers, who might feel they're being treated as cash-cows. But that doesn't mean businesses should ignore the need to make a profit. It just means it's also important to be driven by something deeper, something that's now often referred to as *'Purpose with Profit'*. While this can often sound like a catchy advertising slogan (and it's often used as such) there is mounting evidence that it has become a significant factor for successful businesses.

The Purpose-driven generation

It's vital to point out, *Purpose with Profit* should not merely be used as some glib marketing tactic or trend. There are tangible motivations (and results) driving this shift, and it's largely being spearheaded by Millennials and Generation Z (GenZ). For example, in the book *Good Is The New Cool: Market Like You Give A Damn*, authors Afdhel Aziz and Bobby Jones point to some compelling developments driving this specific shift in consumer behaviour:

"Younger generations want experiences over products, sharing versus sole ownership, and entrepreneurship over employment." [1]

This is a vastly different consumer landscape than the traditional one—held for decades—where companies advertised their wares and customers simply bought them. As Aziz and Jones highlight:

---

1. *Good Is The New Cool: Market Like You Give A Damn*, Afdhel Aziz and Bobby Jones, Regan Arts, 2016, page 24.

"According to the 2015 Cone Communications Millennial CSR Study, 91 per cent would switch brands to one associated with a cause (versus the US average of 85 per cent). In addition, the report states this group is also more likely to purchase a product with a social or environmental benefit, and volunteer for a cause supported by a company they trust." [2]

They cite influential American author and educator, Anna Lappé, to hit home the point:

"Every time you spend money, you're casting a vote for the type of world [you] want to live in." [3]

Why is this important for businesses to recognise? Because it relates to a wider perception of *trust*—or the lack of it. Although a genuine sense of Purpose can dramatically increase trust, a business or brand cannot simply assume trust. It must be earned—through consistent actions and behaviours. And while some businesses might identify these emerging consumer groups as an important—or a potentially profitable—target audience, approaching them using traditional marketing, rather than being Purpose-driven, isn't connecting with them, and won't. But does that matter? There are businesses and brands who might argue their customer demographic doesn't (currently) include Millennials or GenZ and therefore might be less inclined to respond to these emerging market shifts. But that's short-sighted, because it's an enormous and maturing customer base. In fact, according to *FastCompany*:

"Millennials and Gen Z are expected to account for 45% of all luxury spending by 2025", which is why brand heavyweights *"Louis Vuitton, Gucci, and Hermès are battling for young consumers."* [4]

---

2. *Good Is The New Cool: Market Like You Give A Damn*, page 25.
3. *Good Is The New Cool: Market Like You Give A Damn*, page 25.
4. *Inside the luxury industry's fight for millennials' hearts, minds, and wallets*, Elizabeth Segran, FastCompany, online article, 22 July 2019.

•

"Every time you spend money, you're casting a vote for the type of world [you] want to live in."

•

It's worth noting, Millennials and GenZ are also future business owners and leaders who will shape the world according to their Values. Indeed, they're already doing so. And, as consumers, they have the means and motivation to talk about businesses and brands on numerous digital platforms, whether or not they're customers of those brands. This ability to 'call out' or discuss a brand's behaviour is now so powerful, even young children are in a position to impact a company. The pressure that can be applied to mega brands and organisations is unprecedented, and cannot be ignored. But how much pressure can younger people really apply? Quite a bit, as it turns out.

The new power of public pressure

In 2019, sisters Caitlin and Ella McEwan (aged 7 and 9 respectively) approached *McDonald's* directly about their concerns around something they had learned at school: the devastating ecological implications that small plastic toys given away with *Happy Meals* were having. When they received no response, they set up a *change.org* petition which very deliberately presented their call-to-arms:

"We like to go to eat at Burger King and McDonald's, but children only play with the plastic toys they give us for a few minutes before they get thrown away and harm animals and pollute the sea... We want anything they give to us to be sustainable so we can protect the planet for us and for future generations." [5]

In early July, 2019, the petition had over 399,000 signatures, with a goal of 500,000. Although the sisters' direct approach to *McDonald's* (appealing for them to do the right thing) had failed, these two concerned kids—at the helm of nearly 400,000 people—didn't give up and instead pressured *McDonald's* into listening. What was the brand's response to the children's petition?:

---

5. *McDonald's might make Happy Meals a little happier, and not because of 'The Lion King'*, Melissa Locker, FastCompany, online article, 19 July 2019.

"In the UK over the next six months our Happy Meal promotions will include a mixture of board games, books and soft toys—which will see an almost 60% reduction in the number of hard plastic toys given away in comparison to the first half of the year." [6]

Two young girls and a petition achieved this change. It's clear the next generations are acutely aware of the impact businesses and brands are having on the environment and social issues. And they understand this will have a direct impact on their own futures, and want to support businesses who are looking to address these problems with tangible solutions. Not because it's good for business, or because it's their obligation, but because it's simply the right thing to do. Truly Purpose-driven businesses and brands understand this and are willing to rise to the task. This is the new reality—and it's more important than ever to build your brand with Values, ethics, with Purpose at its heart, and a determination to do the right thing by society. Younger generations are only going to get more influential as they mature. And if that's not compelling enough, consider this: Millennials and GenZ are already employees, and they're making decisions on vastly different criteria than before. According to Aziz and Jones:

"Increasingly, Millennials want to work for companies that have a higher purpose than just making a profit—the kind of ethical stakeholder-driven companies that think about people and the planet, not just profit. According to Deloitte's 2015 Millennial Survey, [for] a staggering 84 percent of Millennials making a positive difference in the world is more important than professional recognition. And six out of ten Millennials said a sense of purpose (more than just making a profit) is part of the reason they chose to work for their current employer." [7]

---

6. *McDonald's might make Happy Meals a little happier, and not because of 'The Lion King'.*
7. *Good Is The New Cool: Market Like You Give A Damn,* page 26.

Now, before you think I've drunk the kool-aid and have dusted off my soap box, let's take a deep breath. While being Purpose-driven is becoming increasingly common—or, at least, awareness of it is growing—there are very good reasons why we need to proceed with caution. Skepticism is warranted because Purpose is already being overstated, co-opted, misrepresented and misunderstood by opportunists seeking to (smoke and) mirror businesses and brands who are genuinely committed to conscious capitalism; those who rarely—if ever—call their organisations Purpose-driven but, instead, allow their actions and behaviours to consistently present visible and tangible evidence. So, when it comes to being Purpose-orientated, not all businesses and brands are equal. According to British marketing, communications and brand strategist, Tom Roach, there are three different versions of businesses we should be aware of:

1. **Born Purposeful:** *These are often founder-led and typically began with a societal Purpose already embedded within—and across—their entire organisation.*

2. **Corporate Converts:** *Have often only recently adopted a Purpose-driven approach, but who genuinely want to make a positive difference in the world—alongside making money. They might need to correct past transgressions, or just want to become a better corporate citizen. However, they may not yet have a business model built around their Purpose, and their culture may still be in transition.*

3. **Pseudo-purposeful:** *These tend to adopt Purpose purely for a new ad campaign, claiming to solve some social issue, which they have identified as being important to whatever demographic they're currently targeting. They will embrace whatever dominant issue is likely to paint them in a good light but it's unlikely that any suddenly declared Purpose will take root within the organisation.*[8]

---

8. *Brand purpose. The biggest lie the ad industry ever told?*, by Tom Roach, online blog article, 13 November 2020.

Obviously, being pseudo-purposeful is short-term, short-lived and short-sighted. And while we shouldn't view every declaration of Purpose with skepticism, we absolutely should judge a business or brand by their actions and behaviours. We *should* hold them accountable for the promises they make.

Redefining 'Good'

With so much focus on being Purpose-driven, but not much definition around it, confusion is inevitable. This could be due to a genuine lack of understanding. Or perhaps it's fuelled by a deeper cynicism, where businesses see 'Purpose' as novel, but not really a core business requirement. So, what might be influencing business owners to think like this? Well, for a start, the idea of being Purpose-driven has traditionally been understood as the purview of *Non-government Organisations (NGOs)*. The *Oxford Dictionary* definition of an NGO is: *"A non-profit organisation that operates independently of any government, typically one whose purpose is to address a social or political issue."* This doesn't sound like the definition of an average traditional business. In commercial terms, addressing a social or political issue has previously been low on most businesses' list of objectives—outside of any CSR activities— due to a stronger motivation to make a profit, to grow the business, to deliver shareholder value, and a fear of taking sides. But all of this is changing significantly, as we'll see from a number of examples throughout this chapter. For example, I asked David Ohana (who spent 11 years at the *United Nations*, five of them as global Chief of Brand Building at *UNICEF*) whether he was optimistic or suspicious about the rise of Purpose-driven brands and businesses:

"I am incredibly optimistic about the idea of Purpose-driven brands. Gone are the days when [brands and businesses] would hire a Corporate Social Responsibility (CSR) person—often a team of one— essentially to tick a box and create tokenistic change. Purpose has to be in the absolute DNA of an organisation. If not, it becomes harder and harder for brands to engage consumers, to hire the best and the brightest, and then to retain them. Millennials and Gen Z have finely-tuned 'BS-detectors', enormous purchasing power and most

will switch for a good cause—so if I'm a brand, or an employer, that's pretty hard to ignore. If you're doing good, you're no longer seen as an 'outlier'. Purpose is becoming mainstreamed, and that's good for our kids, our businesses, and our planet." [9]

Essentially, Ohana is suggesting that big brands can make a big difference by being ethical. But his view isn't idealism. With exponentially more resources, larger budgets and numerous paypoints within their supply chain, the *UN* is learning from observing brands like *Coca-Cola* about new ways to distribute aid to the farthest reaches of the globe. So, when it comes to being Purpose-driven, Ohana believes there are obvious crossovers between the NGO world and the private sector. This new relationship is now steeped in a more engaging and mutually beneficial arrangement, and it's all being underpinned by having a clear (and bigger) Purpose at its heart. Whether a business partners with an NGO, or whether it's driven by a belief in a cause or an issue, the Purpose must genuinely show up in the actions and behaviours of the business. It can't be superficial. As Ohana points out:

"A clearly defined Purpose can't just be a list of words on a poster in the boardroom. It has to be at the heart of everything the brand does— both the compass and the map. From each decision made, to supply chains and partners, to the way in which staff conduct themselves— the purpose has to be ingrained in the fabric and character of the organisation and anyone who represents them." [10]

The business of Purpose

Aside from the benefits of attracting—and retaining—the best and brightest staff, which has a direct impact on productivity, being Purpose-driven can also positively impact a business' bottom line. To illustrate, Ohana offers a striking example of how businesses partnering with *UNICEF* has helped enormously while offering additional insight into consumer trends and preferences at a societal level:

---

9. David Ohana, interview by author, April 2019.
10. David Ohana, interview by author.

•

"Purpose has to be in the absolute DNA of an organisation. If not, it becomes harder and harder for brands to engage consumers, to hire the best and the brightest, and then to retain them."

•

"We had a team who worked to measure UNICEF's brand value in financial terms. In conversations with potential partners it's always helpful to have case studies showing not only significant social impact—but also partner results above and beyond just the 'feel-good' factor. One example is Pampers nappies. UNICEF has had a longstanding relationship with P&G to eliminate maternal and neonatal tetanus which has helped save nearly 1 million newborns. While UNICEF never endorses any product or service, there was an increase in sales of the Pampers packs which bore the UNICEF logo and partnership information. Both a compelling impact and business case. The best and most sustainable relationships require all parties to benefit. And if a great deal of good is achieved in the process, everyone wins." [11]

There is an obvious correlation between nappies/diapers and *UNICEF*, because they're both relevant to children. And while this example might not suggest *Pampers* is Purpose-driven, per se, just because of its partnership with *UNICEF*, it does clearly show how *aligning* with a Purpose can positively impact the business, the NGO and, ultimately, children in need. The significant spike in sales also illustrates how this is resonating deeply with customers, and society, in general. In short: Purpose must have genuine impact and it's often the impact model that will ensure a Purpose-driven business has the required reach. However, as Ohana suggests, Purpose *must* be in a brand's DNA. And Anne Miltenburg agrees:

"The trend of businesses led by Purpose has been gaining incredible momentum in the past decade. And the success of certain brands like Patagonia or TOMS leads to a lot of anecdotal evidence that Purpose is key to commercial success. I have two big points to raise there though. First, I think we need to be very sharp on definitions: what does that actually mean and, second, we need to be a little more critical about the standards we set (or fail to set). For example, in a major piece of research into the effect of Purpose on performance, the list of companies that are supposedly

---

11. David Ohana, interview by author.

Purpose-driven is pretty surprising: a champagne brand that 'exists to turn every occasion into a celebration'. Is that truly a Purpose-driven company? It's great copy writing, and it could probably just narrowly pass the requirements of a Purpose bigger than your own self-interest. But still, you have to wonder.

The Purpose-driven trend has been around for [over] a decade, but our thinking around it hasn't really matured. There is a difference between being Purpose-driven and being a social enterprise. A social enterprise is created to develop a sustainable business model that can address a social or environmental issue at a systems level. These organisations are trying to solve the complex financial constructions that charities and NGOs struggle with. TOMS Shoes is often called a social enterprise. But I'd say it's more a business with a philanthropic arm: for each shoe that is sold, one is given away. The TOMS model doesn't really tackle the causes of poverty that lead to people needing a pair of free shoes to begin with. They undermine the local shoe market. And they don't provide jobs at a local level.

The companies that I would call true to the definition of social enterprise would definitely fall in the innovative category. They want to create change, but they start with where people's needs are not being met. If you are an animal rights activist, and you want people to stop killing and eating animals, you want meat eaters to embrace a plant-based diet. Yet for decades, the vegetarian/vegan food industry was focussed on vegetarians, and their brands were based on the absence of meat. But that's not appealing to meat eaters. What does appeal to them is flavour and health, and that's where new innovative companies have focussed. If we want to change the trajectory of our planet, we need to meet people where they are. And brands are a great vehicle for that. We shouldn't be selling vegetarian burgers to vegetarians. We should be selling them to meat eaters—and as many [of them] as possible. If done ethically, brands could play a major role in these transitions." [12]

---

12. *Branding for change (part 2)*, Anne Miltenburg in conversation with Kevin Finn for DESIGNerd, online article, April 2018. Revised slightly in 2022 by Anne Miltenburg.

The big end of town

Let's be clear. None of this is easy. It takes clarity and effort to be Purpose-driven. Indeed, I've had conversations with business leaders who confess that the idea of being a social enterprise or Purpose-driven business from the start sounds easier than transforming an existing, often traditional business that's set in its ways. The thought of having a blank canvas appeals to them, and while their ambition might be to become more Purpose-driven, sometimes those hurdles can be used as an excuse for avoiding a more Purpose-driven path. Well that's all about to change. We're no longer looking to the social enterprise sector to forge a way forward when it comes to being commercially Purpose-driven. That requirement has now broadened to include the biggest and most significant enterprises in the world. And whether those enterprises take up the mantle or not will determine how some of the most influential business leaders will view them in the future. Not convinced? Well, in 2018, Larry Fink, Chairman and CEO of *BlackRock* (the world's largest asset manager, with US$9.5 trillion in assets under management, as of October, 2021[13]) used his annual Letter to CEOs to drive home this point.

"We also see many governments failing to prepare for the future, on issues ranging from retirement and infrastructure to automation and worker retraining. As a result, society increasingly is turning to the private sector and asking that companies respond to broader societal challenges. Indeed, the public expectations of your company have never been greater. Society is demanding that companies, both public and private, serve a social purpose. To prosper over time, every company must not only deliver financial performance, but also show how it makes a positive contribution to society. Companies must benefit all of their stakeholders, including shareholders, employees, customers, and the communities in which they operate.

"Without a sense of purpose, no company, either public or private, can achieve its full potential. It will ultimately lose the license

---

13. *BlackRock,* Wikipedia.

•

"Without a sense of purpose, no company, either public or private, can achieve its full potential. It will ultimately lose the license to operate from key stakeholders."

•

to operate from key stakeholders. It will succumb to short-term pressures to distribute earnings, and, in the process, sacrifice investments in employee development, innovation, and capital expenditures that are necessary for long-term growth. It will remain exposed to activist campaigns that articulate a clearer goal, even if that goal serves only the shortest and narrowest of objectives. And ultimately, that company will provide subpar returns to the investors who depend on it to finance their retirement, home purchases, or higher education." [14]

It's worth noting, Fink wasn't 'jumping on the bandwagon'. This is a position he's held for over two decades. However, his 2018 Letter to CEOs signals a turning point in his campaign, and due to the significant standing *BlackRock* commands in the business community, Fink has put CEOs on notice. And it's being echoed by the groundswell from Millennials, GenZ and societal shifts.

Building Purpose-driven brands

This is another bow in the argument that a brand is not built on things such as logos, websites and branding alone. Becoming a brand is a whole-of-organisation commitment, fulfilled over the long-term. And one that now needs to include being Purpose-driven as a priority. Branding designers can provide businesses with a blueprint, a path forward and a clear direction. They can develop tools and frameworks, supported by appropriate messaging that will focus a business on specific objectives. However, it's still just a pathway. The business or brand must follow and build upon it—well after the branding designer is out of the picture. It's the business, as a whole, that must take ownership and responsibility for building its brand through providing value, but also by living its Values, ethics and Purpose.

However, for businesses struggling to express their bigger Purpose, setting time aside to figure it out, to articulate it properly, isn't easy. But it's incredibly important to get right. It needs to be clear—and

---

14. *A sense of Purpose, Larry Fink's 2018 Letter To CEOs,* Larry Fink, BlackRock, online article.

genuine. As Fink stated in his 2018 Letter to CEOs, Purpose is now central to a business' licence to operate. This illustrates, once again, just how important it is for a business to identify its Purpose because it needs to be embedded in its Values and behaviour; it should be visible in the organisational culture, and tangible in its actions. Still, it can be difficult for businesses to articulate their bigger Purpose, primarily because most business owners are in operational mode, grappling with numerous issues on a daily basis. Equally, identifying a Purpose can be interpreted as a management decision, where staff are excluded by not being engaged or included in that conversation. Naturally, this is a flawed approach. In fact, it's frightening how many business owners are missing the point (and opportunity) when it comes to Purpose. As *Forbes* highlighted:

"79% of business leaders surveyed by PwC believe that an organisation's purpose is central to business success, yet 68% shared that purpose is not used as a guidepost in leadership decision-making processes within their organisation... Fresh consumer data shows that customers view purpose-driven brands as being more caring and, as a result, are more loyal to them. Yet, there is a gap between what business leaders believe their purpose to be and what their behaviors suggest their purpose truly is." [15]

Leading by example

Considering the importance of all this, it might be worth defining what being Purpose-driven actually means. Here's my definition:

Being Purpose-driven means putting something incredibly important—something that has a bigger and wider positive impact in the world—above and before making a profit.

While that might sound simplistic—or even idealistic—it gets to the heart of the issue. But how does that play out in practical terms? Well, let's take *Patagonia* as an example. Their alignment and

---

15. *Purpose-Driven Companies Evolve Faster Than Others,* Caterina Bulgarella, Forbes, online article, 21 December 2018.

concern for the environment has been baked into their business from the beginning. Over time it has become one of the brand's defining characteristics, supported, pursued and championed by legions of customers. *Patagonia* has simply been consistent on their Purpose, and have made a number of significant decisions because of it. For example, from a marketing point of view, while many companies have adopted 'built-in obsolescence' within their products, or they bombard customers with new versions of the same products, *Patagonia* is well-known for adverts that suggest customers repair their *Patagonia* clothing rather than buy new ones, since this is better practice for the environment. (*The North Face* has since followed suit.) Again, on 8 November 2016, during the U.S. Presidential election, *Patagonia* closed all of its stores, urging staff and customers to vote for candidates who expressed explicit support for clean water, clean air, and renewable energy. Obviously, while the decision to close stores had an impact on their profits for that specific day, cynics will point out it was just for one day. However, while other companies also closed their stores that day, *Patagonia* were explicit in their request for people to vote for environmentally-minded candidates. And, of course, critics could also justifiably claim the adverts, which suggest mending clothes, is just a smart marketing tactic. So, let's look further into how *Patagonia* puts Purpose before profit.

From the outset, President Trump's 2018 company tax reform wasn't something *Patagonia* supported. Their view is that companies should pay taxes—because taxes serve a broader societal function. True to form, Rose Marcario, *Patagonia's* then CEO, was uncompromising:

"Taxes protect the most vulnerable in our society, our public lands and other life-giving resources. In spite of this, the Trump administration initiated a corporate tax cut, threatening these services at the expense of our planet. Being a responsible company means paying your taxes in proportion to your success and supporting your state and federal governments, which in turn contribute to the health and

*well-being of civil society. Taxes fund our important public services,
our first responders and our democratic institutions. We are giving
away this tax cut to the planet, our only home, which needs it now
more than ever."* [16]

Patagonia received a considerable tax cut ($10 million) from the
newly enshrined tax reform. However, rather than just criticise the
tax reform (but keep the money, anyway) *Patagonia* donated all of
it to a number of environmental groups. That's an incredible—but
consistent—decision to take, and again puts a clear Purpose before
profit. Now, perhaps some readers might think: *"Well, Patagonia
can afford it."* Okay, let's address that. Think about the last tax
returns your business received. No matter how large or small, did
you consider donating it to something bigger than you, bigger
than your business, or something more important in a societal or
environmental way? This isn't about whether we can *afford* to do
something or not. It's about whether we *decide* to do something,
and whether that decision is consistent with our Values, our beliefs,
our Purpose, our behaviour and our desire to support something we
think is important, and which has a wider societal impact. However,
for argument's sake, let's say *Patagonia's* $10M tax windfall
decision was an isolated incident and might have been a marketing
ploy to grab positive PR headlines. But that just doesn't stack up,
because below is yet another example of how *Patagonia* is putting
Purpose before profit.

Over the years, co-branded *Patagonia* fleece and puffer vests (also
referred to as fleece jackets) have become incredibly popular in
corporate uniform wardrobes, particularly in the finance and
tech worlds which, as *Bloomberg* observes, is *"an odd turn for
an outdoor brand that sells everything from wetsuits to sleeping
bags."* [17] However, in early 2019, *Patagonia* publicly shifted their
client focus to "mission-driven companies that prioritise the planet,"

---

16. *Patagonia's $10 million donation: Why they gave away their US tax savings,* Caterina
    Bulgarella, Forbes, online article, 29 November 2018.
17. *Patagonia Is Cracking Down on the Wall Street Uniform,* Kim Bhasin, Bloomberg, online
    article, 3 April 2019.

•

Being Purpose-driven means putting something incredibly important— something that has a bigger and wider positive impact in the world—above and before making a profit.

•

particularly companies with *B Corp* status (businesses who meet specific environmental, social and transparency standards and who are certified by a private organisation). No doubt, this shift has had a significant impact on *Patagonia's* sales—and initially, it was probably a negative one. But by putting their Purpose well and truly before making a profit, this move has further cemented their reputation—and their brand status. According to *Bloomberg*:

"Patagonia was reluctant to sell co-branded gear with companies they consider 'ecologically damaging,' such as the oil and mining industries. It also singled out religious groups, political-affiliated organizations and financial institutions." [18]

Whether this resonates with you or not, it is an incredibly clear articulation of their Values, beliefs and ethics. It's also a clarion call for like-minded people. *Bloomberg* went on to report:

"Late last year [2018], Patagonia updated its mission statement, saying, 'We're in business to save our home planet.' [19]

That is an enormously ambitious Mission, and one that has clear implications for the types of clients, customers, products and suppliers *Patagonia* is willing to do business with. But it's a position many of its customers will continue to support. Not only is this statement incredibly clear, they've already been pursuing it for decades.

We can see from these examples that decisions have been made for the greater good, from a strongly held belief in the business, and how the returns—not only in reputational capital, but also in customer loyalty—have impacted the business, and the community, in a positive way. With a clearly defined Purpose, and a consistent position on something meaningful, these decisions become far easier to make. They start to define your business or brand—and this becomes your *filter*. How this affects organisational culture cannot

---

18. *Patagonia Is Cracking Down on the Wall Street Uniform.*
19. *Patagonia Is Cracking Down on the Wall Street Uniform.*

be underestimated. When a company is clear about its Purpose—
which is informed by its Values—it attracts like-minded people, in
terms of staff and customers. Without even realising it, what you
stand for becomes central to how you operate your business.

Purposeful decisions

George Lois, one of the original 1960s Advertising *'Mad Men'*, once
shared a wonderfully brave story with me, which again illustrates
how Purpose and consistency of Values—over the pursuit of making
money—can positively impact a business and define a brand.

*"I lost a lot of business by showing who I am. [For example] in 1975,
when I got Muhammad Ali to join me and start raising hell about
Rubin Hurricane Carter, who was absolutely screwed and had
already been in jail for 15 years or so for supposedly killing three
white people. I got dozens of celebrities to back us, and I was raising
hell with getting Rubin Hurricane Carter out of jail. He was being
depicted as this 'crazed nigger.'* [†] *I lost two big accounts because of it.
One client called me in and said, 'Stop working for the nigger.' I said,
'Well, I'm not gonna stop working for him because the guy's innocent.'
He said, 'Lois, I just told you—if you don't stop working for the nigger,
you're fired.' I said, 'Well, I guess I'm fired—so go fuck yourself.'*

*"So, I lost the client, who at that time was my biggest account. It was
a six million dollar account and I walked out. I went back and told
everybody in the agency. You know, when you tell people that you lost
a big account, everybody's scared shitless that they might get fired,
right? I remember I called everybody in, and there was like 60 people.
I told them the story: 'I told the guy to go fuck himself so the account
is gone.' But, you know, 60 people gave me a standing ovation. How's
that for good people? People who understood what I was about;
somehow I picked the kind of people that I wanted to work with, you
know? People who cared about doing good things, about helping the
poor people and helping the disadvantaged, and doing things like
fighting racial injustice—all of the good stuff that I learned from my*

---

†   This word has been included to illustrate the offensive racism Lois was fighting against.

father, to tell you the truth. So I was controversial from that point of view, but it was funny the way I lost accounts but not my reputation... I've got a reputation for being some kind of legend." [20]

That reputation (and leadership) defined his personal brand, and over his career he attracted an incredible array of client work and creative talent. Among many other things, he used that same bravery to create the ground-breaking campaign *"I want my MTV"* with Mick Jagger, which essentially helped bring the pioneering business back from the brink of bankruptcy; he helped make the previously unknown *Tommy Hilfiger* into a household name almost overnight; and he also largely defined the era through his socially informed and politically charged cover designs for *Esquire* magazine. While Lois' decision to take such a strong stand might have been unusual over 40 years ago, it's becoming more common today. Increasingly, organisations driven by deep-set Values and a desire to simply do the right thing, are leading the way—some of them quietly—but with immense impact and, in some cases, with phenomenal reach. They understand they're part of a wider community, and that their actions and behaviours will affect it.

Responding to responsibility
Brands and businesses shouldn't just see themselves as having an 'obligation' to help a community. Instead, they should see themselves as *part* of the community, and if they're in a position to contribute to the wider wellbeing of that community they should want to do so—willingly. No matter how big or small your business is, partnering with people on the ground (local organisations who have a better grasp of what's needed) not only brings more relevant information to the table, it shares the burden and co-owns the solution, which in turn empowers far more people within a networked community to act. That's the basis of a genuine impact model. David Ohana touches on this exact point:

---

20. *George Lois: The Man and the Myth,* George Lois in conversation with Kevin Finn for Open Manifesto Issue#6: Myth, 2012, page 235.

"[A purpose-driven brand] needs to understand what they're good (and not-so-good) at. For private sector brands hoping to change the world, or end poverty—there's plenty to be learnt from organisations and professionals who've been working on these issues for years, who know what they're doing but often don't have the resources. So, we just need to work better together. I've seen numerous examples of well-meaning actions gone wrong—but equally, when a public/ private partnership 'works', the results can be truly world-changing— and the world needs more of these collaborations right now." [21]

As Ohana points out, good intentions are admirable, but they're not enough on their own. In some cases, they could even unintentionally end up making things worse. By partnering with others, solutions can be identified and then actioned appropriately. And rather than beating ourselves up, or giving ourselves guilt-trips about how we're now *expected* to be Purpose-driven, we could try revising our approach. Instead of: *"This is something we're expected to do"*, we could change to, *"This is something we decide to do."* That simple shift will foster a completely different mindset and approach. Striking a similar tone, Hamdi Ulukaya (founder of yogurt brand *Chobani*) says:

"Companies shouldn't approach communities with their hand out. Instead, businesses should go to struggling communities and ask, 'How can I help you?'... Go search for communities that you can be part of. Ask for permission and succeed together." [22]

Can you scale Purpose?
Successfully scaling a culture is a difficult task. What might be working smoothly at the early stages of a business can become undone as the company grows. So, scaling a Purpose-driven culture must be especially hard. And yet, there are cases that prove this is not only possible, but that it's beneficial on many levels. It just takes a different approach and mindset. Once again, it comes down to making a deliberate decision to simply do the right thing—even

---

21. David Ohana, interview by author.
22. *The anti-CEO Playbook,* Hamdi Ulukaya, TED Talk, online video, April, 2019.

when you're taking a leap into the unknown. For example, in 2012, Michael Lastoria launched *&pizza* in Washington D.C. with self-confessed zero experience in the food industry. Instead, he was driven by a belief that he could positively impact the community in which his business was embedded. As it happens, his lack of experience and relative naivety became the driving force behind turning the traditional business model upside down—an approach that was built upon a deeply held set of Values: to simply do the right thing by people. From a practical point of view, when *&pizza* launched, Lastoria was incredibly nervous. But, in a video for *Inc.*, he shared how his motivation helped position the business with a Purpose-driven mindset from the outset:

"We were paying too much [to staff], we were using ingredients that didn't make sense economically. And I remember when we opened up our first pizza shop, we had one of the most inflated—both food and labour—costs that I've ever seen in an actual restaurant, because we were paying a living wage, [and] we were literally making everything from scratch with the highest quality ingredients that we could find. But fast forward to six months later, the word got out in the community that there was this really cool pizza shop, led by an amazing group of people that really cared about wage, and humanity, and community, and what it meant to be a good neighbour. And the lines started forming. And then the lines started going around the block. And all of a sudden, we couldn't make enough pizzas to sell, and that was the springboard that brought us from a single location in 8th Street, North Eastern Washington D.C., to well over 35 locations in six different markets, doubling the size of the company in the next 18 months, [because of] the fact that we did the right thing and we got rewarded for it, not just internally but externally... It's worth doing the right thing. It's worth putting humanity into a company because what you get out of it is the day-in, day-out reward of feeling good, and the day-in, day-out support from all of your people wanting you and the company to win, and having your back through thick and through thin." [23]

---

23. *When This CEO Shifted His Focus From Dollars to Employees, Things Changed Dramatically,* Michael Lastoria, Inc, online video, 20 December 2019.

Lastoria and *&pizza* are on a mission to do the right thing through leading by example. But also through on the ground activism, attending rallies, as well as addressing the 'Living Wage' issue in person on *Capitol Hill*, campaigning to raise it to $15 an hour. As a result, the staff and customers have rewarded the business through loyalty. But it doesn't stop there. During the 2018 US government shutdown—the longest shutdown in history—around 800,000 government employees were impacted. So, *&pizza* decided to step up:

"When the federal government shut down in December, I felt a responsibility to support Washington, D.C., and its greater community. They embraced my company when we launched back in 2012. They didn't have to. Now, it was our turn. As roughly 800,000 government employees and numerous contractors were left wondering when their next paychecks would arrive, we quickly offered free pizza to furloughed federal employees simply because it was the right thing to do." [24]

Now, when all is said and done, altruism is a wonderful thing, but from a commercial business perspective, Lastoria's decision was also an incredibly risky thing to do, right? And according to Matt Higgins, *&pizza* investor and Board Member, the decision was made abruptly by Lastoria alone.

"There wasn't even a planning meeting on it. Michael [Lastoria] just felt like it was the right thing to do, that we should support this community that supported us. [He said] 'We're just going to give away pizzas.' I said, that's all well and good, but did anybody model this out? How many pizzas are we going to give away? What's the plan? When will this end? And Michael's thought was: 'Don't worry about it. These are the same people that supported us. This is their greatest time of need and it'll work itself out.' And he was right." [25]

---

24. *3 Powerful Lessons From the Entrepreneur Who Gave Away 30,000 Pizzas During the Government Shutdown,* Michael Lastoria, Inc, online article, 11 February 2019.
25. *This Pizza Company Is Fighting to Raise Minimum Wage—And It's Made Them Profitable* Michael Lastoria, Inc, online video, 9 May 2019.

The reason Lastoria has made such unorthodox decisions is because they're part of the business' DNA and they're all consistent, in terms of the Values and beliefs underpinning them, because they're borne from a Purpose-driven mindset. As Lastoria explains:

"The common denominator for every brand during times like this is social responsibility. Activism is in &pizza's DNA. We're part of a community, and members of a community should look out for one another. That's what good people do, and that's how brands and private companies should behave: like people." [26]

Lastoria also knows that, for this to be truly genuine, authentic and actionable, it needs to be deep within the culture; it needs to be a whole-of-business belief:

"I knew our support would be meaningful only if my employees backed the decision and were willing to shift schedules to accommodate the increased demand and lines [of customers]. The timing of the shutdown also presented operational challenges, as many workers were out on vacation for the holidays. We were able to make it happen thanks to the fact that our employees were on board and aligned with our mission. Together, we're proud to have donated more than 30,000 [pizzas], to date." [27]

A Purpose-driven mindset

Fostering a genuine Purpose-driven mindset can help truly transform your business—and this can happen at any stage within a business' journey. Often, that transformation comes from personal life experiences. For example, in 2012, at the age of 25, Jessica Walsh became a partner in the influential New York-based design practice *Sagmeister Inc.* The business honoured this new partnership by changing its name to *Sagmeister & Walsh* and in less than a decade, the business grew even further in size and reputation, with Walsh taking an equal lead in the business.

---

26. *3 Powerful Lessons From the Entrepreneur Who Gave Away 30,000 Pizzas During the Government Shutdown.*
27. *3 Powerful Lessons From the Entrepreneur Who Gave Away 30,000 Pizzas During the Government Shutdown.*

While this sounds like an incredibly successful journey, like most things, it was marred by some challenging moments, and for Walsh, many of them were personal. It was some of these moments which, in 2019, prompted Walsh to set up her own creative agency—&Walsh—coinciding with Sagmeister's decision to take a step back from the business to work on more self-generated projects (a decision Walsh supports and says she will continue to collaborate on with Sagmeister). But what's interesting is the bigger Purpose and drive behind Walsh's decisions and the focus underpinning her practice. She says:

"As women, we are constantly told what we can or cannot do. It's been happening all our lives. At every step of the way, forces tried to tell me 'I couldn't' or 'I wouldn't.' My elementary school teacher told my parents I was too fearful and introverted and would never make it in this world. When suffering from severe depression and eating disorders as a teenager, a woman in the hospital told me she could tell I was one of the ones that would never recover. Even when we achieve success, our legitimacy is doubted. When I was named partner with Stefan at the age of 25, many men and women said (publicly!) that I only got the position because I [must have] slept with him. Can you imagine them saying that about a man? Then as a partner, I was ignored and talked down to by older men in more meetings than I care to remember." [28]

Sagmeister and Walsh's relationship remains strong—professionally and personally. But it's our life experiences which shape us and become our guiding principles. They make us who we are. For Walsh, that meant tackling some significant issues:

"The lack of representation in leadership [and] the pay gap for women and non-binary people has been a focus of mine through our non-profit initiative 'Ladies, Wine & Design'. This initiative was born out of personal experiences I had with sexism in our industry, not only

---

28. *&Walsh launches, joining the .1% of Women Founded Creative Agencies,* Jessica Walsh, &Walsh, online article, 23 July 2019.

from men but from other women. I found that sometimes women were unsupportive of one another, possibly because our chances of reaching the top are much slimmer than for men. The numbers say it all: 70% of design students are women, but only 5-11% of creative director positions are held by women. Only 0.1% of creative agencies are women-owned. POINT. ONE. PERCENT. How does this make any sense when women drive about 80% of consumer purchasing? Diversity in leadership at agencies drives profit.

"While we've made strides towards equality in the last few decades, we still have a long way to go. I'm determined to use &Walsh to expand on these social initiatives such as 'Ladies, Wine & Design', and I also want to implement these principles within our studio. I'm excited to build an agency that provides mentorship and equal opportunity for all to learn and grow creatively and climb the ranks towards leadership, if that's their desire. I also recognize that the career success or leadership track does not have to be the path for everyone, and I will implement paths for those who prefer to focus on their individual craft." [29]

Clearly, Walsh is determined to tackle some serious societal and business issues, including inequality for women and the struggle for genuine diversity more broadly. These values come from personal experiences and observations, not just an acknowledgment of what needs to be addressed. But rather than shift the business to align with a specific NGO or a not-for-profit with similar concerns, Walsh has simply embedded her principles and beliefs into the culture and DNA of the business (in a similar way as Michael Lastoria has done with *&pizza*) publicly declaring her position, and backing it up with action. She continues her client work as before, but with clearer intent, culture and Purpose embedded within the business itself. This was a decision that Walsh made—and then acted on. Yet, while Walsh's decision is Purpose-driven, it's also a reflection of smart business leadership. Her understanding of the female market isn't just about solidarity or blanket feminism. It's incredibly astute. According to the *Harvard Business Review*:

---

29. *&Walsh launches, joining the .1% of Women Founded Creative Agencies.*

"Women now drive the world economy. Globally, they control about $20 trillion in annual consumer spending, and that figure could climb as high as $28 trillion in the next five years. Their $13 trillion in total yearly earnings could reach $18 trillion in the same period. In aggregate, women represent a growth market bigger than China and India combined—more than twice as big, in fact. Given those numbers, it would be foolish to ignore or underestimate the female consumer. And yet many companies do just that, even ones that are confident they have a winning strategy when it comes to women." [30]

The article goes on to cite a 2008 *Boston Consulting Group* comprehensive study, which explored how women felt about their work and their lives, but also how they felt they were being served by businesses:

"It turned out there was lots of room for improvement. More than 12,000 women, from more than 40 geographies and a variety of income levels and walks of life, responded to our survey... Women feel vastly underserved. Despite the remarkable strides in market power and social position that they have made in the past century, they still appear to be undervalued in the marketplace and underestimated in the workplace. They have too many demands on their time and constantly juggle conflicting priorities—work, home, and family. Few companies have responded to their need for time-saving solutions or for products and services designed specifically for them. Although women control spending in most categories of consumer goods, too many businesses behave as if they had no say over purchasing decisions. Companies continue to offer them poorly conceived products and services and outdated marketing narratives that promote female stereotypes." [31]

With women driving approximately 80% of purchasing decisions, Walsh has highlighted a glaring business opportunity, one that's still being mishandled. Her Purpose serves to directly address this,

---

30. *The Female Economy,* Michael J. Silverstein and Kate Sayre, Harvard Business Review, from the September 2009 issue.
31. *The Female Economy.*

while also being aligned with potential business opportunities—in a collaborative, smart and sensitive manner. Focusing her business from a female perspective isn't a shallow tactic. Walsh is the same person she was before founding her independent firm, but her decision to actively pursue an openly Purpose-driven approach has led to a completely different intent for her business—one that is built into the DNA, and which, in its fledgling moments, is already a beacon for female leadership, equality, diversity and smart business. In the design and business worlds, Walsh is increasingly becoming an inspirational figure because she hasn't given up (on herself or her work). She's allowed herself to be vulnerable, she's practiced what she preaches, and she's taken risks. Her design work is a result of this, but I believe it's her Purpose-driven mindset that has fuelled her success as a designer and as a business leader.

Calling out bullshit

Ironically, cynicism and skepticism won't necessarily kill off Purpose, but enthusiasm might. With such strong and public pronouncements about being Purpose-driven, businesses and brands become far more visible. Unsurprisingly, this makes them more accountable for their actions—and justifiably so. Marketing spin aside, there are some businesses and brands who readily embrace the idea of being Purpose-driven, but only at a superficial level. For many of them, their Purpose might be genuinely in the DNA of the culture, but it's not embedded in the business model. This becomes problematic when the company is under pressure— and even more acute in times of crises. All of this can attract strong criticism from the wider community. Take *Everlane's* 'Radical Transparency' positioning as an example (which we'll revisit in more detail on page 160). One of the most prominent Purpose-driven startups in recent years, the Coronavirus pandemic exposed some glaring contradictions in the brand. As Rob Walker, writing for *Marker,* pointed out on *Medium*:

"One minute you're a virtuous and apparently successful company out to make the world a better place. The next, no less than [US Senator and 2020 Presidential hopeful] Bernie Sanders is calling

your business decisions 'morally unacceptable.' That's the whipsaw moment being experienced by Everlane, one of the more prominent 'mission-driven' startups in recent memory. And it's a telling example of the perils of the mission-driven strategy, particularly as companies are forced into crisis mode.

For consumer retail brands, and maybe startups, in particular, having a Mission that transcends maximising profits is a useful tool to attract employees as well as customers. Who doesn't want to work for a company whose purpose goes beyond selling more than stuff? And who doesn't want to purchase something that makes them feel like they are doing something good for the world? But what happens when profits evaporate? What happens when consumers, employees, and even erstwhile presidential candidates start critiquing your every frantic move through the lens of your highfalutin 'mission'? And if you can't uphold that 'mission' when it really counts, how much of a strategic misfire was declaring it in the first place?" [32]

This might sound harsh. And it might wrongly dismiss good intentions, which may well be still present within the business at a time of crises. But if those good intentions aren't embraced properly—not just within the business, but also in the business model—things can begin to fall apart quickly. And *Everlane* is not alone in this. *The Wing* (a network of women-focused clubs and co-working spaces) has faced even more scrutiny. Having been hailed as a shining light of the new wave of Purpose-driven startups, and having secured significant funding by venture-capital powerhouse *Sequoia Capital*, among others, *The Wing* appears to have fallen well short of its lofty aspirations. According to *The Wall Street Journal*:

"Today, the company is reeling, a casualty of both the Coronavirus pandemic and, before that, the enormous challenges for a business built on ideals trying to live up to its aspirations." [33]

---

32. *The Recession's Calling Bullshit on 'Mission-Driven' Companies Like Everlane,* Rob Walker, Marker/Medium, 13 April 2020.
33. *The Wing Aimed to Build a Business on Values. It Was a Struggle Even Before Coronavirus Hit,* Katherine Bindley, The Wall Street Journal, 20 April 2020.

•

"More than 9 out of 10 employees, we found, are willing to trade a percentage of their lifetime earnings for greater meaning at work. Across age and salary groups, workers want meaningful work badly enough that they're willing to pay for it."

•

Reports suggest *The Wing* has made a series of missteps, including vague directions over whether male guests could be admitted into the women-only club. A litany of accusations have ensued, including one member who said she heard a male voice at the door of the shower rooms where she was undressing, and when she turned towards the door it was closed quickly. Other members have reported complaints or concerns around racial harm and discrimination.[34]

Being Purpose-driven isn't easy, and it becomes even more difficult if the business or brand is more invested in promoting their Purpose than they are in implementing, managing and protecting it. Lofty ideals might sound attractive but, understandably, they also set expectations.

What now?

But that doesn't mean being Purpose-driven is purely a marketing tactic—unless that's how it's being deliberately deployed and promoted. In fact, those that have fallen short are a cautionary tale for anyone thinking of jumping on the bandwagon for purely opportunistic reasons. And for any skeptics who believe being Purpose-driven is a passing fad, there is enough evidence that this approach is not only a good strategy, or offers a competitive advantage, but that it brings a deeper sense of empathy, of community, of humanity, and that this is genuinely connecting with staff and customers alike. The successful examples in this chapter just scratch the surface of a movement that's steadily gaining momentum. In 2018, *BetterUp* (an organisation dedicated to "helping professionals everywhere to pursue their lives with greater clarity, purpose, and passion") produced a report focusing on *Meaning and Purpose at Work*, which surveyed the experience of 2,285 American professionals, across 26 industries and a range of pay levels, company sizes, and demographics. The results stunned the authors.

---

34. *The Wing Aimed to Build a Business on Values. It Was a Struggle Even Before Coronavirus Hit.*

"More than 9 out of 10 employees, we found, are willing to trade a percentage of their lifetime earnings for greater meaning at work. Across age and salary groups, workers want meaningful work badly enough that they're willing to pay for it. The trillion dollar question, then, was just how much is meaning worth to the individual employee? If you could find a job that offered you consistent meaning, how much of your current salary would you be willing to forego? We asked this of our 2,000+ respondents. On average, our pool of American workers said they'd be willing to forego 23% of their entire future lifetime earnings in order to have a job that was always meaningful. The magnitude of this number supports one of the findings from Shawn [Achor's] recent study on the Conference for Women. In a survey of attendees, he found that nearly 80% of the respondents would rather have a boss who cared about them finding meaning and success in work than receive a 20% pay increase. To put this figure in perspective, consider that Americans spend about 21% of their incomes on housing. Given that people are willing to spend more on meaningful work than on putting a roof over their heads, the 21st century list of essentials might be due for an update: "food, clothing, shelter—and meaningful work." [35]

Regardless of company size or sector, it's clear that having a Purpose-driven mindset, with a tangible impact model built into the DNA of your business, is not only ethical, it's essential. The statistics, data and evidence in support of this movement is becoming overwhelming, and its depth and range is increasing at a staggering rate. When we consider the importance of Purpose to consumers, employees, society and a growing number of business leaders, it's hard to argue where the trends are heading. From Larry Fink's annual letters putting CEOs on notice, to Jessica Walsh championing gender equality, female leadership and opportunity in her business model; whether your similar in scale to *Patagonia* or *&pizza*; or regardless of whether you're a seasoned veteran CEO or a seven-year-old child; being Purpose-driven is now expected. And

---

35. *9 Out of 10 People Are Willing to Earn Less Money to Do More-Meaningful Work*, Shawn Achor, Andrew Reece, Gabriella Rosen Kellerman, and Alexi Robichaux, Harvard Business Review, online article, 6 November 2018.

●

"Purpose is not the sole pursuit of profits but the animating force for achieving them."

●

where some have fallen short of delivering on this promise, enough have proven that it's more than achievable. In many cases, deciding to take a Purpose-driven path has been a deliberate decision—a *mindset*. Think of it this way: Bruce Mau (author, designer and global leader in innovation) once said:

"Companies don't need a CSR department, a department of 'good'. If CSR is a 'department', what does that say about the CEO's office, or the rest of the organisation?" [36]

But there is yet another important factor at play in all of this, and which relates directly to doing good and remaining profitable: it's about being—and remaining—relevant. Afdhel Aziz and Bobby Jones sum it up perfectly:

"Thus it is clear that building purpose-driven companies and brands that practice purpose-driven marketing is not only crucial for survival today but for ensuring you 'future-proof' yourself for the next two generations of customers and talent." [37]

Brands fail or die when they begin to under-perform, or when they start to lose relevance. So, from a *Purpose with Profit* perspective, there are obvious opportunities and benefits for businesses and brands if the right Values, motivation and mindset are in place. Echoing this, in his 2019 *Letter to CEOs*, Larry Fink doubled down on the importance of Purpose for all business leaders who are invested in navigating the future:

"I wrote last year that every company needs a framework to navigate this difficult landscape, and that it must begin with a clear embodiment of your company's purpose in your business model and corporate strategy. Purpose is not a mere tagline or marketing campaign; it is a company's fundamental reason for being—what it does every day to create value for its stakeholders. Purpose is not the

---

36. Mentioned in a keynote presentation at the *Semi Permanent Conference*, Auckland, 15 August 2019.
37. *Good Is The New Cool: Market Like You Give A Damn*, page 27.

sole pursuit of profits but the animating force for achieving them. Profits are in no way inconsistent with purpose—in fact, profits and purpose are inextricably linked. Profits are essential if a company is to effectively serve all of its stakeholders over time—not only shareholders, but also employees, customers, and communities. Similarly, when a company truly understands and expresses its purpose, it functions with the focus and strategic discipline that drive long-term profitability. Purpose unifies management, employees, and communities. It drives ethical behavior and creates an essential check on actions that go against the best interests of stakeholders. Purpose guides culture, provides a framework for consistent decision-making, and, ultimately, helps sustain long-term financial returns for the shareholders of your company." [38]

Just think about what that world will look like—the problems we will collectively solve, and how businesses and brands will be rewarded for doing so; where NGOs, the private sector and the public will work in collaboration to build a better future—one that is as profitable as it is positively impactful. And just think about how you might be able to contribute to that world, a world that is currently being deliberately designed from top to bottom. It leaves us with one obvious question: Where do you see yourself in this new emerging reality?

---

38. *Purpose & Profit, Larry Fink's 2019 Letter To CEOs,* Larry Fink, BlackRock, online article.

15 Brand Principles

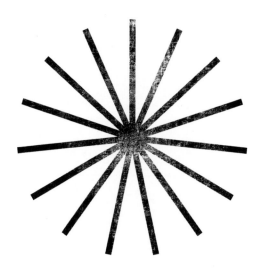

Great businesses and brands rarely just 'happen'. They are designed *deliberately*, whether that's consciously or intuitively. No matter what business you're in, every staff member contributes to how you build the brand, how it's experienced and how it's championed; from administration through to finance, product development to customer service, reception to CEO. More than that, great brands are clear and intentional about their core focus. They also have an understanding of how they're perceived in the minds of others. But it's an ever-changing and dynamic context, so let's take a closer look at what's involved.

In nearly 30 years working as a branding and identity designer I've observed common themes and patterns in the field. As a result, in 2013, I compiled a variety of observations as a list of 15 principles, using them in my work with clients as a means to shape an approach to thinking about brands and branding. From the outset, the response was really positive. To further test and validate this thinking, two years later—in February 2015—I posted the Brand Principles as an article on *LinkedIn*. Again, the response was incredibly positive and generated an engaging discussion around the simplicity and benefit of these principles. More importantly, working directly with clients, I've seen firsthand the practical value of these principles, whether that relates to a start-up or an established business. These 15 principles have helped business leaders re-frame their understanding of a brand, while also highlighting their role and ability in building one.

But before we move onto these principles, let's do a small exercise. Think of a brand, one that you're very familiar with but which you are *not* a customer—and are never likely to be one. Choose any brand, from any industry sector, but make sure you're reasonably familiar with it and what it stands for.

Ready?

1. A brand is the most valuable real estate in the world—*a corner of someone's mind* [1] *and a relevant place in their life.*

1. *Hegarty on Advertising: Turning intelligence into magic,* Sir John Hegarty, Thames & Hudson, 2011, page 39.

No matter which brand you chose, and for whatever reason, you've clearly given it space in your mind. That means you're acutely aware of this brand, what it does (or doesn't do), what market sector it inhabits and what value it provides (or doesn't). You're probably also familiar with its branding—or its logo at the very least. And you feel the brand is important enough to remember, or to reference, or you've acknowledged its relevance in today's world. So much so, you've given it some space in your consciousness. All of this despite our incredibly overcrowded minds, which are constantly navigating our busy day-to-day activities. And you're not even a customer, nor are you likely to be one! The fact there are countless other businesses and brands you've encountered in your life, and which you don't easily recall, speaks volumes about the ones you do. So, what's going on here? How can brands be this powerful?

This can be hard to fathom, but looking at it from a practical perspective it becomes obvious. It's partly due to a brand's ability to broadcast far and wide, since this provides *exposure*. But exposure alone won't be enough; a brand also needs absolute *clarity of message*, a way for us to process its meaning and to understand its value—which builds *awareness*. This brings us to the next vital element: *relevance*.

Being relevant is essential to a business or brand's success. Obviously, it needs to be relevant to customers who receive the value, but also to non-customers, who acknowledge the relevance of the brand in today's society through their understanding of it. This could be as simple as the brand being a market leader, or as complex as the brand being the antithesis of someone's personal values. Either way, it brings us back to clarity, because clarity allows a brand to communicate its position, its beliefs, and its value propositions. But, as world renowned advertising guru Sir John Hegarty points out, this isn't just important for customers' understanding:

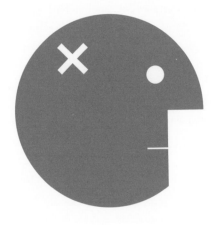

"A brand isn't only made by the people who buy it, but also by the people who know about it. When managing and promoting your product, this is probably the most important lesson to bear in mind. Even though a person may never buy what you sell, the fact that they know about what you are selling adds value to it." [2]

By this reasoning, the more people who know about (and understand) a business or brand, the greater collective importance we bestow upon it. The aggregation of this wider significance increases the perceived value of the brand in the minds of others (which broadly speaking means society at large) making it immediately recognisable. This awareness includes customers and non-customers because it can translate into what we traditionally refer to as being a *household name*, a brand that's become synonymous with something specific and which we use as reference against other similar 'things'.

There are many factors contributing to this. For starters, it has to do with reputation, which can be as practical as being 'a reliable product', or as nebulous as defining our personal identity, or a means to convey a sense of status. In every instance it relies on people having a clear and collective understanding of the brand, which then needs to be backed up by our experiences of the brand itself, whether that's direct or indirect. Furthermore, and perhaps surprisingly, it's also still the result of an age-old promotional tool: *word of mouth*. The more people who are aware of your business or brand—meaning, the more they understand it; the more visible it is to them; the more value they receive from it; and the more relevant it is in their lives—the more they will talk about it *in their own words*. It stands to reason, then, that whether their opinion of the brand is positive or negative becomes increasingly significant, because what they say will be trusted far beyond what a brand or business promotes about itself.

---

2.   *Hegarty on Advertising: Turning intelligence into magic*, page 43.

All this places added importance on how brands communicate—
and to whom—which can be a challenging mindset for traditional
business leaders to adopt, particularly those who are more
comfortable broadcasting to a rigidly defined customer segment
or market sector. So let's do another little exercise: what if you
tried promoting the value and relevance of your product or service
specifically to people who are *not* your customers? What might that
look and sound like? You might be thinking that's a novel idea, but
a pointless exercise. Yet, there is a very practical aspect to it. When
you're looking to grow your customer base, to expand your market,
to scale your reach, or to build your profile, is there any sense in
'preaching to the converted', or to a limited customer group? Isn't
the objective to always widen the influence? If so, Hegarty suggests
thinking about it this way:

*"According to the Bible, when Christ stood and made his Sermon
on the Mount he preached to the masses. He didn't get up on
that rock and say, 'I'd like to talk to 18-25-year-old ABCs, with a
predisposition to change and a disposable income of X.' No, he got up
and preached to as many people as possible. He was in the business
of recruitment, building loyalty and getting people to change their
behaviour. If I'm not mistaken that's the function of a great many
brands today."* [3]

Religious references aside, there's an important lesson in Hegarty's
observation: don't define who you should communicate to based on
an assumption that you know what people are looking for. If your
message is clear and compelling it will attract those who see value
in your offer. This applies to attracting new employees, as much
as customers. In short, being front of mind (for the right reasons),
and being clearly understood by a wide group, is the pinnacle of
successful brand communication.

---

3. *Hegarty on Advertising: Turning intelligence into magic,* page 44.

Absent minded

Sadly, the incredibly valuable mental real estate we all possess has traditionally been seen by businesses as an exploitable resource, something to mine in order to increase their profits, earnings and revenue. But, as we've seen from Chapter 6 in particular, all this is now changing. In our new emerging world, that valuable real estate has become more about a brand's responsibility, obligation, transparency and accountability. With societal trends shifting, people are actively seeking out brands and businesses who deliver on this. And that includes employees, because this mindset extends to the whole organisation—those who are charged with delivering the promise, as well as maintaining it on a regular basis and in a consistent manner.

The death of any business is to first be absent from our minds— which is the result of being invisible, irrelevant, unable to provide genuine and tangible value, misunderstood, or losing trust. This idea of being absent from our minds is so significant, it cannot be overstated. If customers don't believe your brand or business merits a second thought, the impact on the business is enormous. And it's even more important for businesses who are seeking to build a brand, as much as for established brands seeking to maintain their market position. Consider Hegarty's insight, based on decades of international experience working with a swathe of high-profile brands:

"In reality, a brand only ever exists in the minds of consumers." [4]

---

4. *Hegarty on Advertising: Turning intelligence into magic,* page 42.

2. **Successful branding is based on truth**—*it's also the easiest way to implement and maintain your communications because truth is natural, genuine and memorable. It's also expected.*

There are many cases where brands and businesses have been caught out stretching the truth, or worse—outright lying—to staff, customers and society. In a lot of cases, the repercussions have been enormous because news travels exceptionally fast in our digitally connected world.

For example, consider *VW's* emissions scandal, something they're still desperately trying to crawl back from and which cost the brand over $30 billion;[5] or the financial sector, which prompted the Global Financial Crisis as a result of their greedy practices and which ushered in new levels of distrust for banks; or *Facebook's Cambridge Analytica* debacle, which caused the closure of *Cambridge Analytica* and in 2019 cost *Facebook* a $5 billion fine (which may be pocket change for an organisation that made $16.9 billion in the second quarter of 2019 [6] but the ongoing impact to its reputation is still playing out in real time); not to mention *BP's* mishandling of the 2010 Mexican Gulf oil spill. Each example involves various levels of deceit.

When it comes to truth, we can assess a business or brand by what it says (words) and how it behaves (actions). How these two add up determines our perception of that organisation. Aside from ethical reasons for being truthful, there are perhaps more practical reasons for doing so in terms of communications and branding: *truth is easier to remember.* Now, that might sound painfully obvious, but truth is based on more than just words and actions. It's based on experience—something that's lived. We remember the context, and the circumstances. We recall how a 'truth' came about: what was involved, when we experienced it, with whom, and how we felt in that moment. When communication (and branding) is based on truth, the business can position itself in the market with confidence— in the knowledge they can back it up through products, services, words, actions, behaviours and history. In other words: *proof.*

---

5.   *Volkswagen's CEO and chairman charged in Germany over diesel emissions scandal,* by Charles Riley and Mark Thompson, CNN Business, online article, 24 September 2019.
6.   *Billion-dollar fines can't stop Google and Facebook. That's peanuts for them,* Siva Vaidhyanathan, The Guardian, online article, 26 July 2019.

This is equally vital for staff. With clarity and truth, they avoid having to remember or recall fabricated stories for marketing purposes. If that clarity aligns with their own experiences then staff will remember it in visceral terms, allowing them to express or convey it in their own words—rather than scripted versions imposed upon them by the Marketing Department. Combined, these stories and experiences from each individual get consolidated within the business. When that truth shows up consistently in products, services and customer relations, it becomes embedded in the minds of people inside and outside the business. It then becomes enshrined in the brand DNA.

While this is something branding designers can help identify and articulate, a 'truth' must first come from *within* the business. It must be compelling and validated beyond clever words, logos or marketing campaigns. As a designer tasked with the challenge of translating what a company stands for, its aspirations and its business strategy, unless I'm working with truthful and tangible information I'm simply guessing. It's like throwing suggestions against the wall—based on assumptions—to see what sticks. This approach essentially asks whether the business 'likes' the proposal, rather than challenging whether or not it's an honest portrayal of them—one that they can embrace and live up to (in terms of actions, behaviours, culture, products, services and Purpose). Put simply, anything short of truth is dangerous, because it presents and propagates deceit. All professional designers should be expected to challenge anything that's misleading or vague. And while branding provides assistance (meaning it won't build a brand on its own), it should lay clear foundations and a blueprint for the business to leverage and build their brand with confidence, clarity—and truth. As Simon Sinek says:

"Being right doesn't make us trustworthy. Being honest makes us trustworthy."[7]

---

7.   *Notes to inspire: A dose of inspiration in your inbox every weekday,* Simon Sinek, e-newsletter series, 9 July 2019.

3. **A brand is internal before it's external**—*your staff need to be your greatest ambassadors. The mistake is to think branding is purely about external broadcasting.*

There is a common misconception that branding is primarily about external marketing and communications. While these *are* vital aspects of building a brand, it's essential to first ensure that everyone inside the business fully understands and supports what it stands for, what their individual role is, and whether or not they genuinely believe in the company. It sounds obvious, right? And yet, it's amazing how often this is overlooked. But is it really all that important to get everything—and everyone—aligned inside the business first?

Well, since most businesses are knee-deep in operations, and most staff are focused on their day-to-day tasks, it's easy for everyone to presume they're all heading in the same direction. In situations where internal communications aren't regular or clear, there is ample opportunity for individuals to *assume* they understand the business—it's Purpose, it's focus, it's expectations, it's value proposition to customers, etc. However, an independent and objective assessment can quickly identify whether everyone really is on the same page, because if there is any disconnect, confusion, or misunderstanding, the ramifications can be severe.

Think of it like this: employees—at all levels—drive the business or brand. Their actions and behaviours directly reflect how the business performs and how it's perceived, internally and externally. Culture is the organisational motivator which binds it all together. So, when an employee is in a social setting—for example, at a dinner party, or a barbecue—and someone asks what they do for a living, their response is a good indicator for how they understand the business and their role in it. These casual settings don't require the employee to rattle off Mission, Vision or Values statements, or to deliver an 'elevator pitch'. Instead, their responses will be natural and (ad-libbed) in their own words. It's usually unfiltered and raw. In some cases it may be light or evasive. Yet, their response provides an insight into the business, not only because of *what* they say, but also *how* they say it.

How they respond will likely reflect the feeling which the business or brand provides to them on a daily basis. Why is this important? Because it impacts culture, morale and productivity; because how they talk about the business or brand contributes to perceptions that other people will then establish (internally and externally); and because all this is, in fact, *branding*. In other words:

- If an employee is disengaged at work—for whatever reasons—this will be reflected in how they behave *at* work and also how they talk about *where* they work;
- If an employee is unclear or misinformed at work—for whatever reasons—this will be reflected in how they behave *at* work and also how they talk about *where* they work;
- If an employee feels positive, energised and motivated at work—for whatever reasons—this will be reflected in how they behave *at* work and also how they talk about *where* they work.

You get the picture. Essentially, how staff feel and behave at work will be reflected in how they treat their colleagues, how they deliver customer experiences, how productive and engaged they are and, fundamentally, how they represent the business. All of this is internal branding—which eventually translates into external branding, where perceptions are shaped and where marketing messages are validated—or discredited.

But there is another important aspect to all of this. If external branding is at odds with staff's understanding of the business—its messages, its promises, its behaviours—those marketing messages can compound or exacerbate any disconnection staff might have, or which they might begin to foster. In simple terms, they might see external marketing messages and wonder if they actually work for the same company. Or worse, they might end up using external communications to develop a better understanding of the company that they work for. What message does *that* send to staff? What does *that* say about the business or brand? Maintaining clarity, and ensuring there is unified understanding internally first, will ensure any external communications are more likely to resonate accurately with the people who are tasked with delivering on those specific messages. If you're clear about your Values, consistent with your behaviors and mindful of your internal communications to ensure everyone is on the same page, staff will know whether or not they fit in. Allowing a strong culture to thrive is in everyone's interest because when staff are happier (and on board) productivity will be higher and more consistent. Make no mistake, all of this feeds into branding and has a direct impact on the brand. When there is trust, belief, clarity and a Purpose within a business, it makes everything else easier and smoother. As Simon Sinek once said:

"Customers will only love the company once the employees love it first." [8]

People are people

As we all know, 2020/21 presented incredible challenges for businesses, brands and individuals. Sadly, too many didn't survive. While the numerous restrictions doled out around the world actively helped fight against spreading Covid-19 they also ushered in an unprecedented 'work-from-home' global movement. With so many people now working remotely—or in a hybrid model—does this notion of internal branding still stack up? If staff are 'scattered', does it still apply? Well, the short answer is yes—and more than ever.

Without daily contact with colleagues, meetings have been recast as *Zoom* calls. Of course, that's not necessarily a bad thing, but without consistent and continuous interaction with their colleagues and culture (either physically *or* digitally) there is more chance for people to feel isolated, to feel left out, and to feel uncertain about the direction of the company. Ensuring that everyone is crystal clear about where the business is heading, how important their role is in delivering on the business' promises—and in building the brand— reduces the opportunity for staff to disengage, or to go off range, or to interpret things in their own way. A disorganised, disconnected,

---

8. *Notes to Inspire,* Simon Sinek, online newsletter, 26 February 2021.

possibly dysfunctional understanding will undoubtedly show up in how customers and clients experience the brand, even if it's unintentional, because it will quickly find its way out into the world. But so too will a clear, organised, energised, unified and cohesive understanding. And remember, brands exist in people's minds—first of all with staff, who *deliver* what the brand represents, and then by customers, who *experience* what the brand represents.

4. A brand is not a department—*it's the responsibility (and the representation) of your entire organisation, from receptionist to CEO.*

Business owners, and perhaps even branding designers, often fail to impress upon staff that building a brand involves *each and every employee*; that it's not limited to a marketing exercise, a logo, or an advertising campaign. Nor is it an Executive dictate, where staff are left wondering why the stationery looks different and the website has been revamped. The reality is that every staff member contributes to building the brand and how it's experienced—internally and externally—whether that's how they answer the phone, how they treat their colleagues, how they make customers feel, how Accounts, Admin and Finance ensures the smooth running of the business, right through to how Executives and Management lead by example. Everyone is important to the brand; everyone contributes to how it's built and delivered. *Everyone.* So, why doesn't it feel that way?

Every business has a visible hierarchy of perceived importance and some roles may be valued more highly than others. For example, 'top-tier' roles may be those that directly deal with clients and customers or positions which visibly advance revenue: Executives, Account Managers, Sales, etc. The 'value creators', like product developers, ideas or solutions generators, may be 'second- tier roles'. Everyone else sits beneath these and are largely seen as 'support'. It's often the case that staff are constantly reminded of where they sit on that scale.

However, businesses and brands wouldn't function without all of these various, specialised and different roles. At the very least, they would struggle to operate effectively. A diverse range of roles ensures the business is maintained, and the brand is developed, sustained, and protected. While some positions may be more visible than others, it takes every role to deliver on the brand promise—every day, and over the long-term. Why is this even important to acknowledge? Well, aside from the ugliness of deliberately looking down on colleagues, it's the difference between a business full of people with 'jobs' versus a brand filled with people

bound by a common set of beliefs and a genuine understanding that they're all contributing to something bigger—*through* their role. It recognises that each individual is a very important part of a larger (brand) picture.

Some enduring lessons

When I graduated from design school I began my search for a job. Unfortunately, my Honours Degree gave me no confidence that I was actually ready for the real world—even though this was merely my own self-inflicted doubt. Nevertheless, I convinced myself to persevere. Through a personal connection I ended up in the boardroom of a 'real' design studio, sitting across the table from the owner—*a real designer*. I was terrified. In an attempt to take the edge off, I reassured myself I wasn't likely to get the job anyway, so there was no need to panic. But the owner had other ideas. He was interested in me working directly with a senior designer, whom he was also considering. The senior designer had years of experience, and he always worked alone, but the owner was only willing to hire us as a team. He felt that, while I was clearly inexperienced, I could bring some fresh thinking to the partnership. And while the senior designer was very experienced, there was a sense he may be set in his ways. It all made perfect sense. It also had an immediate and direct impact on my increased anxiety levels. But what he said next changed me forever.

He said, if I was offered the position, each of the other six people in the company—including him—would rely on me living up to expectations, giving it my best *every day*, and requiring my commitment to not letting anyone down. It was rather blunt, and felt a little overstated. However, he reassured me that, in fact, I had the better end of the deal: while six people would be relying on me, I could always rely on six people. That meant, if I ever needed help, guidance or assistance I could ask any of the other six people in the business—from our receptionist right through to him, the owner. It was a simple equation, but it shaped my thinking from that moment on: about working in teams; about treating all colleagues equally and with respect; about the fact we are all part of a collective effort; and that we are all equal in our own different ways. Needless to say, I accepted the position, despite still being terrified. And even though it didn't always work out the way it was pitched, we all worked a lot harder to foster that collaborative culture, that mindset.

Now, while some readers might dismiss this as a cute story, it had a profound influence on me and helped shape my observations in every company I worked in, thereafter. For example, for the majority of my tenure at *Saatchi & Saatchi*, Sydney, the agency had two receptionists, a role that's regularly taken for granted— either unwittingly or intentionally. It's often seen as a 'supporting' position, being both necessary and useful, but perhaps not particularly instrumental in helping to build the brand. I've always found this an incredibly frustrating oversight.

However, at *Saatchi & Saatchi*, Sydney, both receptionists at the time were male, which was a welcome break from the more narrow-minded tradition. One of those men was larger than life. His name was Semi—a singing and guitar-playing tireless entertainer, with a huge smile to match. It's an understatement to say he was a personality, but it was a personality that absolutely fit the *Saatchi & Saatchi* brand, attitude and culture. He was allowed to be himself and, as a result, he personified the brand. So much so, he had a crucial role in the agency, not just because he was one of the first points of contact, but also because he was a great motivator for staff, and an amazing ambassador for the dynamic, creative culture. Without question, his contribution to the local *Saatchi & Saatchi* brand during my tenure was significant.

Now, remember: he wasn't in the Marketing Department; he wasn't an Executive; he wasn't a Manager, or in the Business Development team. *Yet*, he was just as important as all of them. In his role as receptionist, his impact on the brand was both internal and external.

It was also a constant reminder that building a brand isn't confined to the Marketing Department, or the Executive suites, or to the more 'important' positions. And it's further proof that every single employee, no matter how their role might be perceived, contributes to building the brand—regardless of whether or not you recognise and acknowledge it.

5. **A brand is about culture**—*it's the collective attitudes and ideas of a group of people. Your brand is as much about individual behaviour as it is about collective behaviour.*

While the importance of culture has gained traction in the business world, it's still often considered as a *soft* element, something for HR to oversee, or perhaps something the Executive understands helps 'keep morale high.'

As a business leader, you're always juggling multiple situations in tandem. In these instances, you base your judgments on experience; you consult colleagues, experts, and/or any available information that's relevant to the situation in order to make informed decisions. These are clear and conscious decisions you make on a daily basis. However, are you taking the same approach with how you attract talent and how you consider the environment you oversee to help foster your culture, among other 'softer' aspects of your organisation? Those decisions are just as important because they have consequences for your business—good *and* bad. How you value your culture can impact the productivity of your team, and the perceptions around your brand, because culture is about shared Values and collective behaviour. Entrepreneur and author Blair Enns sums it up neatly in his book *Pricing Creativity*:

"When it comes to culture, one viewpoint will ultimately dominate the other because culture is a set of shared assumptions that guide what happens in organisations by defining appropriate behaviour for various situations." [9]

No doubt, at some point in your career you've experienced a situation where an individual in a team hasn't been the right fit and has upset the entire culture of a previously harmonious and productive group. It's never pleasant. However, being acutely aware of your culture can help minimise this. Let's take recruitment as a case in point. As Joint Creative Director of *Saatchi Design*, Sydney, my colleagues and I regularly interviewed applicants for various roles. Potential candidates were generally qualified for the positions, or had the relevant experience, or were referred by trusted peers.

---

9. *Pricing Creativity: A guide to profit beyond the billable hour,* Blair Enns, Rockbench Publishing Corp, 2018, page 15.

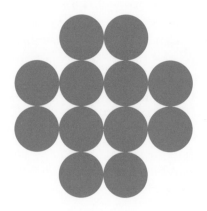

However, after pretty much every interview—regardless of the candidate's experience or qualifications—we would first ask each other one question: *"Do you think they're a Saatchi person?"*

We didn't have specific criteria for this. It was more about a *feeling*, rather than a list of bullet points to reference. Now, that might sound a little vague, but it was a deliberate question, nonetheless. We based the answer on whether we *felt* the candidate would fit comfortably into our immediate team culture, but also into the wider *Saatchi & Saatchi* culture. We considered what it might be like working with them in close proximity—eight or 10 hours a day, five days a week, plus overtime—and whether we *felt* they were the right fit, whether we *felt* they would be willing and able to contribute to our culture—not just *slot in*. Why? A healthy culture grows and expands with like-minded people, those who are the right fit and are on the same page as the rest of the business. That means it's not *just* about qualifications. It quickly becomes a brand decision.

Hiring for the brand, not the job
Rather than just hiring a qualified 'body to fill a job', it's important to attract people who are the right fit, those who are looking for a career step, not just another role. The likelihood is they will *still* have the qualifications (or the drive, desire and passion for your business) but they'll also be more likely to fit better with the rest of your staff. That's critical when fostering, protecting and nurturing a healthy organisational culture.

Of course, if the candidate doesn't have the specific qualifications or experience you're looking for, it might be worth assessing their potential instead. For example: *Why did they apply for this role? Why are they interested in your company? What else can they bring to the position?* This is a conscious shift in approach. Remember: you can pretty much teach anything to smart, motivated people. Here's a specific example. At *Saatchi Design*, my co-Creative Director, Julian Melhuish, and I were recruiting for a young designer and received a landslide of applications from qualified candidates. We saw a conveyor belt of similarly styled portfolios, none of which were terribly inspiring. However, towards the end of our interviews, one candidate, Christopher Doyle, stood out, but not for his portfolio. Throughout the interview he was polite, friendly and exceedingly nervous. Like other candidates, we dismissed his portfolio as being 'much of the same' and finished up the interview. Then, before leaving, he handed me his business card. I had never seen anything like it before. It read:

YOUNG MALE
GOOD SENSE OF HUMOUR
INTERESTS:
LONG WALKS
SUNSETS
GOOD CONVERSATION
PLS SEND PHOTOGRAPH

The card included his contact details, but it eschewed all the other usual business card details in favour of something more courageous—and ultimately more memorable. In essence, he'd created a short personal columns advert—perhaps unconsciously canvassing for the right design studio *relationship*. Whether he was aware of it or not, it was deliberately designed for a specific culture. *Ours.* This simple, confident and understated business card felt totally inconsistent with the entirety of his portfolio. And it gave us pause. It also gave us an insight, not only into his abilities to think outside the square, but also into his personality. We immediately saw potential. Here was a creative thinker who—when pursuing his own style and approach—was capable of stopping people in their tracks in an unexpected way and making them smile. It answered our advertised role, but not in any way we had anticipated.

Needless to say, we hired him—and taught him everything we knew. Within six months he won his first design award. Not only that, he stayed with *Saatchi Design* for over five years, contributing significantly to the culture and output of the business, bringing his own style of humour and goodwill. Even better, he taught us different ways to consider things, ways we hadn't done before. It was incredibly refreshing. Everyone benefited.

Had we interviewed purely on qualifications, we probably would have missed out. But instead, we were intuitively hiring for the (*Saatchi & Saatchi*) brand, and for our culture. This underpins the need for and importance of clearly understanding your culture (in *Saatchi & Saatchi's* case, it was always to lead with creative thinking). From there, the culture, which will grow organically if populated with like-minded people, begins to define the brand. It becomes the guiding principle which should be openly encouraged and celebrated to ensure that it's a visible metric. And, while recruitment might seem like one of the softer aspects of a business, it's vital to ensure *all* candidates for *all* roles are considered in the same light. Ensuring everyone aligns with the business—your Values, your culture, your commercial focus and your Purpose— can help attract people who resonate with your culture and commercial objectives.

Hiring the right people for your business or your brand increases productivity and contributes to your culture because a healthy culture thrives in environments that are designed for staff who are encouraged, yet challenged; who are supported, yet accountable. These are all conscious decisions, within a healthy culture, where every person in the business is naturally contributing towards building the brand.

Designing culture
When it comes to fostering culture, branding designers are well placed to help articulate and craft language and communications to shape perceptions around a business, right through to developing effective recruitment adverts to attract the right candidates. According to some schools of thought, there are those who argue designers are even in a position to design the actual organisational culture itself. But this is a dangerous road. Instead, it's more

important to design the *environments and the situations* that can nurture a growing, organic culture. Business leaders are in a better position to design and shepherd those circumstances through crafted language and communications, helped along by designers where needed. But all of this needs to fit hand in hand with the objectives of the business, in terms of the team it wants to attract and keep—as well as the culture, attitude and Values it wants to uphold. However, the business and staff must then *live it* every day, backed up with consistent actions and behaviours. Otherwise, a business is vulnerable to operating in its own echo chamber, one based on superficial marketing spin.

Hamdi Ulukaya, founder of *Chobani,* has very specific opinions about the importance of culture and why it's vital to foster a positive environment for staff. He sees it as a critical component of business and his incredible success is proof that his approach has a positive impact on business.

"Today's business books say businesses exist to maximise profit for the shareholders. I think that's the dumbest idea I've ever heard in my life," Ulukaya says. If businesses shouldn't try first and foremost to make money for their owners, what should they aim for [instead]? "Businesses should take care of their employees first," he insists. In 2016 Ulukaya took the unusual step of giving his 2,000 employees shares in the company. "Some people said it's PR. Some said it's a gift. I said, 'It's not a gift'... They earned it with their talent and their hard work." [10]

Ulukaya isn't alone in this view. In 2010, *Japan Airlines* was on the brink of bankruptcy. Desperate to save their national carrier they reached out to Kazuo Inamori, an entrepreneur, management guru and Buddhist priest. Inamori refused their advances on numerous occasions because he had no experience in the aviation sector. But *Japan Airlines* were convinced by his track record and

---

10. *Kyocera founder's secret: Make workers happy,* Jessica Stillman, The Japan Times / Bloomberg, Takako Taniguchi, online article, 5 November 2015.

•

"Company leaders should seek to make all their employees happy, both materially and intellectually. That's their purpose. It shouldn't be to work for shareholders."

•

his methodologies (based on having established the electronics giant *Kyocera Corp.* and *KDDI Corp.*, a multi-billion dollar phone carrier). That said, when he eventually agreed to come on board, they encountered his unorthodox thinking firsthand. In response to questions around how he planned to increase shareholder value, he said he would do *nothing*. Instead, he suggested it would be more beneficial to look after staff, because staff look after customers and customers look after shareholders. It's a profoundly simple approach. In Inamori's own words:

"Company leaders should seek to make all their employees happy, both materially and intellectually,' Inamori said. 'That's their purpose. It shouldn't be to work for shareholders...' While that might not impress some investors, [Inamori] himself sees no conflict. 'If staff are happy, they'll work better and earnings will improve', he said. 'Companies shouldn't be ashamed to make profits if they're pursued in a way that benefits society.'" [11]

Shigenobu Nagamori, another Japanese billionaire and CEO of *Nidec Corp.*, has a similar view. According to *Business Insider*:

"When I'm asked by investors, I tell them they're No. 1, but it's not what I really think,' he says. 'I speak my mind if shareholders ask strange questions at the annual general meeting. I tell them it would be better if the likes of you didn't own our shares. I say I can't choose my shareholders, but you can choose the company you invest in.' Nagamori says... he's unwilling to fire employees if they're putting in the hours, instead choosing to find them another position where they might perform better. He eats every meal with his staff." [12]

For any remaining cynics, consider the heading of the *Business Insider* article about Shigenobu Nagamori: *This Japanese CEO cares about his employees more than investors, and his stock is still up 457%*. With Inamori, we also see reference to a greater

---

11. *This Japanese CEO cares about his employees more than investors, and his stock is still up 457% since the crisis*, Rachel Butt, Business Insider, online article, 12 August 2016.
12. *Kyocera founder's secret: Make workers happy.*

Purpose—*making profits that are pursued in a way that benefits society*—which is central to business success, driven from the inside, and based on a culture that is clear, aligned, like-minded and appreciated. Put simply, attracting the right staff protects the culture; a healthy culture helps staff to look after customers; and customers look after shareholder value. Combined, they all help build the brand.

6. Mission, Vision and Value statements are great internal guides—*but no one outside the organisation really cares. They will only be interested in the value these statements deliver.*

Take a moment to think about your favourite brand—but also why you like it. Now, can you recall their Mission statement, or their Vision statement? Probably not. Can you recite, with certainty, their core Values? Probably not. Do you care that you can't? Probably not. However, you probably *do* have a sense about what these statements represent: how the brand behaves, what it stands for (and stands up to), and how you experience their products or services. Why? Because everything they do is influenced and informed by their core Mission and Vision, and this is backed up by the Values instilled in their employees. That means these statements are simultaneously very important, and not very important at all. How so?

Lots of brands and businesses make a point of articulating their Mission, Vision and Values. Many of them actively broadcast these statements publicly or feature them proudly on their website. They do this because those statements are important to them. And rightly so. Now, since they're important to the brand they must also be important to their customers, right? Well, not so fast. You see, customers are more interested in how a brand's story shows up in their own personal story—how it aligns with their world view and how relevant it is in their life. So, these company statements generally don't mean much in isolation because people experience brands in so many different ways. How we broadly interpret what a brand is about, and what it represents, is far more important. This understanding is generally derived from individual experiences and observations. And if a customer happens to be aware of any of these company statements, it usually serves as a way for them to hold the brand accountable, to assess whether it lives up to what it professes, and to gauge whether or not it delivers on its promises. I'd argue, these finely crafted statements aren't all that important for customers—*until* they become unquestionably important.

Okay, hold up! Are these company statements important to customers, or not? Well, let's address their function first. From a business' perspective, these statements *are* incredibly useful

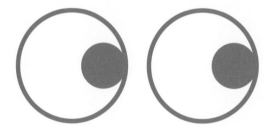

because they clearly state the brand's core focus, their long-term ambition, and the behaviours and beliefs underpinning their organisational culture. See—very important! But they are essentially an internal guide to help everyone inside the business remain aligned, while also providing the means to measure success. In essence, they contribute to the smooth running of a sustainable business. As ex-Advertising Creative Director for *Apple*, Ken Segall, once shared with me:

"It's about guiding a company to avoid standing over people's shoulders telling them they're doing it right or wrong. If staff understand the Values of the company, or they understand there's a clear Mission, then when they're creating products or making decisions in marketing, or whatever, they're all consistent. They're all moving in the same direction." [13]

So why do brand's and businesses publicly share their Mission, Vision and Values? Well, it's partly to remind staff about where the business is heading, and the expectations it has of employees; it's partly to attract and recruit like-minded talent with more accuracy; and it's partly to provide partners and investors with specific guidelines to reference. But, from a purely external perspective, the intention of these statements is also often an attempt to differentiate the brand from competitors, with the deliberate objective of hopefully connecting more deeply with customers and society at large (on ethical, emotional, societal and practical levels). Logical as this might sound, unfortunately it's unlikely that customers will go out of their way to research and remember these statements. (Have you ever done that?) And while promoting these company statements might make a brand more understood, it also makes them incredibly vulnerable—particularly if the brand defaults on those commitments. So, when customers get a sense that perhaps a brand is being misleading or untrustworthy, these statements become unquestionably important for them. Which brings us to *Everlane* and its promise of 'Radical Transparency'.

---

13. *The transformative power of simplicity,* Ken Segall in conversation with Kevin Finn for DESIGNerd, online article, March 2018.

Hype and hubris

In 2010, *Everlane's* refreshing and exciting Vision—casting them as a guiding light in reshaping the fashion and retail industries as ethical, honest and ultra transparent—quickly garnered positive attention from customers, venture capitalists and celebrities alike. This enthusiasm was further underpinned by a commitment to shun predatory and greedy behaviour by honouring a more open 'direct-to-consumer' business model and a pledge to share details on pricing markups, clothing suppliers, and its ecological footprint, among other things. A decade ago, with the emergence of Purpose-driven brands at a tipping point, *Everlane* was taking a stand—loud and clear. As we heard briefly in Chapter 6, as inspiring, welcome and much-needed as *Everlane's* 'Radical Transparency' was, fast forward 10 years and their spectacular overreach sadly became all too apparent. It also became radically public. So much so, after more and more staff began to speak out about the toxic culture, an investigation was opened into the brand's practices. According to *The New York Times*:

"Investigators found that insensitive terms were used while discussing Black models; that leaders violated employees' personal space by touching them, and used inappropriate terms when referring to people of color; that new hires felt isolated and unwelcome; that there was lack of consistent policies around promotions; [and] that there were no formal processes to effectively escalate harassment or discrimination.

'A good chunk of us were zealous fans, because we really, really did believe in the mission,' said Toni Kwadzogah, 28, who was laid off this spring [of 2020]. 'When you cultivate an image in such a progressive style, you attract people, workers and customers alike, who have those progressive values. And when you fail them, well, good luck.'" [14]

---

14. *Everlane's Promise of 'Radical Transparency' Unravels,* by Jessica Testa, Vanessa Friedman and Elizabeth Paton , The New York Times, online article, 26 June 2020.

•

Staff are essentially the
delivery mechanism for a
brand's Mission, Vision and
Values, whereas customers
are the beneficiaries of
the value which these
commitments provide.

•

Everlane's breathtaking fall from grace left the business haemorrhaging on two fronts. Firstly, the brand's public image—which it had carefully created and aggressively promoted—was shattered inside and out. Ranging from accusations of employee inequality through to body-size discrimination, *Everlane* was quickly becoming the antithesis of everything it promised to uphold. Secondly—and for skeptics who might feel that defaulting on your company Mission, Vision and Values isn't all that significant—*Everlane's* founder and CEO, Michael Preysman, confirmed that the business would lose over $15 million in 2020 alone, as a result of the exposure. In other words, customers were listening, observing—and shunning the brand. Now, whether or not customers could recite *Everlane's* company statements, it seemed they had a pretty good sense of what the brand apparently stood for and what the promise of Radical Transparency meant for them. Unfortunately, at some point along the way, *Everlane* seems to have got caught up in its own hype and hubris.

"Everlane puts a great deal of focus on 'radical transparency' and has made it a key selling point," said Luke Smitham, a sustainability expert at Kumi Consulting in London. "But fundamentally, what they do is not any different from most mass-market fashion brands who do exactly the same, or more. They do some good work, but I wouldn't describe it as radical. The most radical thing about Everlane is the marketing." [15]

So what?

There are plenty of organisations and brands whom we may not agree with—ethically, morally or commercially—including those with questionable reputations, who nevertheless continue to operate and, in some cases, thrive. So, what's going on here? Well, it's possible people may not be aware of the brand's promises in the first place, meaning they're simply oblivious to the fact the brand might be defaulting on their stated commitments. (Though this

---

15. *Everlane's Promise of 'Radical Transparency' Unravels.*

should be obvious through the brand's actions and behaviours.) Then there are people who just don't care, which is an unfortunate reality. In other cases, it depends on whether or not there is a viable choice or alternative in the market.

Either way, it's vital that businesses and brands express their Mission, Vision and Values because it serves as a public declaration of their aspirations and beliefs. But as a business owner, don't assume (or expect) customers will look for those statements, or remember them. Making these statements public is more about expressing a willingness to be accountable, about being confident in your beliefs, and conveying a sense of clarity around what's important to the business, meaning there is a direct relationship between the internal and external functions of these company statements. But this is not for marketing reasons. It's far more visceral than that. In other words: staff are essentially the delivery mechanism for a brand's Mission, Vision and Values, whereas customers are the beneficiaries of the value which these commitments provide. It's really that simple—and that complicated.

7. The logo doesn't make your brand; the brand gives your logo its value—*your logo is the quick, shorthand visual reminder of all the individual associations, experiences and perceptions people have with your brand.*

As this book has illustrated, your brand is much bigger than your logo. While logos and branding play a vital role in how we distinguish companies and organisations, a simple fact still remains: *Brand is who you are and how you behave— branding is how you look and how you're recognised.*

But it goes even deeper than that. When a widely recognised brand is continuously relevant in our lives it becomes more about meaning and belonging, rather than just products or services. As we know, the most successful brands often become absorbed as part of our personal identity. It's a powerful place for any business to land. Now, for some readers that might sound sad, tragic or even overreaching, but whether it's cars, jewellery, technology, fashion, sport, digital platforms, hotels, phones, energy drinks, or even our jobs (and everything in between), brands influence how we're perceived by others. In many cases, intentionally so. And, of course, the quickest and easiest way to be visually associated with a brand of choice is via their logo. This is why logos are regularly referred to as 'brands'. But logos need context. They don't exist in isolation; they don't exist in a vacuum. As I discussed in Chapter 2, there is little-to-no context at the inception of a business, but it builds and expands over time as the business evolves and matures. This means a logo can communicate multiple complex meanings in tandem, in a succinct and efficient way, and at different points in a business' journey. In fact, the influence of context cannot be underestimated— or overstated.

For example, on 7 January 2021, after a mob insurrection on the United States Capital Building, *Facebook* took the unprecedented— and perhaps long overdue—step of suspending then President Trump's account. This was an effort to take a tougher stance on his misleading *'Stop the steal'* campaign, which questioned the 2020 election results, refused to acknowledge President Biden's legitimacy, and helped mobilise a violent response from Trump supporters and conspiracy-laden *QAnon* followers, among many others. Interestingly, *Facebook* wasn't alone in taking this action.

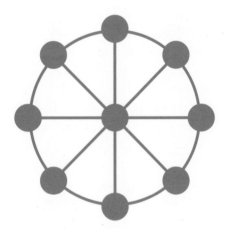

Twitter, along with various e-commerce websites and other influential social media platforms, made a similar determination. And while *Facebook* was already the cause of consternation for many from both the Left and Right of the political divide—in a highly charged political environment—*Facebook* leadership recognised how company branding (their logo, in particular) could actually endanger staff. Less than a week after suspending Trump's account, *Facebook* sent a memo to all staff, which included a very specific and chilling warning:

"In light of recent events, and to err on the side of caution, global security is encouraging everyone to avoid wearing or carrying Facebook-branded items at this time." [16]

In this instance, the *Facebook* logo was very much about individual identity, where the idea of supporting the brand simply meant working for it. It meant that the logo both represented and communicated the brand's actions and beliefs (including suspending Trump's account); it meant the logo ensured individual's would be recognised as 'belonging' to—and presumably agreeing with—*Facebook*; and, ultimately, it meant the logo put *Facebook* staff at personal risk. All this, and yet, *Facebook's* logo design—in and of itself—doesn't mean that much. But what it represents absolutely *does*, because context matters.

It's the same for every other familiar brand, and it's a primary reason why logos are often referred to as 'the brand'—even though they are merely an open canvas for associations, meaning and belonging. Unsurprisingly, as context and awareness of a brand grows, so too does its interpretation. This, in turn, elevates the significance and impact of their logo. It also increases a brand's collective value.

---

16. *Facebook reportedly tells employees to avoid wearing company logo in public,* by Carrie Mihalcik, CNet, online article, 12 January 2021.

What's a brand worth?

The phrase 'brand value' is often mentioned when seeking to express the importance and influence of a brand. However, as we know, it's notoriously difficult to establish a figure to quantify that value in tangible terms—specifically a financial value. But that doesn't stop people from trying. Nevertheless, brand value is a 'thing'. Part of that value is calculated based on products, services, systems, processes, databases, recognition, revenue, business models, general and specific assets, and other *tangible* items. It can also include measuring the value of the logo or branding, which is less straightforward.

But things get really tricky when trying to assess how people *perceive* the brand; and what the brand means in people's lives. Obviously, that's incredibly valuable. Unfortunately, it's just not very tangible. So, you can see how quantifying brand value with accuracy becomes problematic. And yet, how people *feel* about a brand is probably the best measure of brand value, because it explains loyalty, it explains how people forgive a brand for its transgressions, and it explains the feeling of 'belonging'—specifically how a brand contributes to a person's identity. This, perhaps more than anything, goes some way towards expressing how valuable a brand can become. One such brand is *Supreme*.

Now, you may recall from Chapter 2 that influential fashion platform, *Lyst*, crowned *Supreme* the industry's most powerful logo in 2018. We also learned that the logo can turn almost anything into a collector's item and that, at the time, *Supreme* was valued at a cool $1 billion. But things have changed since Chapter 2—*Supreme's* value has risen significantly. In fact, it has doubled. In November, 2019, footwear giant *VF Corporation* bought *Supreme* for over $2 billion, and the logo played an important role in that valuation. Indeed, a *Christie's* auction catalogue explicitly supported this assessment by stating:

•

Wherever your
brand moves, your logo's
meaning will follow.

•

"Equally at home on both the sidewalk and the catwalk, the [Supreme] Box Logo is the pumping heart of the brand, and is now more highly coveted than ever before." [17]

Supreme illustrates how appropriate, intelligent branding can reflect the philosophy of a business. Although simple, the 'Red Box' logo design is very deliberate in paying homage to Barbara Kruger's art and subject matter: culture, power, identity, consumerism, and sexuality. What better representation of youth culture and skateboard attitude? And while these themes in the logo might not be immediately visible or recognised by some people, they absolutely set the tone for the business from the outset. As the brand matured and evolved, the logo became a central means for conveying *Supreme's* intangible (yet very real) brand value— something that more established, mainstream and conservative brands wanted to be associated with. Through numerous successful collaborations with influential brands and artists, *Supreme* managed to monetise its rapidly growing cache of 'cool'. As brand commentator James I. Bowie once put it:

"The box logo serves a secondary function [...] allowing Supreme to confer its imprimatur of coolness on its lucky collab partners—like Hanes, Lacoste, and even the likes of Brooks Brothers—by placing it adjacent to their less hipster marks." [18]

Some might argue that *Supreme* 'sold out' by deliberately associating its brand with these 'less hip' and perhaps more mainstream or conservative collaborators. After all, these are the antithesis of *Supreme's* original Kruger-esque street philosophy. But others might see the irony in a perceived anti-establishment brand leveraging its 'cool factor' in order to upstage those mainstream brands in desperate need of some relevance with youth culture. It's a contradiction in terms, and yet *Supreme* has navigated

17. *How Supreme Created the Most Valuable Logo of All Time,* by James I. Bowie, Marker on Medium, online article, 7 January 2021.
18. *How Supreme Created the Most Valuable Logo of All Time.*

it deftly, while adding immense value to the brand in the process. Indeed, James I. Bowie went on to question this thorny conundrum:

"It's not always clear who is in on Supreme's joke. Are the hypebeasts, the enthusiasts of the brand who stand in line for hours to cop some pickups from the latest Supreme drop (as the kids say), earnest or ironic in their fandom? Supreme has gamified their consumerism. One intrepid shopper did manage to obtain all 253 versions of the iconic Supreme box logo T-shirt; Christie's was expected to sell the collection last month [December 2020] for $2 million, or eight grand per shirt." [19]

Astonishing as that might seem, *Supreme's* logo ensures the brand is recognised for what it stands for—or, at least, how they want to be interpreted. For many, it exudes culture and street cool. It channels an upstart skateboard philosophy into an attainable identity by transmitting a level of status bestowed by *Supreme* on its community. While the business manufactured this value it was the community who elevated it to an exalted position—and without whom the brand would have little relevance. Yet, the logo itself (the badge) remains a simple red box with the word *Supreme* set in Futura font. It says so much, with so little; it means so much, without saying much at all.

It's worth remembering, *Supreme's* Red Box logo was designed at a specific point in time—for a fledgling business—to reflect those early attitudes. While it has been a beacon of underground street culture, *Supreme* could now be abruptly veering towards a more mainstream market. In turn, the logo's meaning will come to reflect this shift, even though the design hasn't changed—nor is it likely to. Nevertheless, a lot *will* change. A different context will usher in new perceptions and meaning, and this will inevitably impact the brand's value—and its customer profile. The point is: wherever your brand moves, your logo's meaning will follow.

---

19. *How Supreme Created the Most Valuable Logo of All Time.*

8. Branding makes an organisation visible and understood—*the logo and communications material are a window to your brand. Consider how you want to be seen. If you're not clear about your own brand, don't expect that others will be, either.*

It's obvious that branding is vital in the pursuit of differentiating a business, a brand or an organisation in the market. If done right, it can be incredibly powerful and can deliver a swathe of messages instantaneously through one simple logo. I'm sure you can think of a number of brands that achieve this on a daily basis. But in this instance, I'm not just talking about contemporary branding. I'm talking about the 17th and 18th centuries. I'm talking about a movement that was known and understood throughout the world. I'm talking about *pirates.*

Pirates? Yes, pirates! There's a lot that brands and businesses today can learn from these (unexpected) masters of branding. But before we get into this, summon all those images, stories and legends you associate with pirates (including *Jack Sparrow, Captain Hook* and *Blackbeard*). Got them? Right, now let's consider how the pirate movement actually came about—and what motivated them. In his wonderful book *Be More Pirate*, Sam Conniff Allende's opening paragraph sets the scene:

"Three hundred years ago a small group of frustrated and underappreciated, mostly young professionals had finally had enough of living in a society run badly by a self-interested and self-serving Establishment. Disruption had become the constant backdrop to their lives as they faced ongoing uncertainty and mass redundancy in a world plagued by ideologically influenced international conflict. This generation felt entirely abandoned, and they were right. The odds were stacked high against them in every single way, the rules of the day favoured an elite few, and for the majority of people life was unclear, unfair and unfulfilling." [20]

Okay, so what does all this have to do with branding—or logos, for that matter? Well, for a start, 300 years later we have a pretty good sense of what pirates represented, admittedly

---

20. *Be More Pirate,* Sam Conniff Allende, Penguin Random House, first published by Portfolio, 2018, page 3.

skewed by more notorious representations in books and films. However, those books and films do overlook some of their more impressive achievements, which include an innovative approach to organisational structure and some forward thinking on gender and racial equality in the workplace. Not to mention their pioneering work in the field of branding, where they very cleverly, quickly and deliberately, fashioned an unsavoury, sword-wielding, frightening reputation on the high seas, albeit for surprising reasons. As Conniff Allende puts it:

"The majority of Golden-Age pirates tried to create the impression of violence whilst actively trying to avoid conflict wherever possible. I know that sounds counter-intuitive, but hear me out: pirates were heavily motivated to steer clear of actual violence because it made sense financially. For pirates, there was a clear case—fear equals profit and violence equals cost." [21]

I'm sure we can all agree that instilling fear is not the best strategy for any business to adopt in the 21st Century. But pirates provide a clear example of how to build a reputation—and a brand—that could immediately convey a message, while also attracting like-minded people to their movement. All of this was embedded in their world-renowned logo—the *Skull and Crossbones* flag, otherwise known as the *Jolly Roger*. In his book *The Invisible Hook: The Hidden Economics of Pirates*, economist and author Peter Leesen explains:

"Pirates used the Jolly Roger to enhance their profit through plunder. But it was the profit motive that led them to overtake victims in the least violent manner possible. By signalling pirates' identity to potential targets, the Jolly Roger prevented bloody battle that would needlessly injure or kill, not only pirates, but also innocent merchant seamen. Ironically, then, the effect of the death's head symbolism was closer to a dove carrying an olive branch." [22]

---

21. *Be More Pirate*, page 12.
22. *The Invisible Hook: The Hidden Economics of Pirates*, Peter Leeson, Princeton University Press, 2011, page 101.

For a group who initially had nothing going for them, and therefore nothing to lose, pirates were incredibly business-minded, while also adept at marketing, communications and branding. They understood the simplicity of a visible, effective logo. But it didn't stop there. The pirate brand, once established, also communicated a series of very progressive policies which, in those uncertain times, would have acted as an effective recruitment drive based on some strongly held Values and beliefs. For example, any pirate that was injured received a payment from the ship's common funds—all done in a structured and equal manner, specific to each injury. This approach predates modern public policy and was a forerunner of human rights. (Bet you never thought of pirates that way before.) This was embedded in their business strategy—steering clear of violence, wherever possible, in order to avoid hefty payouts. All this was part and parcel of the pirate brand, which:

"Questioned and challenged the established order, rebelled against the status quo and then rewrote the rules. They came up with better alternative ideas and formed powerful communities of people who wanted to reorganize themselves in a new society. In these pioneering groups, the pirates made a point of fighting for fairness and inclusion. As they did this, they weaponised the art of storytelling and anticipated the idea of branding, crafting killer stories about themselves that helped magnify their reputation and establish their legacy." [23]

But maybe you're thinking that was a different time, and a different context. Perhaps you don't see a correlation between how pirates built their brand, designed their logo and developed their reputation. There's a 300+ year gap, after all. Well, let's fast forward to today. In an article for *Forbes*, Jeroen Kraaijenbrink discusses the purpose and power of logos—whether for a movement, a business or a country. It's a strategy that works just as well today as it did 300 years ago:

---

23. *Be More Pirate*, page 18.

"A company's logo and branding express what a company adds and how it wants to be perceived by its customers, suppliers, competitors and other stakeholders. And this is usually made explicit in a company's strategy. Without a clear strategy, there is not much use for a logo because it is not clear what the logo should express." [24]

---

24. *Does A Country Need A Logo? (And Is This One Worth $220,000?)*, Jeroen Kraaijenbrink, Forbes, online article, 11 November 2019.

9. **Your brand is not just what you say it is**—*it's what other people say it is; the challenge is managing the gap. And never underestimate the power of perception because it can be more persuasive than the truth.*

You may be familiar with the phrase: *your brand is what people say about you when you're not in the room*. It's attributed to Jeff Bezos (founder of *Amazon*), which probably affords it some extra weight and credibility. It illustrates how powerfully advantageous, or irreversibly damaging perception can be. Why? Because it involves something frighteningly persuasive: *other people's words*.

Many businesses and brands spend enormous resources broadcasting their messages in the hope they connect with customers, clients and the market. These marketing messages are often very specific. They're also extremely controlled. The intention is to help shape favourable perceptions, whether that relates to price, quality, convenience, status, emotions, experience, or reputation, among many other things. Unfortunately, it's notoriously difficult to gauge how successful these messages might be. And don't forget, they're only part of how we perceive a business or brand. There are so many other factors that people take into consideration and we only really get a sense of this when we hear how they talk about those businesses or brands within their own personal networks. That means how people speak about your business or brand is very much out of your control. The best you can do is to *influence* them with the messages you send, backed up by actions and behaviours that validate those messages. The most effective way to achieve this is by being transparent, consistent, authentic and ethical in everything you do because all of this contributes to something even more important: *trust*. While that sounds logical it's amazing that some businesses and brands still struggle with adopting this approach—despite the power people now wield through social media.

However, 'other people's words' are also incredibly useful because they're a valuable feedback loop to help identify any gaps in perceptions. How a business or brand responds to these shared opinions (whether positive or negative) can make all the difference and can either add to or diminish those views.

Word-of-mouth referrals and testimonials have been used as a tool for as long as business, trade and social structures have existed. But it's now far more pervasive. The advent of resources like *Tripadvisor, Google* reviews and social media, in general, permits people to have immediate access to what others think about a particular product, service, business or brand. And people are less inhibited than ever before about sharing their (often unfiltered) thoughts, which makes their opinions far more potent. It also provides a window into patterns: while there will always be a mix of positive and negative comments, we can quickly average them to get a sense of the dominant view. We tend to believe (rightly or wrongly) that individual reviews are genuine and authentic. At the very least, they add to and influence any other opinions or perceptions we've encountered elsewhere.

This works on both a micro and macro level. It could relate to opinions about a local restaurant through to detailed commentary on global brands. From opinions on *BP* or *Netflix*, through to *Apple* or *Nike*, and from Elon Musk to J. K. Rowling, whether it's *Uber's* rating system, or comments from the *Twittersphere* or *TikTok*, we all have stories about how other people's words have influenced our perception about things within our orbit of interest. Ultimately, all of this affects our decisions about when and where we spend our money.

This also applies to family and friends who offer their casual (sometimes unsolicited) opinions, as well as news articles and films or documentaries, wine awards or simple book cover reviews. Opinions have become an important reference for how we navigate and validate the world. In fact, it's not lost on me that this book features other people's words, ranging from interviews through to referencing reports, research, books, articles and video transcripts. Across the board, other people's words are an undeniable influence. They can prompt change, identify a consensus, encourage support, or incite rage. Unsurprisingly, the challenge is staying on the right side of perceptions.

Managing the gap

If you're still in any doubt about how other people's words can help shape perceptions and impact a business or brand, consider this: in 2004, Morgan Spurlock's documentary *Super-size Me* tracked his month-long experiment where he exclusively ate at *McDonald's*. The resulting impact on his health was shocking and led the fast food mega brand to fundamentally change how they operated, essentially removing the 'Super-size' option from their menu and repositioning the brand in an attempt to appear more health conscious. While a documentary might sound like a large scale or ambitious undertaking, Spurlock only had a reported $65k to make the film—but its reach was vast. That the film went on to gross $22.2 million at the box office,[25] provides a sense of the public pressure *McDonald's* would have experienced as a result. When we take into account what one lone voice can do to impact a brand and shape perceptions, just think what an aggregate of multiple voices can do in a similar situation today.

Of course, the impact of *other people's words* isn't always negative. *&pizza* is a case in point, where word-of-mouth was instrumental in positioning them in the market—and in the community—and where their consistent actions and behaviours built upon (and reinforced) those positive opinions. In short, what *&pizza* said about themselves generally matched what other people said about them. This activity happens on a daily basis, wherever people speak favourably about a positive experience they've had with a business or brand. So much so, they feel compelled to share their stories and recommend their experience to others. Without question, this has shifted the power to influence even more in favour of individuals and groups. We no longer need to make documentaries to have an impact because people are more than willing to share their opinions on digital platforms about the experiences and value they have (or have not) received from your business or brand. And this holds far more weight than anything you can ever say on your own behalf.

---

25. *Low Budget Films That Made More Than Their Money Back,* by James Spiro, Editor Choice, article, 20 December 2018.

As marketing expert Seth Godin so eloquently puts it:

"What you say isn't nearly as important as what others say about you."[26]

---

26. *This is Marketing: You can't be seen until you learn to see,* by Seth Godin, Portfolio Penguin, 2018 / Penguin Business, 2019, page 14.

10. Your brand is your filter—*use it to help decide on everything, from hiring staff to making acquisitions or pursuing initiatives. It's all about finding the right fit.*

Running a business involves juggling multiple variables on a daily basis. This is amplified when building or maintaining a brand. It can often be overwhelming. However, when you genuinely know who you are, what your business stands for—*and* what you won't tolerate—when you're living your Values every day, and delivering on your promises consistently, you have a 'brand clarity' that you can use as your *filter*. All of your decisions can be assessed on whether or not they fit with you, how you act and behave, right through to considering an acquisition, or fielding an investor inquiry. You can't do this with your logo.

The benefit of being a brand—or having a brand mindset—is an understanding that everything you do and influence is a reflection of who and what you stand for. However, approaching this in a random manner breeds a similar culture inside your business: uncoordinated, inconsistent, opportunistic, scatter-shot, confusing. The phrase 'chasing your tail' comes to mind. In contrast, when you use your brand as a filter, everything becomes much simpler because in every scenario you have a singular choice: does this fit with us or not? The clearer you are about who you are—and what your brand is—the easier and quicker those decisions become. For example, if an opportunity doesn't fit with you—your brand, your Values, your culture, your Purpose—you can quickly identify this early in the process and decline the opportunity, no matter how lucrative it might be. On the other hand, if the opportunity is just too good to pass up—even if it's not the right fit—you'll accept that it will change your brand, with an understanding that you'll need to adjust accordingly. But you'll have a very clear grasp as to why—and what that means for your business.

Practically speaking, how does this work? Well, it's highly unlikely that an environmentally-minded brand—for example *Patagonia*—would hire a climate denier, or entertain an opportunity that will produce a negative impact on the environment. While that's a pretty simple example, it serves the point. If your Values and

Purpose are clear, if you and customers completely understand your brand, your culture, and what you stand for, then you can avoid anything, or anyone, that might jeopardise it. As Seth Godin argues:

"Customer development is the act of gaining traction with customers, of finding a fit between what you make and what they want. This traction is worth far more than fancy technology or expensive marketing. That, and only that, separates successful projects from unsuccessful ones." [27]

Of course, achieving clarity can be a work in progress. There may be transition periods which impact your staff, who now feel they don't fit—perhaps discovering that they actually never did fit. But your filter will also attract new talent who align more clearly with you. It could mean losing some customers—those who decide you're not for them. But it will also help you to connect with new customers who feel you're the perfect fit. Either way, having clarity about who you are requires the courage to use your filter, which will ultimately benefit everyone.

---

27. *This is Marketing: You can't be seen until you learn to see,* Seth Godin, Penguin Business, 2019, page 33.

11. Don't just have a positioning—*have a position. Taking a stand will help define your brand.*

Most businesses have a strategic positioning, which clearly outlines where they operate within a market and how they differentiate themselves. However, in branding, a *strategic brand positioning* should convey this as a succinct value proposition—although it can also express an attitude or a personality around how the business delivers value. Regardless, it's best to keep a strategic positioning as a short sentence to ensure it's easier to remember and allows others to expand on it in their own words. This is the opposite of attempting to memorise a 'crafted corporate script'. On the other hand, taking a 'position' is far more pointed and generally reflects a social or political stand the business has taken around a particular issue. So, what might compel a business to 'take a position'—and why are more businesses increasingly doing so?

As we've seen from Chapter 6, in particular, Purpose-driven businesses and brands are on the rise and this shift is encouraging businesses to take sides. According to *Forbes*:

"Brands are increasingly aware that younger consumers want their brands to take a position and to have a purpose. Sometimes brands are compelled to take a controversial position, such as abandoning the NRA [the American National Rifle Association] following the shooting [in February, 2019] at Marjory Stoneman Douglas High School in Florida. Or they voluntarily take a controversial position such as Nike's Colin Kaepernick ad. And, frequently, brands simply adopt non-controversial positions such as fashion brand Everlane promoting manufacturing transparency and sustainability. Expect to see brands of all stripes taking positions on topics meaningful to consumers. Brands can no longer remain on the sidelines." [28]

---

28. *10 Brand Marketing Trends To Watch In 2019,* Michael Stone, Forbes, online article, 28 January, 2019.

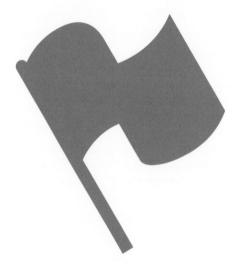

Finding a position

Defining your Purpose (outside of making a profit) can be incredibly difficult. Many people struggle with articulating a bigger picture for their business, one that reflects (and aligns with) their Values. It can be overwhelming to settle on something clear and specific that you can stand behind over the long-term. But *taking a position* on a specific issue or topic can actually be easier, partly because it's often more defined and partly because, initially, it can be a response to a moment in time. In many cases, a position can be tied to a business' bigger Purpose, or the Values which underpin it. Taking a position simply requires being observant of societal shifts, being aware of current affairs and generally having empathy. In short, taking a position is a clear signal (to staff, customers and the world) about what you stand for, or what you believe in—not just as a business, but as part of a group of like-minded individuals.

Taking a position can be the first step in helping to identify a bigger Purpose, to test the waters with staff and customers, and to identify with a wider community who support the same cause or position that you're taking. And while some critics might argue that taking a position at one moment in time hardly makes for a Purpose-driven business or brand, well, they're right. But that's not the point. Taking a position is simply that: *taking a position*. When enough businesses take a position on the same issue (like the environment, immigration, gun violence, domestic violence, LGBTQI+ rights, bullying, a living wage, equal pay, depression, suicide, mental wellbeing, etc), the overall aggregate pushes that topic into the wider public conscience. It facilitates a platform and collectively endorses it as an important issue. And when a business takes that position again, and again, and then again, it serves as a pattern. So, those moments in time add up for that business—perhaps as a Purpose—but definitely in contributing to the aggregate of a bigger collective position. This is the difference between having a *strategic positioning* and *taking a position*. Of course, there are also examples where a market position aligns with taking a stand on the Values which underpin that business or brand. As we've seen, *Patagonia* is a case in point.

Leading by example

In some case, simply taking a position can lead to a bigger impact. For example, in 2015, the Dutch-based file-sharing giant *WeTransfer* opened an office in Los Angeles. According to *FastCompany*, one of the first things [*WeTransfer*] president Damian Bradfield noticed was the homelessness. In 2019, the city had approximately 59,000 people living on the streets, an increase of 12% from the previous year. Another serious challenge facing this vulnerable community was an estimated $35 million in medical debt.[29] Acknowledging this, Bradfield made a startling decision. *WeTransfer* teamed up with *Headspace*, local companies and philanthropists, and partnered with *RIP Medical Debt* (a non-profit organisation) to remove a combined $30 million in medical debt for up to 16,000 people in need.[30] Notably, *WeTransfer* wasn't trying to 'show up' in their market with some socially responsible, ethically minded, Purpose-driven facade. They weren't trying to endear themselves to a current or future customer group in order to increase profits. Quite the opposite. *WeTransfer* was motivated by observing a clear issue, taking a leadership position and simply *doing the right thing*.

Let's look at another high-profile case, where personal values first questioned and then redefined a business. For over a decade, American fashion designer Thakoon Panichgul was the darling of exclusive catwalks, boasting a loyal clientele, which included First Lady Michelle Obama and Anna Wintour, among many others. At his peak, he was designing over 200 looks per year. But he began to question its sustainability—not because of the creative pressure he was undoubtedly under, but because of the impact this had on the environment through materials, supply chains and essentially contributing to luxury 'fast fashion', where garments are worn only once or twice before being discarded for the next 'new' item. According to *Business Insider*:

29. *WeTransfer and Headspace just helped pay off $30 million of people's medical debt*, Ben Paynter, FastCompany, online article, 18 July 2019.
30. *WeTransfer and Headspace just helped pay off $30 million of people's medical debt*.
31. *The fashion industry emits more carbon than international flights and maritime shipping combined. Here are the biggest ways it impacts the planet*, Morgan McFall-Johnsen, Business Insider US, online article, 17 October 2019.

"The fashion industry emits more carbon than international flights and maritime shipping combined." [31]

Fast fashion, and high-end fashion, which dictate trends season after season, have all contributed to overconsumption and waste resulting in 75% of consumers being concerned about the environmental impact of the fashion industry.[32] Observing this shift, Panichgul took two years off at the height of his career to reassess his role in the industry, but also the role and responsibilities of fashion in society. His new business model is now a much simpler direct-to-consumer approach. And where his previous clothes sold for thousands of dollars, his new collection—of just 12 garments— sell for $225 or less. Importantly, each piece is specifically designed to be worn season after season. It's a radical shift, based on market developments and societal observations, and it's the opposite of what he built his brand on. However, at the same time, it conveys a specific attitude and narrative—a position—which, for now, he seems to be embracing for the right reasons. Of course, in many ways, it's also about business survival.

But this change is not confined to individual designers. Large fashion brands like *Prada* are also taking a similar position by embracing a more sustainable business model. Why are they doing this? According to the *Evening Standard*:

"Left, right and centre, brands are clambering to hop onboard the sustainability train, as people are increasingly demanding that their clothes are made in an ethical manner. But now Prada has made history as the first luxury brand to obtain a loan from French banking group Crédit Agricole with stringent sustainability-related conditions attached to it. The first condition of the £42.9 million loan relates to the brand's physical stores: there must be a certain amount of stores that are certified either gold or platinum by the green- building rating system Leadership in Energy and Environmental

---

32. *One of America's top designers quit at the height of his career. Now he's back—with a vision,* Elizabeth Segran, FastCompany, online article, 18 September 2019.

Design, which takes into account the construction of a building, its management, and the number of resources it consumes or waste it produces. Secondly, Prada will have to increase its training hours for its employees, and lastly, the third goal reinforces the luxury brand's pledge to reduce and phase out the use of virgin nylon by 2021, instead moving to Econyl, a recyclable yarn made from upcycled plastic waste." [33]

All this is partly due to commercial pressures, and partly due to consumer preferences. But sustainability is just one aspect of this. The bigger, more important objective is *impact*. This is where Panichgul appears to veer from other fashion brands. He has acknowledged fashion's role in overconsumption (season by season) and has completely changed his business model and philosophy in response—not just through materials or supply chains—and begun building a new 'position narrative' around his brand for the future.

A position of leadership

Clearly, it requires leadership to take a position on something, and the more visible, high profile and influential those leaders are, the easier it is for others to follow with more confidence and certainty. In this regard, Larry Fink (of *BlackRock*) continues to demonstrate clear—and profound—leadership. As reported in the *Financial Review*:

"BlackRock, the world's largest fund manager, is dumping more than half a billion dollars in thermal coal shares from all of its actively managed portfolios, as part of a more active global stance on climate change driven by chief executive Larry Fink." [34]

There are numerous examples of established individuals, businesses and brands who are taking a stand on some of the most important issues of our time, and the list is long and growing.

---

33. *Prada makes history as the first luxury brand to sign a sustainability deal*, Naomi May, Evening Standard, online article, 14 November, 2019.
34. *BlackRock dumps thermal coal*, Toni Boyd, Financial Review, online article, 14 January, 2020.

•

Remember:
action speaks louder
than intention.

•

For example: *Gucci* CEO Marco Bizzari believes sustainability is the company's future;[35] *Google* has bought $2 billion worth of renewable energy, the biggest-ever corporate purchase of this kind to date;[36] *IKEA* has invested in enough clean energy to power all of its operations;[37] *Apple* has bought a 27,000-acre mangrove forest in Cispatá Bay on the coast of Colombia as a means to preserve it;[38] and *Patagonia* did something it never does—they invested in advertising (specifically to promote and support the 2019 *Global Climate Strike*).[39] All this adds up and it's encouraging to see so many influential organisations taking a stand, which clearly illustrates a growing trend.

At the same time—and in stark contrast—governments are actively requesting business to step away from taking a position. For example, in 2019, the Australian government requested *Qantas* and *Virgin Australia* be silent on social issues,[40] something both brands flatly rejected. In an equally pathetic move, the Trump Administration dismantled US environmental regulations and stepped away from the *Paris Climate Accord*, which 186 states and the EU, representing more than 87% of global greenhouse gas emissions, have ratified or supported—including China and India, who are among the largest greenhouse gas emitters amongst the total *UNFCCC* members.[41] Reflecting more responsible global trends, President Biden returned the US to the *Paris Climate Accord* hours after becoming president, seeking to rectify Trump's previous destructive and irresponsible actions.

---

35. *Gucci CEO Marco Bizzari believes sustainability is the company's future*, FastCompany, online video, 18 September 2019.
36. *Google just made the largest ever corporate purchase of renewable energy*, by Adele Peters, FastCompany, online article, 19 September 2019.
37. *Ikea has invested in enough clean energy to power all of its operations (plus extra)*, by Adele Peters, FastCompany, online article, 19 September 2019.
38. *Inside Apple's plan to protect a 27,000-acre forest in Colombia*, by Adele Peters, FastCompany, online article, 22 April 2019.
39. *Patagonia enlists teen activists to speak out for Global Climate Strike campaign*, by Jeff Beer, FastCompany, online article, 19 September 2019.
40. *Qantas and Virgin bosses reject Morrison government calls to be silent on social issues*, by Paul Karp, The Guardian, online article, 18 September 2019.
41. *Paris Agreement*, Wikipedia, https://en.wikipedia.org/wiki/Paris_Agreement

These examples highlight the swift move towards a global tipping point, where businesses are perceiving less action from governments on the most important issues of the day. And rather than taking a position that will just benefit their bottom line, they are also taking a position for a wider good—for our collective future. But remember: action speaks louder than intention. Talking about taking a position, or engaging in marketing spin, won't solve anything. But taking action will, no matter how small to begin with. And even if your position is political, it doesn't mean you've become an activist, in the traditional sense of the word. Instead, think of taking a position more as *actionism*—rather than *activism*. And if you need further reassurance on the benefits of this mindset, consider how *McKinsey and Company*—a bastion of conservative and traditional thinking—has shifted in this direction:

"Purpose-driven brands achieve more than twice the brand-value growth of brands that focus purely on profit generation, and purpose clarity is directly correlated with financial performance."[42]

42. *Our definition of 'success' is holding business back—it's time for a new one*, by Sebastian Buck, Fast Company, online article, 8 September 2020.

12. **A brand is a long-term and evolving objective**—*it requires dedication and commitment. Building and maintaining your brand cannot be outsourced. It's not a short-term exercise.*

Whether you have a business or a brand, it takes time to develop, evolve and sustain. It can take years and significant investment. It means your status, value and reputation needs to be continually earned, and then protected. So, how have successful brands managed to achieve this? Primarily through *clarity.*

Hang on, is it that simple? Not quite. But, if you're clear about your Values, your customers, your value proposition(s) and your Purpose, you'll have the foundations for building something remarkable, even if that's initially from very humble beginnings. You'll have the direction, commitment and tenacity to stay true to who you are and to what you stand for. This also means you can direct your investment with confidence—because with clarity comes focus. Throughout the inevitable change and adaptation your business will experience over the long haul, you should always return to your central point of clarity—at every stage in your journey. Once again, *Supreme* is a good case in point. Remember in Chapter 2 we looked at how logos become a canvas for all the associations we have with a business or brand. We also identified that it's the brand that gives the logo its value. The *Supreme* logo makes this abundantly clear. But don't forget, it took a long time for that value to materialise—for the business to evolve, and for it to progress through its various life stages. At every point (so far), they've been clear about what they stand for; how they remain relevant in their customer's lives; and what they're seeking to achieve. Of course, like most brands, success didn't happen overnight. Yet, their clarity, their culture and their spirit, have remained consistent throughout. Writing in the 25th Anniversary book *Supreme*, Carlo McCormick (American culture critic and curator) lays it out as such:

"Twenty-five years is a long stretch—perhaps not life but enough time to define a life. In a business, as in a relationship, it is something of a milestone, a perhaps arbitrary pivot when the upstart becomes an institution, the contemporary ripens into the historical, novelty cedes into its impetuous will to longevity, and the iconography of

identity is no longer something you just try on for size but consider for its durability.

Twenty-five years: not the end of the story by any means; it seems now just to be getting started... To put it in perspective: Supreme opened because [New York] didn't have a skate[board] shop, and it was what might be kindly called a failing business until they hit on the idea of making and selling their own t-shirts for a bit of desperate cash flow." [43]

Given *Supreme's* phenomenal success, it's perhaps odd to think of the brand as ever having been desperate for cash flow, though many successful businesses and brands are born out of similar circumstances (*Airbnb* springs to mind). But with nothing to lose (and little to leverage), having clarity, embracing who they are at their core—their attitude, their Values, their culture and their aspirations—allowed them to create something raw and honest, something uncompromising and simple: something valuable. From upstart business to internationally influential brand, *Supreme's* trajectory defines many of the most successful brands, whether that's *Virgin, Nike, Facebook, Vice, Apple, Mambo* or *Netflix*, to name a few. Throughout each business' journey—on their way to becoming a brand, where they became understood, valued and loved—they remained true to who they are, leveraged it and allowed it to define the brand. This took time, and a willingness to be flexible and to evolve within the constraints of their strongly held beliefs. In *Supreme's* case, McCormick explains:

"Twenty-five years into an impromptu yet intuitive project that has grown from cottage industry to international trade, the success of Supreme has earned it widespread recognition as a major force and paradigmatic apogee in myriad fields, including design, fashion, art, street style, and branding identity, but putting such accolades aside, Supreme was and will always remain a fundamental, unflinching expression of skate culture. These are its roots, gnarled

---

43. *Supreme*, Carlo McCormick, Phaidon Press, 2020, page 7.

and gritty enough to show through whatever posh 'dot it dons, but more than that this comprises its ethos, what makes everything it does inherently subversive and anti-authoritarian no matter how established it becomes.

[...] The brand strategy is precisely that of the skaters it represents: subversive and invasive, anti-authoritarian and iconoclastic, about velocity and elevation, mischief and magic, the moment of gravitational defiance and that of sudden impact. This is search-and-destroy, trespass, impolite, and in-your-face yet born of an infinite grace." [44]

Dramatic language aside, the core of *Supreme's* spirit—their brand—is the skater's attitude, and everything which that stands for. This simplicity, this clarity, has allowed *Supreme* to evolve over 25 years with consistency and flexibility. Their attitude was present at the beginning (as a failing business) and it remains today (as an international powerhouse). And their story continues to evolve; they didn't progress from a *business* to a *brand* overnight. It's another lesson in how to build a brand, specifically with regards to finding your audience and genuinely connecting with them. A huge part of that process is clarity of message, one that will resonate with people and attract them. While every business seeks to offer (and provide) some form of value, many look at this through an acutely commercial lens. But *Supreme's* clarity, and their specific focus— underpinned by their attitude and spirit—offered a different kind of value. In McCormick's words, that value was more urgent and more important to *Supreme's* emerging target market:

"Supreme, as a site of irascible delinquency—not as a brand or even a store so much as a clubhouse for a new wave of miscreants—was born out of the irrepressible energies and wretched boredom that is youth... Urgency doesn't wait, and when everything around you is fucking boring, that's just permission to find your own fun, even if it means breaking a few rules and bones along the way. A whole lot of

---

44. *Supreme*, pages 7 and 10.

•

"If you don't like change, you're going to like irrelevance less."

•

people didn't get it; they just couldn't fathom the socializing process within the antisocial behaviour. But for those who did, it wasn't just that the kids were still all right; they were the best hope we had."[45]

Change is inevitable

While the core of your brand or business might remain the same—with regard to Values, belief and Purpose—things inevitably do change over time: the world advances; circumstances shift; contexts evolve; and society moves in tandem. Uncertainty is probably the only certainty we have, and things are now moving (and changing) at lightning speed. While we can learn from actions, strategies and outcomes which have been successful in the past, they don't always work when trying to navigate the future. This is the conundrum of change: *understanding the need to change, while at the same time not wanting to change at all.* So, if we know change is inevitable why do we resist it? According to Ellen Jackson (psychologist, internationally published writer, speaker and consultant), there are three main reasons:

"1. It's a shock and we're not ready. If a change is big and unexpected our first reaction is shock, then denial. It's the emotional equivalent of singing 'la la la la la' with our fingers in our ears. We carry on as we always have, telling ourselves that nothing has changed, denying that we've been told anything about a change and making excuses for non-participation. Even if, deep down, you knew this change was coming, you might still linger in denial for a while until you've worked through some fear and discomfort and wrapped your head around what's happening.

2. Change brings feelings and feelings are uncomfortable. As humans we're happy and safe in our comfort zone. Push us near the edge and we get anxious. Push us over the edge and we can fall apart completely. Even when we complain about not being happy with the status quo, it doesn't mean we're ready to launch into something different. Not yet.

---

45. *Supreme*, page 7.

3. We don't know what the future looks like and that's scary. This is important if you're helping others to change." [46]

Having clarity—about your customers, about your value offer, about your communication, about the positive change you're seeking to make in a customer's life—means you're actually not looking to serve everyone. You're looking for a specific type of everyone. In other words, as Seth Godin argues:

"As soon as you ask yourself about the change you seek to make it becomes quite clear that you have no chance of changing 'everyone'. Everyone is a lot of people. Everyone is too diverse, too enormous, and too indifferent for you to have a chance at changing. So you need to change 'someone'. Or a group of someones." [47]

Remember, it's customers and clients who are increasingly dictating how brands need to continuously evolve over time in order to stay relevant, and where complacency and resistance to change can have dire consequences. But change for the sake of change is also futile. It needs to be clear and focused, and in response to contexts and customer expectations. *Supreme* is proof that you can change and adapt while staying consistent over the long-term. But, if you still dislike change, and if you're in any doubt that your business or brand needs to evolve, to adapt and to change over time, consider the words of Eric Shinseki (former United States Secretary of Veterans Affairs):

"If you don't like change, you're going to like irrelevance less." [48]

---

46. *3 Reasons Why Humans Hate Change*, Ellen Jackson, Potential Psychology, online artcicle, 3 June 2019.
47. *This is Marketing: You Can't be Seen Until You Learn to See*, Seth Godin, Penguin Business, 2018, page 28.
48. Quoted in Mackubin Thomas Owens, *"Marines Turned Soldiers"*, National Review Online.

13. **More than ever, your customer or end user is at the heart of your brand**—*whether you like it or not. Put simply: "Brand is the promise you make; customer experience is the promise you keep."**

---

* Proto Partners, www.protopartners.com.au/about

It's not uncommon to hear businesses and brands state how customer-centric they are. Yet, how many truly put their customer at the heart of their business or brand? Well, if they do, it will show up in their products and services, in their culture and strategy, in how they communicate (internally and externally), in their actions and behaviours, and—ultimately—in how *we* experience them.

While it makes absolute sense to put your customer at the heart of your business—simply because without them you don't have a business—the competitive cut-and-thrust of today's commercial world, coupled with our passion for what we do, often means our focus tends to be on managing the day-to-day challenges of operations and delivery. Translation: we're actually more focused on ourselves. In some cases, we're on auto-pilot, or we don't have the time, resources or know-how to understand our customers better. Then, there are the navel gazers, those who are caught up in their own perceived self-importance and who are bound to an outmoded view that customers are essentially cash cows. They're not really interested in their customers' lives, and they are oblivious to the fact that things have changed dramatically, leaving them to wonder why things aren't as successful as they used to be. So what's changed? Well, put simply, the positions of power have flipped. And it's a radically different reality. Businesses and brands are no longer in control—or at least no longer in complete control. Navigating this has now become key to success. As Sir John Hegarty says:

"Today, owing to new technology, brands are controlled by consumers more than ever. The consumer's part in a brand's success is now even more fundamental and indeed precarious. Misunderstand that relationship and a brand is doomed to failure. Great brands that continue to be successful are so because they don't think like a conventional brand owner who is obsessed only with themselves and the belief that the world revolves around them and their product." [49]

---

49. *Hegarty on Advertising: Turning intelligence into magic*, page 42.

Harsh. But true.

Customers and Clients

But before we explore this a little further, it's important to first address another set of definitions. The words 'customer' and 'client' are often interchangeable (and sometimes used in the same sentence to describe the same individual). Yet, how we speak to a customer is very different to how we might speak to a client, because what a customer wants or needs is very different to what a client seeks and expects. While this might sound like splitting hairs—a mere semantic quibble—distinguishing customers from clients is critical to how we place them at the heart of our business or brand. How so?

Customers seek transactions.
Clients seek consultation.

This is an important distinction because the first is usually about the value inherent in a product or service, delivered through one-off transactions, whereas the second is about the value inherent in a relationship, delivered through a deeper consultation (or a series of consultations). Let me put it another way.

Sam is keen to get fitter so she purchases a membership at a local gym. She's a little apprehensive, but she's committed, nonetheless. She does some online research to prepare her workouts and after a few weeks starts to see some tangible progress. But then, she begins to plateau and she feels her workout needs variation—and some motivation. However, she's reluctant to use a number of the machines because she's unfamiliar with them. During her workouts she tries to quietly observe how other people are using the equipment and then starts trying them herself. But she still feels unsure, and that ache in her shoulder is new.

Soon, it becomes apparent that she needs additional help. She decides to speak with a Personal Trainer, to get professional guidance on her workout routines and technique. Sam is introduced to Liz, one of the gym's experienced Personal Trainers. Liz discusses Sam's background, her goals and her objectives. Essentially, Liz wants to know what success looks like for Sam so she can prepare a personalised workout routine. Sam agrees to engage Liz for a series of sessions. She sees immediate results, her technique improves, her fitness increases and that shoulder ache disappears. During one of her sessions, Liz brings up the topic of nutrition and how this can impact fitness and wellbeing. She talks about how the overall health benefits of a nutritional plan can be integrated into Sam's lifestyle and workout routines. At this stage, Sam trusts Liz so she's happy to explore this topic further, with the intention of getting maximum return on her health and fitness goals.

This fictional example traces Sam's arc from *customer* (purchasing a general gym membership) to *client* (engaging a Personal Trainer for ongoing personalised consultations). Of course—just like real life—there are lots of potential variables in this story: perhaps Sam could have attended some group sessions; perhaps she was put off by Liz's casual chat about nutrition, potentially seeing this as an uninvited 'upsell'; etc. Regardless, the point is Sam started as a *customer* and evolved into a *client*. This is significant because the way the gym would have communicated *to* Sam when she was a customer would be very different to the way Liz communicated *with* Sam when she became a client. This can be applied to numerous scenarios. Just think of your everyday life and distinguish between when you're a customer (transaction based) versus when you're a client (consultation based), whether you're buying a carton of milk, engaging with your accountant, getting petrol, ordering take-out, visiting your doctor, or grabbing an *Uber*. In each instance, how the business or brand communicates with you is specific—and it entirely depends on whether you're their customer or client. Indeed, sometimes you might be both, but for different reasons and at different points.

Who buys your products or services?

Okay, all this makes sense, right? But it's nuanced, so clearly identifying how to approach communicating with your customer or client is critical in branding. It can also help you assess whether or not you actually are a customer (or client)-centric business or brand. For example, if you really know your customer or client, then you're clear about the specific value you provide to them, what messages they need to hear from you, how you connect with them, and what their expectations are. If you're *not* clear about any of this, then it's hard to claim you're customer-centric. On this issue, Hamdi Ulukaya provides some food for thought. According to *Inc.*:

"'Today's playbook says the CEO reports to the board. In my opinion the CEO reports to the consumer,' says Ulukaya. He takes this point so seriously that, in the early days of Chobani, the telephone number on each pot of yogurt was his own personal line. Customers could literally phone up the CEO to chat.

'If you're right with your people, if you're right with your community, if you're right with your product, you'll be more profitable, more innovative, and you will have more passionate people working for you and a community that supports you,' he concludes." [50]

The stories we tell

With so much noise in the world it feels like everyone has to shout louder, just to be heard above the fray. Often, businesses and brands jostle to tell their story in the most compelling way expressing: how genuine they are; how sustainable they are; how experienced they are; how their heritage provides status; how successful and results-driven they are; or how customer-centric they are. The instinct is to tell your story as best you can, to connect with your market in a clear and relevant fashion. But there is a problem with this approach—*it's all about you.* It's your story. It's not your customer or client's story. *"But our story is important."* I hear you say. *"We need to communicate our value, and connect with people based on the*

---

50. *Chobani Billionaire Hamdi Ulukaya: To Be Truly Successful, Break These 3 Stupid Business Rules,* Jessica Stillman, Inc, online article, 18 July, 2019.

reasons they may choose us over someone else. Otherwise, how else will they know, or learn about us?" This is true. But that approach is still flawed, because the story is still about you.

The truth is, people generally have one question in their mind when they're seeking a product, service or experience: *What's in it for me?* If you're honest, you have this question in mind when you're looking to engage a supplier, purchase equipment, or when buying a product, etc. The question may not be explicit, but it's in your mind. Sometimes you're looking for reassurance, sometimes quality, sometimes a bargain, sometimes status. Other times you might be seeking change, or transformation, or validation, or impact. Whatever it is—you're looking for something. You want to know: *What's in it for me?* As a business or brand, how do you reconcile this? On the one hand, you want to tell your story and in many cases, *you need to.* It could be your brand story, your approach, your history, or your experience. Whatever it is, it's likely to be an important message for you to communicate. On the other hand, your customer or client is asking what's in it for them? Let's be honest, they're probably not all that interested in a well-crafted text presenting *your* deeply considered story—however genuine it might be. Instead, they're only really interested in knowing *where your story shows up in their story.* So, how might that look and sound?

- *We know your decisions are made based on cost and quality. That's why we've spent years perfecting our systems and handpicking our suppliers to provide the best-quality products at the most cost-effective prices—because that's just as important for us as it is for you.*

- *Like you, we're passionate about being health-conscious. That's why we only source ingredients directly from our trusted producers and prepare our products within 24 hours of harvesting. Free from preservatives and additives, and with no added sugar, our products are fresher, healthier and more nutritious for you and your family.*

•

Your customer is probably not all that interested in a well crafted text presenting *your* deeply considered story—however genuine it might be. Instead, they're only really interested in knowing *where your story shows up in their story.*

•

These fictional examples illustrate how those businesses might tell their story, but in a way that's relevant to their customer or client. By shifting the focus—and the language—there's more chance that a customer will see themselves in your story; more chance that they understand how you show up in their lives; and more chance of them seeing how you reflect what's important to them. This is only possible if you truly know your customer, and if you genuinely put them at the heart of your business or brand, because the promise you make will show up in the customer experience, which should clearly answer *what's in it for them*.

Shifting the focus

But perhaps you're still not convinced. Maybe you're adamant that your story is compelling enough for customers to connect with your business, your products and your services. Maybe they already are. If so, you're probably wondering: why change anything? Well, the science and research might convince you otherwise. Writing in the *Stanford Social Innovation Review*, Ann Christiano and Annie Neimand present it as such:

"Organizations often aim their communication efforts toward building their own profile with messages and tactics that are more about them than about the issue they've set out to address and the audience they are addressing. They are essentially walking into a party, announcing their presence, and asking people to pay attention. Research from multiple disciplines tells us that people engage and consume information that affirms their identities and aligns with their deeply held values and worldview, and avoid or reject information that challenges or threatens them. This requires advocates to move beyond a focus on building and disseminating a message to stepping into the world of their target community... Does it help them solve a problem? Does it make them feel good about themselves or see themselves as they want to be seen? Does it connect to how they see the world and provide solutions that are actionable? If we want people to engage and take action, we have

to connect to what they care about and how they see themselves...
People seek information that makes them feel good about themselves
and allows them to be a better version of themselves. If you start with
this understanding of the human mind and behavior, you can design
campaigns that help people see where your values intersect and how
the issues you are working on matter to them." [51]

The evidence—which science and research supports—confirms
not only how businesses generally broadcast about themselves, but
also how people tend to view that approach. So, the more you know
about your customer or client, the more you can relate to their
world—and their world view—and then add value to it. Essentially,
it's about shifting the focus from you to them. Genuinely showing
up in your customer or client's story means that you've taken the
time to understand them, and proves you're building your business
or brand around them and their needs. It's evidence that you care
enough to put them at the heart of everything you do.

But this doesn't mean 'the customer is always right'. Nor does it
mean customers or clients should dictate your brand. It simply
means you need to identify who your customer or client is,
understand them deeply, and then provide them with genuine
value—whether obvious or latent. They should influence the
innovations and value propositions you develop for their benefit.
All of this will drive perceptions and, ultimately, attract like-minded
people into your fold, whether they're staff, customers, clients,
stakeholders, partners, or investors. Allowing your customer to see
themselves in your business or brand will fundamentally shape how
you engage them, how you communicate your story—and how they
interpret your relevance.

---

51. *The Science of What Makes People Care,* Ann Christiano and Annie Neimand , Stanford Social
    Innovation Review , online article, Fall 2018 (Volume 16. Number 4).

14. If your brand is to have value, what you do must have value—*because this will determine and define your relevance.*

I imagine most brands and businesses will say they're focused on creating value for customers, clients and shareholders. And why wouldn't they? It makes absolute sense, right? In any transaction people want to ensure they're receiving some form of value—whether that's quality, convenience, reassurance, expertise, status, information, a 'return', or simply 'value for money' (where the perception is they've received more than they've paid for). So, creating or providing value is—or should be—a cornerstone of modern business. But is our interpretation of value too narrow?

Businesses and brands invest a lot of effort in conveying their value to customers—but also in what makes them valuable for investors. Research and statistics featured in this book repeatedly prove that being Purpose-driven—or taking a position—can add immense value to customers, communities, and society, as well as contributing to a business' reputation and its bottom line. This golden union, where everyone wins, is beginning to shape how the future is unfolding. And it's a welcome development. But in order to stay financially viable, businesses and brands also need to explore different ways to create value—not just for customers and the community, but also for themselves. To achieve this, the focus is usually on external efforts. But what if you looked internally, instead? Is there a way to create value and also have a wider positive impact in the world simply by finding 'efficiencies'? It sounds inviting, and yet it appears the hardest people to convince are CFOs. According to Tensie Whelan and Elyse Douglas, writing in the *Harvard Business Review*:

"By now most companies have committed to improving their environmental, social and governance performance. Such sustainability efforts have increasingly become table stakes. And yet many CFOs still see them as a cost rather than a source of value. That makes it hard to unlock the internal financing needed to scale them up." [52]

---

52. *How to talk to your CFO about sustainability: Use this tool for measuring the financial return on ESG activities*, by Tensie Whelan and Elyse Douglas, Harvard Business Review, January/February 2021, page 88.

There are usually two sides involved in these particular discussions: the *sustainability* camp and the *financial* camp. Whelan and Douglas argue that hesitation from CFOs is largely down to language and the different metrics being used by both sides. Where the sustainability folk focus on reductions in wastewater or emissions, the financial folk talk about EBIT and ROI. The fact that each camp has a separate reporting structure just adds to the problem and further fractures any connection between the two. While this divide is understandable on a number of levels, it doesn't anticipate the change that's coming:

"As the links between sustainability and economic performance becomes clearer, pressure will mount from investors, boards and executive leadership to track and report the payoffs." [53]

So, how can these two camps successfully collaborate in order to help generate value for a business in tangible, measurable terms, while also ensuring a broader positive impact? Well, Whelan and Douglas have developed a tool called *Return on Sustainability Investment (ROSI)*, which identifies ways for businesses to create value and secure returns by generating new revenue, reducing costs—or both. In one company alone, the result was more than $5 billion in net benefits in a single year. But it's not limited to any one specific industry sector, nor is it simply about uncovering ways to save on costs. Their approach looks at costs, value creation and impact—in tandem.

For example, using new green chemistry principles, a pharmaceutical company was able to reduce water and energy consumption, reduce waste generation, and avoid carbon emission charges. It also retained a larger-than-usual share of revenue in markets where it had lost exclusivity, keeping 65% of its revenue from the previous year.[54] A Canadian utility company also reduced

---

53. *How to talk to your CFO about sustainability: Use this tool for measuring the financial return on ESG activities*, page 89.
54. *How to talk to your CFO about sustainability: Use this tool for measuring the financial return on ESG activities*, page 93.

their greenhouse gas emissions by 20% to 30%, while minimising regulatory risks, particularly those associated with forecasted carbon prices, and saved $3 million in the process. This accelerated their decision to move away from coal, resulting in their stock price increasing by 10%. For the remainder of that year [2019] the company's stock increased more than 50%, faster than the average growth of the Dow Jones utility index.[55]

These are just two examples where, with the right mindset and approach, businesses and brands can look at creating value in a more holistic and deeper way. But it would be a mistake to interpret these figures purely as savings from implementing efficiencies. The reality is, the value created is a byproduct of a more sustainable model being introduced into the business, resulting from using environmentally conscious materials and more responsible practices. The business wins, their customers benefit, and the wider positive impact is tangible. However, this needs to be considered in everything you do. It is an inter-generational pursuit, building on previous innovations and considering future developments, finding efficiencies that provide a wider positive impact—to the community, to society and to the business—while being genuinely conscious of your impact on the environment. As *The Economist* reports, these new behaviours—particularly in the retail space—are reshaping consumer behaviour:

"All around the world the new shoppers are not just value-conscious, but also increasingly project their ethical and political values onto their decisions about what to buy. So, for example, they select firms on the basis of their environmental credentials and supply chain standards. Shoppers are using their power to support trends from veganism to Xinjiang-free cotton. Fashion is increasingly conscious of its carbon footprint. Even Kraft Heinz, the hardest-nosed of Western food giants, is trying to rebrand itself as a force for environmental clean-up, as well as ketchup. It is a mistake

---

55. *How to talk to your CFO about sustainability: Use this tool for measuring the financial return on ESG activities*, page 93.

to view these trends as mere virtue-signalling, or a fad. One way capitalism adapts to society's changing preferences is through government regulation and laws, which voters influence, at least in democracies. But the dynamic response of companies to the signals that consumers send is a force for change, too." [56]

Given these societal shifts, the value you provide—and how you provide it—will ultimately help define who you are and determine your relevance to customers, staff and the wider community. While this can often increase the burdens, responsibilities and expectations for businesses and brands, it's also ushering in numerous opportunities, as well. But it's critical you don't lose sight of being a profitable enterprise in the process, because then no-one wins. By its very definition, a business or brand must itself be sustainable before it can continuously provide a wider value and benefit to others. And this includes being financially sustainable. So, how you generate value, how you communicate and deliver your value, and how we collectively measure that value, will be critical for businesses and brands—and vital for the future.

---

56. *H21st-century consumers*, The Economist, 13 March 2021, page 11.

15. **It helps if you can explain your brand in a few words—** *this makes it easier for staff and customers to remember.*

It's only natural to be excited and enthused about your business or brand. You want to tell as many people as much about it as possible. Perhaps you often do. But it's a crowded, noisy field. This tsunami of information—and choice—makes it increasingly important to communicate in a manner that's not only compelling and relevant, but also memorable. And it starts with how you articulate your business or brand.

Of course, when promoting your business or brand, the temptation is to pack in as much information as possible. There's a belief that when we have someone's attention we need to capitalise on it—in spades. However, this approach can feel like a firehose. It's not very pleasant and can be difficult for people to get a handle on any one central message. A simple succinct sentence about your business will more than suffice to start an interaction with clarity and respect. You can then expand on this incrementally. Rather than a firehose, it's like offering one glass of water at a time.

Meaning and memory

There are a number of ways you might approach articulating your core message. For example, the advertising world often refers to this as the *single-minded proposition*, which conveys a compelling reason why a customer would want to buy your product or use your service. Others might refer to this as their *strategic positioning*, or *value proposition*, which focuses on a benefit to the customer, as opposed to explaining the features in very literal terms. Others still might prefer to use their *Purpose statement* as a way to connect with customers on a deeper level. Either way, you need to decide what you want people to remember most about you. A quick way to consider this is by identifying how that message is relevant in their lives—or, if not, how it might be. Essentially, you want to promote meaning and memory.

The importance of being memorable and understood is central to the success of any business or brand. Without getting too scientific, humans retain different types of memories for different lengths of time. Short-term memories last from seconds to hours

whereas long-term memories can last for years. But we also have what's referred to as a 'working memory,' which helps us retain something in our minds for a limited time by repeating it.[57] This can be achieved when using one, simple, compelling message—consistently and over time. Unfortunately, a lot of businesses end up speaking to themselves or in overly technical terms. This not only makes it difficult for the uninitiated to understand—and to remember—it can also make them feel excluded, or worse, stupid. It's condescending and lacks empathy. In fact, how you make people feel is what people are most likely to remember about you.

The catch

Over the years, I've heard different versions of a particular story explaining—in wonderfully simple terms—how effective communication works. These anecdotes all stem from the advertising industry, but in each retelling the principle is the same. It relates to a request from a client to feature a number of key messages in an advertisement, while the advertising executive explains why it's better to include less information, rather than more. One rendition of this story was shared by a legendary and influential advertising figure, Frank Lowe, in Hermann Vaske's book *Standing on the shoulders of giants*:

"[Lowe:] People, in 30 seconds or 60 seconds, find it very difficult to grasp more than one idea. And if you feed them more than one idea, then they don't get any of it. [This] is a question that has been asked a hundred times and the best way I can describe it is: here's a tennis ball, catch it, thank you. Here's four. Catch them.

[Vaske:] I got one.

[Lowe:] Right, so even though I threw you four, you only got one." [58]

---

57. *Human memory: How we make, remember, and forget memories,* by Michael Greshko, National Geographic, online article, 5 March 2019.
58 . *Standing on the shoulders of giants: Hermann Vaske's conversations with the masters of advertising,* Hermann Vaske, Die Gestalten Verlag, 2001, page 18.

Whether it's tennis balls—or messages—we tend to catch only one or two at a time when a number of them have been thrown in our direction. And the ones we don't (or can't) catch literally fall by the wayside. It ends up being a wasted effort and not a pleasant experience for the recipient. With a constant flow of new messages being hurled at us daily, there is only so much we can grasp and retain. In fact, according to a recent *Microsoft* study people now tend to have an attention span of eight seconds, which has decreased from 12 seconds since 2000. Compounding this, the report suggests that the human attention span is decreasing by 88% every year. [59] But that doesn't mean people are getting dumber, or that we need to appeal to the lowest common denominator. It's simply the result of increased information overload, which is being amplified by smartphones and social media platforms, meaning our busy days don't provide much time to ponder messages from businesses or brands. Now we need to register, decipher, understand and judge a message quickly and accurately—one tennis ball at a time. While this may be occurring at an individual level, it's also happening at a collective level, where the information flow has become more densely packed and trends rarely last long. For example, in another recent study from the *Technical University of Denmark*, Philipp Lorenz-Spreen of *Max Planck Institute for Human Development*, who worked on the study, suggests that:

"Content is increasing in volume, which exhausts our attention and our urge for 'newness' causes us to collectively switch between topics more regularly." [60]

This means, in order for people to catch your tennis ball, to easily consume, connect and make sense of your core message, with context and relevance, it needs to be expressed in just a few words. It's not in anyone's best interest to make people work unnecessarily

59. *The Number One Thing Marketers Need To Know To Increase Online Sales*, by Jia Wertz, Forbes, online article, 31 August 2019.
60. *Global attention span is narrowing and trends don't last as long, study reveals*, by Dream McClinton, The Guardian, online article, 18 April 2019.

hard to grasp the information you're seeking to convey. Not only will this make it difficult to cut through the noise, it will either shape negative perceptions about you, or encourage people to edit you out of their consciousness. And don't forget Brand Principle #1: *a brand is the most valuable real estate in the world—a corner of someone's mind, and a relevant place in their life.*

Brand Principles
in action

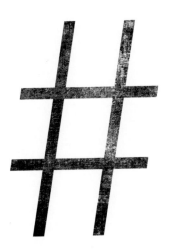

There really is no formula for brand success. What works in one sector might not work in another; what gained traction in one market, could fail utterly in a different region; what is appropriate for a large enterprise probably won't be as relevant for a small business. It's like comparing apples and oranges. Despite this, there *are* specific patterns that can be applied across the board because they're based in an *approach* and a *mindset*; they're not bound by sector, market or size. The seismic societal and commercial shifts currently underway are also impacting how the business world is rapidly changing and adapting. All of this underpins the Brand Principles. So, how do they stack up with an established brand? Well, let's take a look

Of course, we tend to use well-known brands as case studies, primarily because they are familiar to most people but also because there is usually a lot of available information for us to reference. This provides us with an informed understanding about the totality of the brand, including how it acts and behaves in the world. Even so, we don't have a complete picture of everything behind the scenes, so it's hard to avoid using assumptions and conjecture when filling in the blanks.

But there are usually fewer gaps to fill when assessing familiar brands. We also know case studies aren't templates because they won't be applicable to most other businesses or brands. However, in this instance, our example is simply being used to illustrate how the Brand Principles can be applied across one brand. With that in mind, let's revisit a little exercise: think of a sports apparel brand— one you're very familiar with, even if you're **not** a customer.

Got one?

Did you choose *Nike*?

Maybe you chose *Adidas* or *Reebok*. Perhaps it was *Lululemon* or
Under Armour. Either way, let's proceed with *Nike* for the purposes
of this exercise—but also because, when I've done this in group
settings, most people tend to choose *Nike*.

**Brand Principle #1: A brand is the most valuable real estate
in the world**—*a corner of someone's mind and a relevant place in
their life*

There are many reasons why *Nike* pops into most people's minds.
This is partly the result of an enormous investment in marketing—
over decades—but also due to early clarity in the business. From
the outset, *Nike* has been deliberate and strategic about building
the brand, and their success is evident from their near ubiquitous
global visibility. This has been heavily assisted by *Nike's* simple logo
(or *swoosh*), which has remained relatively unchanged since the
early 70s and has driven continuous recognition and consistency
over the long-term. Of course, people are also walking billboards—
whether it's world-class professional athletes or regular people.
When people are wearing *Nike*, we see it in our environment and
this adds to our recognition—of the brand, its reach, its relevance.

Essentially, *Nike* has saturated the landscape, visually and
physically, adapting their communications and products as they've
evolved the brand. Through an on-going and ever-expanding
dialogue *Nike* has connected with (and often represented) people
from all walks of life and socio-economic backgrounds. It has
embraced diversity and choice and, in many ways, has either been
ahead of the curve or leading the charge. We've been updated
on their innovations and informed about their transgressions.
And *Nike's* products and services have been deemed valuable by
generations of consumers. All of this represents the brand and
has ultimately earned them a corner of our mind—regardless of
whether or not we are customers.

Brand Principle #2: All successful branding is based on truth—*it's also the easiest way to implement and maintain your communications because truth is natural, genuine and memorable. It's also expected.*

It's true to say that *Nike* was founded on Phil Knight's passion for running, and for sport in general, which he sees as the means for every individual to push themselves for their own personal benefit—and to have fun doing so. Inevitably, this was underpinned by a sense of competition: if you're not beating your opponent(s), then you're always trying to beat your personal best. But it does require a certain mindset:

"Few ideas are as crazy as my favourite thing, running. It's hard. It's painful. It's risky. The rewards are few and far from guaranteed. When you run around an oval track, or down an empty road, you have no real destination. At least none that you can fully justify the effort. The act itself becomes the destination. It's not that there is no finish line; it's that you define the finish line. Whatever pleasures or gains you derive from the act of running, you must find them within. It's all how you frame it; how you sell it to yourself.

"Every runner knows this. You run and run, mile after mile, and you never quite know why. You tell yourself that you're running towards some goal, chasing some rush, but really you run because the alternative, stopping, scares you to death." [1]

That sounds a little dramatic, but given *Nike's* trajectory Knight's description of running could also easily be interpreted as his approach to business: this idea of defining your own finish line, about pushing oneself and finding justification for it from within, and about staring down the spectre of "stopping"—because of what that might mean. Taken on face value, it suggests that his mindset was in a perpetual state of motion: always going that bit further, always pushing past his personal best, and driven by the constant need to believe in oneself—no matter what:

---

1. *Shoe Dog*, Phil Knight, Simon & Schuster, 2016, page 5.

"So that morning in 1962 I told myself: Let everyone else call your idea crazy... just keep going. Don't stop. Don't even think about stopping until you get there, and don't give too much thought to where 'there' is. Whatever comes, just don't stop." [2]

This wasn't some glib personal motivational pep talk. As a runner himself, he intimately understood the customers he wanted to serve. From the earliest days, Knight was keen to align his fledgling business with college athletes, and then professionals. His objective was to provide the best possible running shoes. This transformed into a personal desire to champion sport in general, which eventually evolved into an aim to democratise our general understanding of movement, health and fitness. It was something the 2018 *Dream Crazy* campaign sought to convey, and which was narrated by controversial *NFL* star Colin Kaepernick. In his book, *Nike: Better is temporary*, Sam Grawe describes it as such:

"Tellingly, not only did Dream Crazy feature top Nike athletes, such as [Serena] Williams, LeBron James, and Eliud Kipchoge, but also ten-year-old wrestler Isaiah Bird, who was born without legs; wheelchair-bound basketball star and gold medalist Megan Blunk; and Alice Woollcott, who was not only named homecoming queen as a high school senior but also played linebacker on the American Football team. Dream Crazy was by no means the first Nike film to elevate the inspirational efforts of everyday athletes. Encouraging each of us to push our limits, to realise personal goals, and to define success by our own standards has long been a hallmark of the brand's ability to engage its customers." [3]

But there was another motivation for Knight, a more profound truth, which seems to have driven him: something bigger than sport, bigger than business, and bigger than 'success':

---

2. *Shoe Dog*, Phil Knight, page 5.
3. *Nike: Better is temporary*, Sam Grawe, Phaidon Press, 2020, page 92.

"I had an aching sense that our time is short, shorter than we ever know, short as a morning run, and I wanted mine to be meaningful. And purposeful. And creative. And important. Above all... different. I wanted to leave a mark on the world. I wanted to win. No, that's not right. I simply didn't want to lose [...] I saw it all before me, exactly what I wanted my life to be. Play." [4]

Brand Principle #3: **A brand is internal before it's external**— *your staff need to be your greatest ambassadors. The mistake is to think branding is purely about external broadcasting.*

At the start of most businesses, the founders are usually fired up about the possibilities and challenges ahead. It's this passion and energy, coming from within the business, which guides and directs every decision and becomes part of the culture—the DNA. In Phil Knight's case, this appears to have been an active conversation from early in the venture. But he wasn't just interested in what the business might be, he also wanted to be clear about what it absolutely shouldn't be:

"I remember that we took turns describing what our little company was, and what it might be, and what it must never be." [5]

It's difficult to imagine *Nike* as a 'little company,' but all brands start out as businesses first—and they're usually small. The fact Knight was actively seeking to articulate what the company 'would never be' illustrates the importance of developing the brand from the inside first. No doubt this description changed over the years— perhaps drastically—as *Nike* grew and evolved, but this internal articulation and understanding would no doubt have continued over decades. Being clear about who you are internally ultimately helps how you communicate it externally. In Knight's case, this involved fostering an attitude that would define the brand. The notion of taking risks, pushing the boundaries and always looking to the future translated into how staff and the business approached

4. *Shoe Dog*, Phil Knight, Simon & Schuster, 2016, page 3.
5. *Shoe Dog*, page 149.

their calling. It permitted everyone in the business to try things—even if those things might not work. While this was specifically an internal approach, it resonated with the market, and *Nike's* customers, in particular. As Knight describes it:

"No other shoe company was trying new things, so our efforts, successful or not, were seen as noble. All innovation was hailed as progressive, forward-thinking. Just as failure didn't deter us, it didn't seem to diminish the loyalty of our customers." [6]

As courageous and inviting as all of this sounds—and obviously it was paying dividends, from a brand point of view—how was this approach being fostered internally? What guidance, direction, or leadership was Knight implementing to create a thriving culture with the 'permission to fail'? Well, apparently he was inspired by a quote from George S. Patton, a general in the United States Army:

"Don't tell people how to do things, tell them what to do and let them surprise you with their results." [7]

Perhaps this resonates with you. You might have a similar approach in your own business or brand. Or maybe you're currently articulating a different approach. In Knight's case, this translated into something deeper—beyond just selling products, pursuing innovation, or building a brand. In fact, it became a driving force from inside the business, a way to influence the culture, which eventually found its place in the world:

"I wanted to build something that I could point to and say: I made that. It was the only way I saw to make life meaningful." [8]

Like any business or brand, there has been success and failure along the way. But in Knight's pursuit to make his life meaningful,

---

6. *Shoe Dog*, page 311.
7. *Shoe Dog*, page 36.
8. *Shoe Dog*, page 124.

Nike's internal attitude and culture—it's DNA—has surely helped the brand to stay on track, to remain focused and to drive its success. However, Knight couldn't have done this alone. It's not an understatement to suggest that this would have been impossible to achieve without the belief, support and understanding of *Nike's* staff. So, how has this shown up inside the brand?:

"Founded on the idea of athletic drive and pursuit of ever greater achievement, the company's inherent brand is progression... "If people are expecting what's new and better from Nike, it's because there is a culture here—within ourselves—where we just believe that [the work] can always be better," says [Nike's Creative Officer Gino] Fisanotti... To him and the marketing teams at Nike, that means being anchored to your DNA and values while always staying ahead of the game." [9]

Brand Principle #4: A brand is not a department—*it's the responsibility (and the representation) of your entire organisation, from receptionist to CEO.*

Obviously, *Nike* places a heavy emphasis on marketing, but also on innovation, retail, and digital experiences, among many other areas. Structurally, there are numerous departmental divisions within *Nike*, all operating across various regions globally. Of course, it's easy to assume the 'brand' sits solely within the Marketing Department, given how active *Nike* is in this area. But that would be a mistake. In *Nike's* case, we can only assume how efficiently and collaboratively each department works to collectively express and represent the brand. Jorie Goins, writing for *Bizfleunt*, offers a glimpse:

"Already known for its innovative footwear, swoosh logo and 'just do it' slogan, Nike is also making strides in the workforce management arena. Nike's flat structure is unique among legacy companies, making this brand an excellent study of the inner machinations of a big business. The company uses this flat structure to maximize transparency and agility among employees and sub-divisions while

---

9. *Nike: Better is temporary*, page 97.

minimizing bureaucracy and deployment time for new ideas [...]
Nike's many divisions operate pseudo-independently within the
overall Nike brand name. This controlled autonomy keeps Nike's
brand consistent and ensures a certain standard of customer
service and product delivery, while also affording separate regional
and product brands the flexibility to satisfy niche customer needs
and demands." [10]

It seems clear that *Nike* has a pretty good sense that everything inside the business contributes to the brand at some level and that, structurally, the business has been designed to amplify this. Whether that has been broadly understood and implemented at an individual level is hard to gauge, but it does seem to have been integrated into the culture. For example, Mark Parker, *Nike's* Executive Chairman, shared an inspiring story about how one individual used the same personal approach, across different divisions and different sporting codes, to successfully represent the *Nike* brand:

"Over the years, a person who excelled at building communities for
Nike relationship by relationship was Sandie Bodecker. In the mid-
1990s he took on the challenge of making Nike authentic in football.
He took us from outsider to leader one victory at a time, earning
respect by being genuine with everyone he met, content to keep his
head down until he conquered the ultimate goal. A few years later, he
took the same approach with the skateboarding community. Sandy
and the Nike SB team built the trust of shop owners and athletes. He
could make a believer out of anyone because he himself believed that
both Nike and skateboarding would be better if they worked together.
He was right. Sandy later joined a Special Projects team within
our Innovation team to create a product that was all about making
athletes measurably better—significantly better—which turned into
the epic Breaking2 project [with the objective of breaking the two-
hour barrier for the marathon]. It was one of Nike's most ambitious
works ever." [11]

---

10. *Nike's Flat Organizational Structure*, by Jorie Goins (Reviewed by Michelle Seidel, B.Sc., LL.B., MBA), Bizfluent, online article, 4 December, 2018.

From departments, divisions and organisational structures, through to individuals at all levels, *everyone* contributes to how a brand is built, developed, understood and perceived—internally and externally. While marketing, design, advertising and communications perform a crucial *assist*, believing that the brand sits solely within the Marketing Department is a clear misunderstanding of what a brand is and how it's developed. Put simply, your brand is much bigger and more collective than just one department.

Brand Principle #5: A brand is about culture—*it's the collective attitudes and ideas of a group of people. Your brand is as much about individual behaviour as it is about collective behaviour.* Knight knew he needed to develop the right culture in order to achieve his goals. He also knew it needed to reflect an attitude and that it should convey an approach:

"We were trying to create a brand, but also a culture. We were fighting against conformity, against boringness, against drudgery. More than a product, we were trying to sell an idea—a spirit." [12]

It's interesting to note that Knight understood a business isn't automatically a brand. He embraced a 'brand mindset': a spirit. This spirit—this attitude and approach—was also bound up in fitness, competition and athleticism. Perhaps reflecting simpler times, but also foreshadowing some of the challenges that *Nike* would face as the business evolved and grew, *The New York Times'* described the culture as such:

"Since Nike's early days in the 1960s, many employees have been guided by a simple ethos: work hard, party hard, get up for your five-mile run in the morning." [13]

---

11. *Nike: Better is temporary*, page 9.
12. *Shoe Dog*, Phil Knight, page 250.
13. *At Nike, Revolt Led by Women Leads to Exodus of Male Executives*, by Julie Creswell, Kevin Draper and Rachel Abrams, The New York Times, online article, 28 April 2020.

•

"We were trying to create a brand, but also a culture. We were fighting against conformity, against boringness, against drudgery. More than a product, we were trying to sell an idea—a spirit."

•

But culture is hard to scale. While people might assume *Nike* has always succeeded in this endeavour, in his book, *Shoe Dog*, Knight shares a humbling story about his challenges with the brand's culture. It centres around a discussion with Masuro Hayami, former CEO of *Nissho*, when *Nike* was their most profitable client. According to Knight, Hayami was one of the wisest men he ever knew and credits him with bestowing valuable advice at critical moments in *Nike's* evolution. In this particular instance, well after the brand had gone public, Knight was back in Japan seeking advice from his mentor:

'We have so much opportunity, but we're having a terrible time getting managers to seize those opportunities. We try people from the outside, but they fail, because our culture is so different.'
Mr. Hayami nodded. 'See those bamboo trees up there?' he asked.
'Yes.'
'Next year... when you come... they'll be one foot higher.'
I stared. I understood.
When I returned to Oregon I tried hard to cultivate and grow the management team we had, slowly, with more patience, with an eye toward more training and more long-term planning. I took the wider, longer view. It worked. The next time I saw Hayami, I told him. He merely nodded, once, 'hai', and looked off." [14]

Brand Principle #6: Mission, Vision and Value statements are great internal guides—*but no one outside the organisation really cares. They will only be interested in the value these statements deliver.*
Does knowing *Nike's* Mission, Vision or Values statements affect your perception of the brand, or influence whether or not you would purchase anything from it? I'd wager it doesn't. And yet, having a Mission is critical. In *Nike's* case, their early Mission was incredibly simple, and extraordinarily focused. So much so, it was expressed as a two-word statement: *Crush Adidas.* [15]

---

14. *Shoe Dog*, pages 376–377.
15. *Nike: A case study in change and management*, by Ram Chettri, 1 February 2013.

Think about that for a moment. Does your business or brand have such a succinct and clear message? It unequivocally set the tone, the attitude and the objective, ensuring every single decision within *Nike* was made with one singular goal in mind. *Adidas* was the target. Plain and simple. At the time, *Adidas* was the dominant sports apparel brand—by a long shot—so going after them would have been insanely audacious. In Knight's own words:

"I was developing an unhealthy contempt for Adidas. Or maybe it was healthy. The one German company had dominated the shoe market for a couple of decades, and they possessed all the arrogance of unchallenged dominance. Of course it's possible that they weren't arrogant at all, that to motivate myself I needed to see them as a monster. In any event, I despised them. I was tired of looking up every day and seeing them far, far ahead. I couldn't bear the thought that it was my fate to do so forever." [16]

Knight's personal 'unhealthy contempt' for *Adidas* was channelled into a commercial commitment, shepherding every staff member and salesperson to collectively achieve clear alignment. It was singular thinking. However, customers would have been none-the-wiser about the motivation, because they didn't need to be. And yet, it's likely they could see and experience this internal commitment through *Nike's* products and services. Indeed, they were the beneficiaries of that commitment coming to life—every day, by everyone who was working in and with the business. Today, *Nike's* Mission couldn't be more different. For a start, it's much longer and it's far less aggressive. This is a testament to the fact businesses and brands evolve, that they are long-term pursuits (which is Brand Principle #12). When contexts change, so do a brand's objectives and motivations. In *Nike's* case, those contexts are now societal. There is also an acknowledgment that, perhaps, 'crushing' the competition is no longer a healthy aspiration—despite the fact *Adidas* continues to challenge *Nike's* position, and is winning in some instances.

---

16. *Shoe Dog*, Phil Knight, Simon & Schuster, 2016, page 111.

So how is *Nike* navigating this development? Well, perhaps their Mission statement provides some insight into their customer-focused strategy:

"To bring inspiration and innovation to every athlete in the world.
If you have a body, you are an athlete."[17]

Customers and society see this 'come to life' every day in how *Nike* embraces and champions diversity, how it encourages everyone to push past their limitations and achieve their best. It also signals that *Nike* is both speaking to niche audiences on an individual basis (direct-to-consumer), as well as to a global community (not all of whom are customers). In its truest form, it harks back Phil Knight's original ambition: to not just sell products, but to champion a spirit.

Brand Principle #7: **The logo doesn't make your brand; the brand gives your logo its value**—*your logo is the quick, shorthand visual reminder of all the individual associations, experiences and perceptions people have with your brand.*
Nike's logo is instantaneously recognisable and has undoubtedly contributed to how the brand has been built over decades. But the logo wasn't designed by an international designer or branding agency. It was designed in 1972 by a young graphic design student named Carolyn Davidson. She was paid a reported USD$35, which is equivalent to around $250 today. Lovingly referred to as the *'swoosh'*, *Nike's* logo and identity has remained pretty much consistent since inception, although the brand's marketing has been an ever-evolving and dynamic journey, which reflects the brand itself. However, the 'swoosh's' origin story is very interesting—and rather eye-opening; a humbling lesson for business owners when judging design. When Knight asked Davidson to design a logo for his new running shoe she asked what kind of logo he needed. Knight responded with:

---

17. www.about.nike.com

'I don't know,' I said. 'That gives me a lot to go on,' she said. 'Something that evokes a sense of motion,' I said. 'Motion,' she said, dubious." [18]

It was with this vague brief that Davidson provided a few options for Knight and his team to review. Their collective response was tepid, to say the least. There was a consensus that they liked the 'swoosh' *slightly* more than the other options because it looked like a wing, or a whoosh of air, or like something a runner might leave in their wake. One thing that was clear was that it looked fresh, ancient and timeless.[19] But Knight remained unconvinced. Remarkably, his response was:

"'You guys like it more than I do,' I said. 'But we're out of time. It'll have to do.' 'You don't like it?' [Bob] Woodell said. I sighed. 'I don't love it. Maybe it will grow on me.'" [20]

Of course, it's easy to look back on that comment and giggle. But there are a few lessons in this story. For a start, we never know how something is going to work out, and a lot depends on how much effort we are willing to put into making it work. It's also a wonderful insight into the fact that business and brands—no matter how successful—are made up of individual people making decisions on a daily basis to the best of their ability at the time. Plus, it illustrates the *'Just Do It'* attitude, which literally came to define the brand. Equally, it proves that while designers are an incredibly important *assist* in the process, it took Knight and his team to build the brand over decades—long after Davidson had provided the image. More to the point, this anecdote is evidence that the logo doesn't make the brand, the brand gives the logo its value.

Although Knight was initially uninspired by Davidson's 'swoosh' logo, it did provide him with the means to explain the 'attitude' to

---

18. *Shoe Dog*, page 180.
19. *Shoe Dog*, page 181.
20. *Shoe Dog*, page 181.

others, and in a visceral way. For example, in 1972, when a group of salesmen looking curiously at the new *Nike* shoes asked what the logo was, and what it meant, Knight simply described it as: *"the sound of someone going past you."* [21] Nothing more needed to be said.

Interestingly, in 1983 Knight gifted Davidson a diamond embedded gold 'swoosh' ring—and 500 shares in *Nike*—as a token of appreciation and gratitude.[22] He didn't need to do this, and yet he did. For many other business owners, commissioning the 'swoosh' would have just been another transaction. But Knight saw it differently. It's a great example of a business owner recognising the difference between cost versus value, particularly when that realisation is reached with hindsight.

Brand Principle #8: Branding makes an organisation visible and understood—*the logo and communications material are a window into your brand. Consider how you want to be seen. If you're not clear about your own brand, don't expect others will be, either.* Many people will recognise the 'swoosh' and interpret it in their own way. While the 'swoosh' is a central *assist* in building and maintaining the *Nike* brand, we know Phil Knight was less than convinced when he first saw the design. Incredibly, even by 1997, he was still unconvinced about the value of advertising. In Knight's own words:

"I still didn't believe in the power of advertising. At all [...] I'd ask them: Can you say definitively that people are buying Nikes because of your ad? Can you show it to me in black-and-white numbers? Silence.
No, they'd say... we can't say that definitively.
So then it's a little hard for me to get enthused, I'd say—isn't it? Silence." [22]

---

21. *Shoe Dog*, page 202.
22. *Shoe Dog*, page 313.

And yet, as visibility increased—as understanding and associations grew—the more valuable and influential *Nike* became. As a result, Knight began to understand that design and advertising were more than a practical necessity, more than just about boosting sales. They were a key assist in explaining and differentiating the brand: a way to increase awareness, to raise the profile, and to broadcast what *Nike* stood for.

"It's unfair to call it a formula when so much effort has gone into keeping the messages fresh and potent, but Nike's playbook of hard-nosed determination, tongue-in-cheek irreverence, rock 'n' roll attitude, and limitless aspiration continues to propel the brand forward [...] 'Each year there's a new generation of "Just Do It" consumers with new expectations,' says Greg Hoffman, former head of Global Brand Innovation [...] 'Of course, it's about how we want people to feel about Nike,' says Hoffman, 'but more importantly, it's how we want people to feel about themselves.'" [23]

As we know, there are so many ways people experience brands, from products and services, through to experiences and expectations: both online and offline—and everything in between. While design, advertising, marketing and communications, in general, can help people understand—and connect with—a brand, all the messages in the world won't save a bad product or a poor experience. Being visible is essential but it has consequences. The business or brand must always live up to its messages. It's an eternal, never-ending dance which, when done right, propels the brand forward. The challenge is to use your visibility and reach to help people understand your business or brand as clearly as possible— and then to validate that understanding through everything you do.

---

23. *Nike: Better is temporary*, page 91.

Brand Principle #9: Your brand is not just what you say it is—*it's what other people say it is; the challenge is managing the gap. And never underestimate the power of perception because it can be more persuasive than the truth.*

Since the 1970s, *Nike* has been publicly accused of using sweat shops, which has inevitably veered into claims of child labour and exploitation. The impact this had on the brand was significant and dramatic, prompting reduced sales and forcing the business to place more focus on the ethics of their workers. Of course, *Nike* denied the claims and blamed their lack of control over third-party factories as an excuse. However, this was roundly rejected as a poor attempt at resolving a clear and unsettling concern. A tangible and accountable response eventually came in 2002, when *Nike* began auditing its factories for occupational health and safety.[24] For his part, Knight appeared genuinely upset by the claims, although reluctant to accept responsibility for an industry-wide practice. And yet, he acknowledged that change was warranted:

"Though we knew that much of the criticism was unjust, that Nike was a symbol, a scapegoat, more than the true culprit, all of that was beside the point. We had to admit: We could do better. We told ourselves: We must do better." [25]

It turns out *Nike* had to do a lot better because it wasn't just words or accusations, there was evidence. In 1996, *Life Magazine* ran a story featuring imagery of a 12-year-old Pakistani boy stitching soccer balls adorned with the *Nike* 'swoosh'. The following year an *Ernst & Young* report for *Nike* highlighted the fact that 77% of workers at a third-party supplier factory experienced respiratory complications, likely due to being exposed to carcinogens 177 times above the legal level.[26] Even more damaging, influential media channels like *CBS* and *ESPN* broadcast footage from factories confirming as much, which prompted pickets outside

24. https://en.wikipedia.org/wiki/Nike_sweatshops
25. *Shoe Dog*, page 373.
26. *Nike Shoe Plant in Vietnam Is Called Unsafe for Workers*, by Steven Greenhouse, The New York Times, 8 November, 1997.

Nike outlets and a significant decline in revenue.[27] But the brand was listening, either out of responsibility or survival. They hired Hannah Jones, Chief Sustainability Officer and Vice President of *Nike's* innovation accelerator.

"In nearly two decades, Jones has helped to transform Nike from a company that was synonymous with sweatshops to a recognised sustainability leader. Last year [2015], Morgan Stanley ranked Nike the most sustainable apparel and footwear company in North America for environmental and social performance, including its labour record." [28]

Another damaging issue that has been highlighted through recent *Nike* insider accounts depicts a toxic culture where belittling, insulting and ignoring women has been prevalent. Reportedly, some staff outings have ended up in strip clubs and there have been accounts of sexual harassment and gender discrimination, with women being made to feel marginalised in meetings, passed over for promotions or excluded from significant divisions. Despite numerous reports to HR nothing was being done about it, which prompted a revolt from within and resulted in the removal of six senior male executives. As *The New York Times* suggests, *'other people's words'* (from within the business) can be powerful:

"While the #MeToo movement has led to the downfall of individual men, the kind of sweeping overhaul that is occurring at Nike is rare in the corporate world, and illustrates how internal pressure from employees is forcing even huge companies to quickly address workplace problems." [29]

Unfortunately, this came too late for some and a number of women have already left the brand, many of whom were not only highly experienced but also instrumental in some of *Nike's* key successes,

---

27. *Just Fix It: How Nike Learned to Embrace Sustainability*, by Kate Abnett, BOF (Business Of Fashion), online article, 1 November, 2016.
28. *Just Fix It: How Nike Learned to Embrace Sustainability.*
29. *At Nike, Revolt Led by Women Leads to Exodus of Male Executives.*

including: Patty Ross, a Vice President of Workplace Design and Connectivity, who also established a women's mentoring program and had worked at *Nike* since she was 16; Kerri Hoyt-Pack, who had worked at *Nike* for 15 years and helped launch the *Nike* women's brand; and Nikki Neuburger, a Vice President in Global Brand Marketing for running, who was instrumental in developing the *Nike+* app. While these reports are reprehensible, they also left *Nike* exposed commercially. You might recall Jessica Walsh (from Chapter 6) who has, in part, positioned her design business to champion women, arguing that male leadership isn't best placed to appeal to—or communicate with—an enormous female market. Well, as *The New York Times* reports, this is clearly emerging as a consequence within *Nike*:

"In women's products, Nike 'is growing in the low single digits, which means it is a long way away from where it wants to be,' said Matt Powell, a sports industry analyst at the NPD Group. 'Companies like Lululemon and even Old Navy are finding greater success in the women's sportswear market', Mr. Powell said." [30]

Whether it's the result of a public outcry, staff statements, or a major media exposé, *other people's words* can have a deep impact on your business or brand. But the reverse is also possible. Over the years, many positive things have been said about *Nike*. That suggests that giving people reasons to speak positively about you should never be about marketing spin. When a concern is clearly evident a business or brand should simply do the right thing—by staff, clients and society. In *Nike's* case, Jones' reorientation of the brand's practices to be more sustainable led to significant change, not only commercially, but also culturally, all of which has influenced more positive perceptions. For example, the specific impact Jones facilitated helped *Nike*:

"[Move] from being a risk and reputation function to being a business lever function to being an innovation function." [31]

30. *At Nike, Revolt Led by Women Leads to Exodus of Male Executives.*
31. *Just Fix It: How Nike Learned to Embrace Sustainability.*

Brand Principle #10: **Your brand is your filter**—*use it to help decide on everything, from hiring staff to making acquisitions or pursuing initiatives. It's all about finding the right fit.*

Now, we can only assume *Nike's brand filter* reflects their general attitude—most potently expressed in their '*Just Do It*' slogan. Fuelled by Knight's pursuit of cutting-edge technology and innovation, sprinkled with a generous helping of disdain for *Adidas,* and marinated in a willingness for risk (as long as it benefited *Nike* customers) decisions have been made through a clear and consistent lens, as one striking story illustrates.

It was in early 1997, and Knight was attending a meeting he knew very little about. He was only mildly aware that two heavyweight engineers (M. Frank Rudy and Bob Bogert) were about to pitch an idea. With enthusiasm, Rudy said they had devised a way to inject air into a running shoe—pressurized air bags or bubbles. Apparently, Knight dropped his pencil (albeit not out of awe), and simply asked "*Why?*" The duo proceeded to explain it was for greater support and cushioning—for *"the ride of a lifetime."* Knight wasn't convinced and was even less impressed. Eyeing the futuristic-looking shoes, just as much as assessing Rudy himself, Knight dismissed the proposal as a ridiculous Jetson's-style comic book idea. But none of this appeared to matter to Rudy, who simply shrugged and said *Adidas* had also been skeptical. It was all Knight needed to hear. Might this be a way to upstage *Adidas*? He took the shoes for a six-mile run. Being sample shoes they didn't hold up very well, but Knight could feel their difference and was impressed with their potential. On his return to the office his immediate response was:

"I think we might have something here." [32]

As the saying goes, the rest is history—launching a new era of innovation and commercial success for *Nike*. As entertaining as Knight's anecdote is, it also sheds light on the practical nature of a brand filter. Although he was initially skeptical, the mere mention of *Adidas* was the first trigger, followed immediately by a trial

---

32. *Shoe Dog*, pages 305 and 306.

to validate the proposal from a customer's perspective. He then assessed the proposal on its technological merits, and quickly finished with a decision that appears to have been driven by *Nike's* 'Just Do It' spirit. Essentially, it fit with the brand. It fit with *Nike* because it had passed their *brand filter*. And that was enough to pursue the proposal—and change the course of the brand.

Brand Principle #11: **Don't just have a positioning**—*have a position. Taking a stand will help define your brand.*
Over the years, *Nike* has taken a position on a number of issues, but perhaps none have been more public or controversial than supporting Colin Kaepernick's decision to 'take a knee' during the US national anthem in protest about police brutality against African Americans. As many readers will be aware, *Nike's* support translated into Kaepernick being the face of its 2018 advertising campaign—*Dream Crazy*—which featured the line: *"Believe in something. Even if it means sacrificing everything."* The ad campaign also celebrated the 30th anniversary of 'Just Do It'.

Now, some readers might believe *Nike* jumped on the bandwagon by supporting Kaepernick. But that assumption is misplaced. *Nike* has supported African American athletes for decades; it's been central to their brand. *Nike* had also been sponsoring Kaepernick for two years prior, even though they had done little with him. And for those who might feel *Nike* brazenly leveraged Kaepernick's international attention, it's worth noting the brand continued to sponsor Kaepernick long after he was dropped from his *NFL* team— the *49ers*—and when no other team was interested in drafting him. Essentially, the *NFL* abandoned him. In contrast, *Nike* developed Kaepernick's own branded line of apparel, the first of which was an *Air Force 1* shoe featuring *'08.14.16'*—the date of his protest— and which sold out online within a day.[33] Not only that, *Nike* was acutely aware of the potential backlash from supporting Kaepernick, partly due to then President Trump's harsh and vocal criticism of

---

33. *Retail Success Of Colin Kaepernick's Nike Sneaker Shows Martyrdom Is Better For His Brand Than Returning To NFL*, by Alex Reimer, Forbes, online article, 26 December 2019.

Kaepernick's actions. As soon as the ad campaign launched, social media was flooded with images of people burning and destroying *Nike* apparel in protest. But *Nike* was clear and convinced they had done the right thing and they were rewarded, garnering $163 million in earned media, as well as a $6 billion increase in brand value, and a 31% boost in sales.[34] But it was a calculated move. As *FastCompany* reported:

"[The advert] was divisive because it jumped on America's biggest fault lines—race, patriotism, sports, and business. But according to Nike founder Phil Knight, that was kind of the point. 'It doesn't matter how many people hate your brand as long as enough people love it,' Knight told Fast Company last year [2018]. 'And as long as you have that attitude, you can't be afraid of offending people. You can't try and go down the middle of the road. You have to take a stand on something, which is ultimately I think why the Kaepernick ad worked.'" [35]

It's worth noting, *Nike* has taken a position on other equally important issues, but in a far less public manner and, again, for very specific reasons. While many businesses and brands might promote their environmental credentials, *Nike* has taken a different approach, supported by customer insights, as usual. According to the *Harvard Business Review*:

"Over the past decade, Nike has invested heavily in R&D to reduce environmental waste in its manufacturing processes. In 2010, the company launched the Environmental Apparel Design software tool—an open-source version of its Considered Design Index—enabling garment designers anywhere to assess the environmental impact of various materials and explore combinations that reduce material waste before making a selection. In 2012, Nike debuted its flyknit technology, which allows the company to reduce waste by manufacturing shoes with a one-piece upper body.

---

34. *One year later, what did we learn from Nike's blockbuster Colin Kaepernick ad?* by Jeff Beer, FastCompany, online article, 5 September 2019.
35. *One year later, what did we learn from Nike's blockbuster Colin Kaepernick ad?*

Nike could tout these efforts in its customer-facing marketing, but it doesn't. In their purchase decisions, customers look for performance shoes that are comfortable, lightweight, and durable. Reducing manufacturing waste is not an attribute most sports-shoe buyers prioritize. Claims of environmental friendliness are also unlikely to help the brand move into adjacent markets. In fact, people buying performance shoes are more likely to associate green-manufacturing claims with reduced durability. Nike does communicate its environmental benefits to partners and investors—for whom these are important operating practices—demonstrating a wise allocation of its social benefit claims." [36]

But, like other brands, *Nike* doesn't always get it right. A case in point is Allyson Felix—one of the most decorated athletes in history, a seven-time Olympic gold-medal winner and an 11-time world champion—who was forced to leave the brand over its pregnancy policy. In 2018, *Nike* wanted to pay Felix 70% less while she was pregnant, which she felt stigmatised maternity. She requested *Nike* take into account that she would not be able to perform at her best during the months surrounding childbirth. It was a reasonable request. But *Nike* declined,[37] and she left the brand for a more open and understanding arrangement with *Athleta*, a certified *B Corporation* focusing on sustainability commitments and supporting the notion of the strength of the female collective.[38]

This was clearly *Nike's* loss, and it's genuinely hard to fathom the brand's position on this important issue. While Kaepernick's ad was calculated and inspiring, *Nike's* treatment of Felix was ill-considered and disappointing. Not only did it show a complete lack of empathy and leadership, it also dismissed women's activewear as an emerging and powerful market.

---

36. *Competing on Social Purpose*, by Omar Rodríguez-Vilá and Sundar Bharadwaj, Harvard Business Review, from the September–October issue, 2017.
37. *Gap's Athleta brand signs track star Allyson Felix, who left Nike over its pregnancy policy*, by Jeff Beer, FastCompany, 31 July, 2019.
38. *How Shared Values Forged an Olympic Partnership at Athleta*, by BOF Studio, Business Of Fashion, 8 October, 2020.

Brand Principle #12: A brand is a long-term and evolving objective—*it requires dedication and commitment. Building and maintaining your brand cannot be outsourced. It's not a short-term exercise.*

As we've seen from Brand Principle #9, over time *Nike* has moved away from its previously destructive reputation regarding sweatshops and transformed into a celebrated brand which champions sustainability and innovation, eventually becoming a leader in best practice around supply-chain working conditions. But this took a long time to achieve. And it was largely the result of years of pressure. From humble beginnings in the 1960s, *Nike* had reached eye-watering heights with a market value of around $112 billion and annual revenues of approximately $36 billion as of 2018.[39] For decades, *Nike's* position and influence has been largely unchallenged, perhaps driven by Knight's personal mission of toppling *Adidas*. But change is always on the horizon:

"[The] company is facing significant business hurdles. Adidas, one of its biggest competitors, has gained ground in key markets like apparel and footwear. Nike is also struggling to get traction in women's categories, the fastest-growing segment of the market." [40]

When it comes to brands, the idea of success is usually rather one-dimensional. We generally measure them by revenue and their ability to fend off competitors. Of course, many people look to *Nike* as a case study in success, and in many respects it is—despite the inevitable ups-and-downs in the business' long journey towards becoming a brand, and then seeking to maintain that position. It has taken years—and a lot of hard effort. This is a reality that *Nike* not only understands, but one that it embraces. According to John Donahoe, *Nike's* CEO:

"Our journey is often portrayed as the ultimate success story, and it is—because it shows how setbacks can lead to truly great accomplishments. Success, it turns out, is a messy process. It requires

---

39. *At Nike, Revolt Led by Women Leads to Exodus of Male Executives.*
40. *At Nike, Revolt Led by Women Leads to Exodus of Male Executives.*

*hard work, tough decisions, sacrifices, risks and failures [...] It's
why Nike time and again invests in experimental concepts and
technologies. Not all will immediately succeed; far from it. But each
will teach us an unknown lesson—and it is these lessons that will lead
us to something unexpected that transforms our reality."* [41]

It's very easy to overlook what is involved in building a brand, simply
because we usually reference established brands at a mature stage
in the process. Rarely do we understand—or know—what led to
their enviable position. But in his book *Nike: Better is temporary*
Sam Grawe pulls back the curtain, giving us a glimpse of some of the
hurdles (and doubt), which *Nike* has had to face and overcome:

*"It may seem difficult to comprehend in retrospect, but by the mid-
1980s, Nike was in the midst of an identity crisis. The company's
technical, performance-based output was being outpaced by more
casual designs and aerobics-based footwear from the competition.
Nike's attempt to branch out had missed the mark. There were
layoffs and the future was by no means certain.*

*[...] When it came time to launch the Air Max, the organization
knew that it would take more than great design to overcome the
headwinds the business was facing. 'The Visible Air launch was a
critical moment for a couple of reasons,' [Phil] Knight recounted.
'Until then, we really didn't know if we could be a big company and
still have people work closely together. Visible Air was a hugely
complex product with components made in three different countries,
and nobody knew if it would come together. Production, marketing
and sales were all fighting with each other. There was tension all the
way around.'"* [42]

Nike's history is littered with similar stories—of risk, hurdles,
challenges, failures and success. And it continues to be the case in
this ceaseless roller-coaster of effort. But over decades there's also
been been an obvious and clear thread of visionary thinking, a sense

---

41. *Nike: Better is temporary*, page 6.
42. *Nike: Better is temporary*, page 89 and 90.

of reaching for the stars, no matter how lofty and unattainable it might have felt at the time. Given the brand's achievements, it's hard to appreciate the hopes and dreams underpinning it. And yet, this ambition has fuelled *Nike* since their early days; something Knight deliberately injected into the business:

"Watching that shoe [the waffle trainer] evolve in 1976 from popular accessory to cultural artifact, I had a thought. People might start wearing this thing to class. And the office. And the grocery store. And throughout their everyday life. It was a rather grandiose idea." [43]

Brand Principle #13: More than ever, your customer or end user is at the heart of your brand—*whether you like it or not. Put simply: "Brand is the promise you make; customer experience is the promise you keep."*
It's fair to say that, from the outset, *Nike* has put customers at the heart of the business, primarily due to the fact Knight was a runner himself. Essentially, Knight was the template for the type of (perhaps fanatical) customer *Nike* wanted to appeal to—and cater to. Knight also understood the importance of a seemingly small but critical shift in how the business saw itself, and eventually how it operated:

"We used to think that everything started in the lab. Now we realize that everything spins off the customer. And while technology is still important, the consumer has to lead innovation. We have to innovate for a specific reason, and that reason comes from the market. Otherwise, we'll end up making museum pieces." [44]

Essentially this meant shifting from being a manufacturing-led company to being a marketing-led company. While that might sound like a small shift, perhaps even semantic, it changed the trajectory of the business significantly and shaped the thinking

---

43. *Shoe Dog*, page 284.
44. *High-Performance Marketing: An Interview with Nike's Phil Knight*, by Geraldine E. Willigan, Harvard Business Review, from the July–August issue 1992.

behind every decision that *Nike* made: the customer is at the heart of the brand and its innovations. According to Dirk-Jan van Hamerenn, Chief Marketing Officer:

"If the brand is a person in the context of a city, we ask, who would be an interesting person in that city to be right now? What things do you want them to be aware of? Are we a great buddy to play basketball with—or explore the coolest new gym trends with? Are we going to tell you about something new that's going on in music? Is there a marathon coming up? If we can transpose ourselves into the person we want to be for a specific subset of customers, we get to the insights and creative expressions that will have our brand, as a person, be more relevant for that group." [45]

More recently, there seems to be a growing recognition that brands are no longer fully in control and that, now, there is a two-way dialogue with customers. In *Nike's* case, not only does this idea seem to be embraced, it's *deliberately* pursued. According to Christiana Shi, former Chief Operating Officer for Global Direct-to-Consumer:

"By creating a two-way conversation with consumers, Nike gains actionable insight into their needs and as the results show, they don't just listen, they react. 'It used to be just focus groups and then monitoring our sales and that was it. Now it's a dialogue,' Shi said. Explaining further, she added, 'For example, the customer didn't say, "I want a waffle shoe." They said they wanted durability, a certain type of performance, etc.' Putting all this customer input together, and coming up with a product that meets their needs, enables Nike to deliver innovation consistent with what the consumer wants." [46]

This two-way dialogue not only provides insights into how products and services might be developed or improved, it also offers a window into how customers interpret and perceive the brand itself.

---

45. *Nike: Better is temporary*, page 93.
46. *Nike Just Does It - Keeping An Eye On The Customer*, by Greg Petro, Forbes, online article, 8 July 2016.

And this is just as valuable—if not more so. As *Nike's* Executive Chairman, Mark Parker, succinctly puts it:

"As others interpret our brand, we learn from it." [47]

Brand Principle #14: If your brand is to have value, what you do must have value—*because this will determine and define your relevance.*

No doubt, the value that *Nike* provides varies between individuals depending on how they perceive the brand: whether people are availing of cutting edge running shoes or donning the latest casual wear; whether they're brandishing a 'swoosh' tattoo (really, *Google* it) or benefiting from a committed community like the *Nike+* running app; whether it's championing a 'Just Do It' positive attitude, or a flagship store, designed specifically to respond to customer preferences. Either way, from products and services through to experiences, *Nike* has been providing broad and specific value for decades. But perhaps there is something more fundamental binding all of these together: *Nike's* consistent pursuit of innovation and its fierce customer-centered approach. These are hallmarks of the brand, which *Nike* has successfully translated into numerous and diverse expressions, consistently and over time. This has ensured the brand has remained relevant for customers, whether they're professional athletes, or regular folk. But, in trying to decipher what all this means, Knight recalls:

"Many afternoons I'd sit around the office with [Rob] Strasser, trying to figure out why some lines were selling and some not, which led to broader discussions of what people thought of us and why. We didn't have focus groups, or market research—we couldn't afford them—so we tried to intuit, divine, read tea leaves. Clearly people liked the look of our shoes, we agreed. Clearly they liked our story: Oregon firm founded by running geeks. Clearly they liked what wearing a pair of Nikes said about them. We were more than a brand; we were a statement." [48]

---

47. *Nike: Better is temporary*, page 9.
48. *Shoe Dog*, pages 311 and 312.

A 'statement', you say? That's a big claim and it's easy to interpret this as arrogance or hubris; a deep and meaningful discussion locked in an echo chamber of self importance. The thing is, *Nike* really had become a statement, but not just because of the shoes and the origin story and the attitude. *Nike* had become a different kind of statement, one of cultural relevance. It was a transformational leap, but they had significant help in achieving it, involving some very specific associations:

"Some of the credit went to Hollywood. We had a guy out there giving Nikes to stars, all kinds of stars, big, little, rising, fading. Every time I turned on the TV our shoes were on a character in some hit show— Starsky & Hutch, The Six Million Dollar Man, The Incredible Hulk. Somehow, our Hollywood liaison got a pair of Senorita Cortezes [shoes] into the hands of Farrah Fawcett, who wore them in a 1977 episode of Charlie's Angels. That was all it took. One quick shot of Farrah in Nikes and every store in the nation was sold out of Senorita Cortezes by noon the next day. Soon the cheerleaders of UCLA and USC were jumping and leaping in what was commonly called the Farrah shoe. All of which meant more demand... and more problems meeting demand." [49]

Nike was a victim of its own rapid success, fuelled in part by the brand's association with Hollywood and its influential stars. Essentially, this was 'product placement' and 'celebratory endorsement', but the intention was to have wider reach and a more tangible relevance, in cultural terms. It's no different today when we see (and perhaps seek to emulate) the best athletes in the world, many of whom are wearing *Nike*. Or popular culture figures kicking the latest *Nike* hightops. What we see regularly and often suggests wide acceptance and an inevitable relevance, not only in our individual lives but in wider society. But, it's important to note that *Nike* has held up its side of the arrangement by constantly providing new and forward-thinking innovation, which helps support and propel its relevance even further.

---

49. *Shoe Dog*, page 312.

That said, perhaps the greatest value *Nike* offers is connection, but not in some glib marketing way. From the outset, *Nike* has been able to genuinely connect with customers, partly due to the fact Knight was a runner himself but also because the brand has gone out of its way to connect with customers and communities. *Nike* has worked on developing relationships by being humble enough to learn, and with an ability connect the dots—from customer insights, to technology and design, innovation, and community, right through to various shared experiences. For the most part, *Nike* has been able to connect with what matters most for who matters most to them.

Brand Principle #15: It helps if you can explain your brand in a few words—*this makes it easier for staff and customers to remember.*

There are many ways *Nike* has expressed its brand, but few descriptions sum it up better than *'Just Do It.'* More than that, this has become a commonplace phrase—and in a far wider context than perhaps it was initially intended. From sports arenas to board rooms, people channel 'Just Do It' in all sorts of scenarios, either explicit or implied. Its depth and longevity is difficult to ignore. Perhaps it's hard to fathom that it was developed for an advertising campaign in 1988, but 'Just Do It' surpassed the original campaign's intent and almost immediately came to define *Nike*, before eventually taking on a life of its own. These three simple words convey an attitude, which has connected with people across the globe. It has been translated into numerous languages and has even appeared as a braille poster. But arriving at such a simple tagline wasn't easy. According to *dezeen* magazine, Dan Wieden, co-founder of advertising agency *Wieden+Kennedy* (also based in Oregon), struggled to develop a slogan that would bind together various different television ads they had created for *Nike* at the time:

"I was trying to write something that would tie it up, so it could speak to women who had just started walking to get in shape, to people who were world-class athletes—and it had the same kind of connection with them." [50]

True to form, Knight was apparently skeptical about the proposal—and aggressively so. But Wieden pushed back:

"'Phil Knight said, "We don't need that shit",' Wieden said. 'I said "Just trust me on this one." So they trusted me and it went big pretty quickly.'"[51]

Ironically, 'Just Do It' is an accurate reflection of Knight's own attitude. From all accounts, Knight seemed to trust his gut since the beginning of the business, regularly taking significant risks which others might have shunned. 'Just Do It' pretty much sums up Knight's approach and spirit and was inevitably embedded within the brand's DNA, long before the phrase was coined. However, unbeknown to *Nike* at the time 'Just Do It' was inspired by the final words of a local murderer, Gary Gilmore, who, when facing a firing squad, said, *"Let's do it."* Morbid as this sounds, Wieden felt the words *'do it'* had a certain quality. A 'call-to-action'. This was something he connected with and felt could have a wider application. So he adapted it.

It's an unusual origin story, but it has since been eclipsed by how *Nike* has continuously embraced a spirit of commitment, an aspiration of achievement, and how they've constantly shaped and evolved their narrative over decades. Of course, when we're so familiar with a brand it's easy to forget that all brands started out as a business first, and that the success we associate with them rarely happens overnight—or in straight lines, for that matter. In *Nike's* case, the 'Just Do It' campaign launched nearly 25 years after the business was founded, but those three words—along with an unusual 'swoosh' logo and a spirited organisational culture steeped in innovation—helped catapult *Nike* into a global brand. Perhaps *Campaign Magazine* sums it up best in their assessment:

---

50. *Nike's "Just do it" slogan is based on a murderer's last words, says Dan Wieden*, by Marcus Fairs, dezeen, online article, 14 March 2015.
51. *Nike's "Just do it" slogan is based on a murderer's last words, says Dan Wieden.*

"Like all great taglines, it was both simple and memorable. It also suggested something more than its literal meaning, allowing people to interpret it as they wished and, in doing so, establish a personal connection with the brand." [52]

In summary

While *Nike* is a global mega brand, it wasn't always the case. In the journey from business to brand, it's a long and varied adventure for those who are committed to the path, as this chapter has highlighted. Perhaps this fact, and this chapter, has brought you some perspective—and even some encouragement. Hopefully it has provided some guidance. But remember, the Brand Principles can be applied to any business, in any sector, and any size because they're based on an approach, a mindset. From there, it's just a matter of scale. And in *Nike's* case, their journey is far from over—but their attitude remains consistent. As *Nike's* CEO, John Donahoe, says:

"So as we pursue progress over perfection, we will continue to redefine what's possible by giving ourselves permission to try the counterintuitive, to refrain from making assumptions, to occasionally fail, and to keep on failing until we succeed. We will recommit daily to the complicated journey—the messy process." [53]

---

52. *Nike's "Just do it" slogan is based on a murderer's last words, says Dan Wieden.*
53. *Nike: Better is temporary, page 7.*

On simplicity

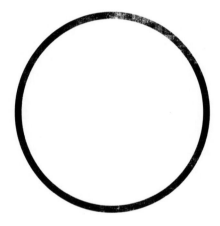

Our world is becoming increasingly complex. Every day, there are new and constant pressures vying for our time and attention, from social media expectations (as well as threats) and concerns about global pandemics, or recessions based on geopolitical movements that we have little control over, through to how our individual consumer behaviour—which is bound into complex and powerful commercial systems— is negatively impacting our climate. And then there are the everyday concerns of running a business, nurturing staff, completing projects on time, delivering on customer expectations—*and* having a life outside of work. Did I miss anything?! All of this makes the prospect of keeping things simple ever more inviting, yet increasingly more remote. It's the reason we see value in simplicity, yet at the same time reject its value out of hand. Why?

Keeping things simple can sometimes sound so easy. But, in truth, it's incredibly difficult to achieve successfully, and it can be even harder to maintain over the long-term. Part of the reason involves perceptions around simplicity. Oftentimes, it's dismissed as being obvious—even *too obvious* at times—and somehow less valuable, as a result. There is a tendency to believe that, for something to have true value and meaning, it must have an *element* of complexity. When assessing simplicity, we might judge the results as something a child could do, equating 'simplicity' with 'simplistic'. But that undervalues simplicity and overlooks the process. The very nature of simplicity means someone has literally removed complexity. They've made things clearer, smoother and/or more intuitive—*on our behalf.* That means the first step in achieving simplicity is understanding the complexity surrounding a specific task, problem or experience, as well as assessing the context in which it exists. It means first making sense of the mess. Only then are we in a position to design a simpler solution—deliberately, and with intelligence.

While all of this is incredibly valuable, it takes effort, time and investment to pursue. And if the cards are already stacked against simplicity from the outset— *"Oh, that's too simple, let's add something to it"*—it can be near impossible to appropriately leverage the value of simplicity for a specific task or outcome. More importantly, this mentality excludes the customer's perspective because we've made the decision that (*for us*) it seems too simple when, in fact, simplicity will actually make someone's experience, or their life, literally more manageable. How does this work in practical terms? Let's look at a well-known product from a household brand name, where Ken Segall discussed how simplicity was a driving factor in the development of the *iPhone*:

"I worked on the original iPhone advertising development and in the initial briefings I remember the first meeting we had with the product manager. He said: 'We all use BlackBerries here.' That was the accepted thing to use in business for email, etc. He went on to say: 'But we don't use around 80 percent of the features in a BlackBerry because we have no idea how to.' So, the idea of the iPhone was that you wouldn't even need an instruction manual. It would just be so obvious how to use it. The idea was you would simply use the features because they're right in your face [and] you don't need a manual for it." [1]

What drives simplicity?
Clearly, simplicity doesn't mean stripping things down to their bare essentials. It doesn't mean removing character or interesting aspects. Instead, it means making things easier to access or absorb. I can't imagine anyone saying: *"I'd really prefer if this was more difficult to understand, or more complex to interact with"*. Nor can I envisage someone thinking: *"I really wish this was more boring."* Keeping things simple is a balancing act between reducing friction, while maintaining or increasing positive experiences.

---

1.   *The transformative power of simplicity,* Ken Segall in conversation with Kevin Finn for DESIGNerd, online article, March 2018.

Furthermore, the notion that simplicity courts the lowest common denominator in an attempt to dumb things down is also a misunderstanding of the underlying intent. This is the difference between being simple and being simplistic. In a similar way to branding, in its most efficient form simplicity acts as the *assist*. For example, the crossword is a complex puzzle made incredibly simple. It's a concept pretty much anyone can grasp. But within that simple construct the actual experience can be either dumb, easy, difficult, or damn near impossible, depending on the content and design (the words, the hints and the size of the crossword, etc). Crosswords are bound by a simple set of rules, applied to a simple framework, which can be designed in multiple ways to foster any number of crossword experiences. It's a perfect interaction between complexity and simplicity. And it's an approach which can become a powerful tool for business, if embraced. In *Apple's* case, Segall describes how Steve Jobs sought to 'weaponise' simplicity as a competitive advantage:

"Simplicity comes along in stages. You look back at things that we thought were simple years ago, but which were actually terribly complicated. We all grow up together and become more sophisticated. But I think it's hard to deny that [simplicity is] one of the most powerful competitive weapons because, if you give the customers a choice of a difficult way or a simpler way, human nature will go with the simpler way. So, if you can make that clear to people, to communicate [that] you're offering simplicity—and in the case of Apple, where there's a lust factor for a cool-looking thing, because the design is so beautiful—it's hard to lose." [2]

The idea of intuitive simplicity has become a hallmark of *Apple's* brand experience—and something many other businesses and brands have been scrambling to emulate. Yet, few have come close to adopting a fully integrated system of simplicity in the way *Apple* has, despite its universal success. So, why don't businesses adopt this approach more readily and more often?

---

2.   *The transformative power of simplicity.*

The value of simplicity

The short answer is, achieving simplicity at scale is incredibly difficult. Within some organisations, people can deliberately hide within complexity, where it's easier to avoid accountability and responsibility. In worst-case scenarios, it can manifest as the primary reason for them to maintain and sustain complexity, because simplicity can be far too transparent.

In other cases, making things more complex has never been the intention. It just... sort of... *happens*. However, as we know, things tend to happen for a reason and, in these instances, it's usually cultural. Whether it's a lack of leadership or a climate of fear, compromises begin to undermine confidence in simplicity, which can impact a system, a business model, a marketing campaign, or the organisation as a whole. Either way, this tends to invite complexity, whether inadvertently or not. As Segall points out:

"I believe, if you really understand the nature of simplicity, and you work hard to create something wonderfully simple, it takes a lot of effort and it needs attention. For example, with a lot of companies I've worked with previously, at the beginning of every project someone would typically stand up, make a pretty strong speech about how they're going to do it 'this' time, how it's going to be so much different than 'last' time. And then it ends up being a pile of crap again because—suddenly—other people get their fingers in it. It's a case of having to please 'these guys' and 'those guys'; and do the research around the country; and revise it three or four times. Of course, before you know it, it's not simple anymore. I believe people who don't truly appreciate the power of simplicity tend to let it go along the way in the form of compromises." [3]

That's not to say collaboration isn't incredibly valuable. But without clear criteria for maintaining simplicity, those compromises can undermine the original intent. Usually, the bigger the organisation,

---

3. *The transformative power of simplicity.*

the more complex they become—or at least the conditions for complexity to thrive increases. In these instances, the value of simplicity can be profound. As Segall observed:

"Pretty much every organisation starts small, in some way—and then it grows. So somewhere along the line it changes. And when it gets bigger, it develops processes. It brings in smart people to 'run the company like a big business' and can lose sight, as a result. Steve [Jobs] was able to straddle this. He built Apple as the world's largest startup. He didn't want to lose those Values. It's that cultural thing again. Your job, your company, it's all about the culture—and within that processes can be created, but the Values [still] show up." [4]

In these circumstances, if there needs to be a guiding thought for businesses with regards to the value of simplicity, think of it this way: *customers are put off by complexity, just as much as staff can be unnecessarily hindered by it.* If something is difficult to use, to engage with, or to understand, we tend to react negatively. Increasingly, our collective intolerance for complexity compels us to seek alternative options—and there is now an abundance of options available to us in most industry sectors. For the most part, customers don't want to invest time trying to figure things out. Adding insult to injury, it gets more frustrating when customers *do* persevere with complex experiences and then realise there was a better, easier and simpler way that the company could have approached the product, service or communication (but clearly decided not to). This forms negative perceptions about the business, which can have a direct—and immediate—impact on the brand's reputation and its bottom line. This is where the contradiction occurs—where we both value simplicity and question it at the same time. How so? The reason is similar to De Bono's view on humour and hindsight; it's about our appreciation of outcomes over process. In Segall's words:

---

4.   *The transformative power of simplicity.*

•

If there needs to be a guiding thought for businesses with regard to the value of simplicity, think of it this way: *customers are put off by complexity, just as much as staff can be unnecessarily hindered by it.*

•

"The arguments I used to have about simplicity were because it's only obvious when you see it done and when you think about it in hindsight. Those kinds of ideas connect with people better. When you look back and think how simple it is, or how simple it seems to others, it's a reminder of how much incredible work, debate and anguish went into it. And yet, it often ends with people saying: 'Oh, that's so simple.' [5]

Simplicity at the core

When we consider how important it is for staff to truly absorb what a business stands for—its objectives, what sets them apart and how its Purpose drives their positioning, etc—simplicity can play a key role in making it easier for the whole organisation to fully understand everything—or not. For example, I've seen businesses produce paragraphs of well-meaning text conveying their Values, their Mission and their Purpose, only to be lost on staff who don't have the energy (nor sometimes the inclination) to remember the script, in full. When interviewing a client's staff, I always ask about the business' Values, yet it's not uncommon for individuals to either guess or struggle to remember what those Values might be. Not only that, I once saw an organisation's Values printed out, laminated and attached to every desk phone as a constant reminder of how staff should behave. While the intention might have been worthy, I actually found it rather draconian. Besides, it didn't really work because, astonishingly, few people even remembered those printed Values. If communicated clearly and simply, Values should be among the primary—and visible—traits which attract staff to a business in the first place. And when it's reinforced on a regular basis, through general conversations, actions and behaviours, as well as proof, it becomes cultural; it becomes part of the DNA. In *Apple's* case, Segall describes how simplicity showed up as an integral part of their culture:

"I was in plenty of meetings without Steve Jobs where people were preparing their presentations. They'd help each other by saying:

---

5. *The transformative power of simplicity.*

'You've got six things on that slide. That's probably a bit more confusing than it should be. Can you get it down to two?' And they would. People were always looking to help one another to do something that was more consistent with the culture. Culture has a lot more than simplicity but having this as a central philosophy is stronger—as opposed to a culture where processes are more important than anything else and where people must follow the process above all other things." [6]

Obviously, having simplicity at the heart of *Apple's* brand DNA—and valuing it—became cultural. This would have been achieved through numerous employee exchanges, broader communications and products, and over a long period of time. So, are there ways a business can employ simple processes that can affect an entire organisation, touching every staff member, keeping everyone on track, and encouraging them to be themselves while also living the Values and philosophy of the organisation? Well, let's look at how *Zappos* has achieved this.

Guiding culture

There are a few simple guiding principles underpinning *Zappos'* success, enabling the online shoe company to challenge its category conventions, while also adding immense value to customers and to the business itself. This success has, in part, been driven from the top, where the late founder and CEO, Tony Hsieh, believed: *"Your culture is your brand."* [7] (Essentially, this is Brand Principle #3: *Branding is internal before it's external.*) By identifying culture as the brand's core motivator, the entire organisation benefits from a simple guiding philosophy—one which clearly states that each employee has a role in delivering on (and building) the brand. But, of course, it's pretty easy to use nice, compelling and motivating words. We've all seen examples of this. However, in too many cases those words often go no further than appearing on a poster in the

---

6. *The transformative power of simplicity.*
7. *Good is the new cool: Market like you give a damn,* Afdhel Aziz and Bobby Jones, Regan Arts, 2016–2018, page 212.

staff kitchen area, or on the website. But following through on those words is where it counts. And *Zappos* is very clear about what their culture stands for in their company Vision: *"Delivering happiness to customers, employees, and vendors."*

"It's just more words!" I hear you say. Perhaps. And it would be easy to dismiss their Vision as being rather generic. So what's different here? While their Vision might sound simple, it actually outlines the playbook for how the culture operates and how it should be fostered, but also why it needs to be protected. And remember: *words have meaning.* The clarity and value of these words has allowed *Zappos* to create a very simple process, one that not only upholds those words but personifies them through every single employee as a lived experience. *Zappos'* Chief of Staff, Jamie Naughton, explains:

"Every single employee goes through call center training. So your first job when you enter our organisation, regardless of whether you are a vice president or on our maintenance team, is to go through four weeks of call center training, learning about our history, values, philosophy, how to work our phones. And then they spend eighty hours on the phone with the customers. So, 100 percent of our team is trained on how to be a call center employee. And when it gets busy for us, during the holiday season, every employee is expected to spend an additional ten hours on the phone—that's how we stay connected to this service proposition we have." [8]

Not only does this employee on-boarding process ensure every staff member has an equal and full understanding of the organisation, they also experience the brand at the coalface. In addition, this simple process ensures every employee understands that they all contribute to the brand, regardless of their role. Plus, through shared empathy, every staff member can appreciate their colleagues on a deeper level, and pitch in, when required. It

---

8. *Good is the new cool: Market like you give a damn,* page 212.

can also break down silos, minimise (and expose) any potential superiority complexes, and facilitate everyone having a more holistic understanding of customers. Essentially, it enables the entire organisation to put the customer at the heart of the *Zappos* brand (which is Brand Principle #13: *More than ever, your customer or end user is at the heart of your brand*). It's worth noting that the evident simplicity here belies the investment, leadership and commitment required to implement the process. And, no doubt, there is a lot more underpinning this approach. However, once again, appreciating and valuing simplicity is very different to acting on it and embedding it as a whole-of-organisation effort, where it's used to build and maintain the brand over the long-term. In *Zappos'* case, their simple principles, systems and philosophy can be revisited and adapted as needed, but with consistency and clarity at every stage. That said, I think we can all agree, none of this is immediately evident in the *Zappos* logo. How could it be? Instead, the results of these simple principles and processes have been embedded into customer associations, where the logo has become the symbol which visually conveys the *Zappos* brand experience as a canvas for all of this meaning to be embedded—to absorb those multiple meanings over time—individually and collectively. That said, can simplicity impact branding and logos, in particular—if at all? Let's take a closer look.

Consistency and flexibility

It's hard to argue against the value of simplicity, particularly when a business, process or system is complex and requires more efficient ways to operate and/or communicate internally and externally. So how might simplicity be beneficial when designing logos and identities? We're all familiar with global examples: the *Nike* swoosh, the *Apple* icon, the *Airbnb* looped 'A', and the *Target* symbol, to name a few. It's their simplicity which allows them to cut through the noise—either in a digital or a physical environment—where images and text are constantly shouting at us. The simpler your branding, the easier it is (for customers) to remember, to identify and to recognise. This is particularly striking in instances where a logo is either intricately detailed or incredibly literal, since this makes it harder to apply any wider meaning and/or expression to it. Nowhere is this more obvious than in the political sphere, a notorious sector that often embraces the lowest common denominator (in visual terms). It's also a sector that's rife with visual clichés and tropes, making it hard to distinguish one logo from another with any real impact. Michael Bierut had to navigate this challenging landscape in order to design Hillary Clinton's *2016 Presidential Campaign* identity. In this instance, the logo's simplicity belies the detailed process sitting behind it; an approach that needed to meet the complex requirements and demands of a political logo. In my conversation with Bierut (at the peak of the 2016 Presidential race) he said:

"From the start we looked at a lot of different elements, and a lot of different aspects. Unlike some of the Republican candidates, we had a candidate who is extremely well known, who arguably has 100 percent name recognition, but who has a disadvantage of this sense of inevitability. Of course she's going to be the candidate. And the competition is using an increasingly gruesome type of entertainment strategy. It's so awful to watch.

"The [Clinton team] realised the combination of things permitted them—or challenged them—to look for certain aspects in the way they handled the candidate's messaging. That made for an interesting challenge. It gave us the freedom to make variations of it over time. In the case of the [2008 President Barak] Obama logo, that aspect wasn't embedded in it at the outset—this idea that it could be adapted for different purposes. But that really became one of its fundamental attributes.

"So, the Clinton logo is the simplest thing in the world: straight vertical and straight horizontal lines, and then the arrow that points forward, which is just created by adding two 45-degree diagonals [pictured overleaf]. Of course, it's been criticized because a four-year-old could draw it. But I have a beautiful picture of a girl,

who looks about four years old, and who wrote on a piece of paper:
'I can be president.' The image has our logo drawn with a red and
blue crayon. It makes me think: Hell yeah! Go for it, four-year-olds!
So, when someone says a four-year-old could draw that logo, I say:
'Thank you very much!'" [9]

The simplicity of the logo was initially criticised (by the media, the
public, the design community and everyone else with an opinion).
However, they all failed to understand how this logo was going to
work across multiple channels, topics and issues—how it *needed*
to work. Not only that, many failed to understand that the logo
wasn't the brand. It was the symbol of the brand: *Hillary Clinton.*
And those dismissive comments—that a four-year-old could have
designed the logo—turned out to be a major benefit. Not because
Bierut anticipated an army of four-year-old's drawing the logo, but
because the simplicity of design helped with accurate recall, which
is a powerful advantage for any logo. Furthermore, the logo quickly
became a simple and consistent canvas for the Clinton campaign to
flex their messaging in an incredibly diverse manner. On that point,
Bierut went on to elaborate on this aspect of the branding system:

"When we were collaborating with the Clinton campaign team one
of the things we wanted to do was just provide an arena for things
that could then evolve and grow. And so that's why today—out
there—you'll see that symbol with lots of photography inside it.
When marriage equality was argued in front of the Supreme Court—
making it legal for gay couples to get married—the Clinton logo
changed from being just red and blue to having the pride rainbow
stripes in them. And it made headlines: 'Hillary Clinton Changes
Logo.' It's a way to show your support for a position." [10]

---

9.   *How to approach design,* Michael Bierut in conversation with Kevin Finn for Open Manifesto,
     Issue #8: Change, 2017, page 85.
10. *How to approach design,* page 88.

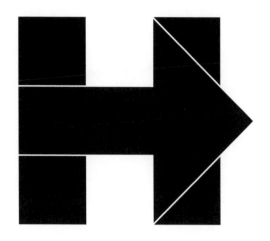

Photograph courtesy of Michael Bierut.
(Originally appeared in Open Manifesto #8: Change)

The benefit of hindsight

Once again, in hindsight—after the *Hillary* logo became a visual system and a canvas for multiple messages, and as more people became familiar with it—the solution seems like an obvious choice. The fact that it was incredibly different to all other logos in that particular Presidential race just added to its presence and visibility. And while the logo is simple, using two basic and recognisable shapes—a forward-facing arrow and the letter '*H*'—it wasn't a typical or clichéd logo. Unlike other political logos, the *Hillary* logo wasn't loaded with images or symbols of patriotism. Unsurprisingly, this was deliberate and intentional. As Bierut pointed out:

"I think [the campaign team] were confident that the candidate's patriotism was beyond doubt. Or that those who doubted it wouldn't be persuaded by seeing a logo. There's a kind of deadening predictability in that language of waving stripes and stars. It really is difficult. In doing that work we generated lots and lots of different options. And it was amazing how quickly people moved away from things that fell back on those clichés of patriotism and nationalism, the type of symbolism where it's preloaded already. One of the reasons people resisted this was because it's a predictable approach, and it's clichéd. But also, the more you load the logo with that symbolism the more it inhibits what you can ultimately do with the mark." [11]

Here Bierut succinctly illustrates the power of simplicity when seeking to have a broader communications platform, one that is both consistent and flexible, and where being literal can hinder you, or worse: *box you in*. Surprisingly, Trump won the 2016 election aided by an even simpler visual tool—a red baseball cap featuring *Make America Great Again* in conjunction with his abrasive but consistent personal brand. These examples are proof of the power of clarity and simplicity—for better *and* worse. Yet, there is a different school of thought embracing the use of literal logos, which aren't always designed with simplicity.

---

11. *How to approach design, page* 88.

More, or less?

In mid-2019, researchers Jonathan Luffarelli, Mudra Mukesh and Ammara Mahmood published the results of seven experimental studies they conducted analysing the effect of logo design on brand equity for 597 companies. Their objective was to gauge the effectiveness of logos which are more literal or descriptive versus those which are more abstract or suggestive. Writing in a *Harvard Business Review* article, the researchers first set the context by outlining the value of logos and branding in clear, tangible terms:

"Logo design choices might seem inconsequential to some. But getting the design right is important for a number of reasons. A well-designed logo can offer substantial benefits to brands. It can help pique the interest of consumers, differentiate brands from competitors, facilitate brand recognition, influence investors' decisions, and convey what a brand is all about. A logo is also a ubiquitous communication tool that might appear on your company's products, website, annual report, entryway, and even on your business cards. It is thus a brand element that is frequently seen by stakeholders, particularly consumers. Furthermore, the design characteristics of logos can considerably impact consumer behavior and brand performance. Prior studies on logos have shown that their simplicity or complexity can influence the funding decisions investors make, and that their symmetry or asymmetry can boost brand equity." [12]

Logos *do* have a real and tangible impact on how businesses are perceived by customers and society, and how this—directly and indirectly—impacts a company's bottom line. But they won't do all this on their own. Their role is to reflect the business and help identify it with associations. Unsurprisingly, this makes the design of a logo incredibly important from a business perspective, not just a marketing one. On that note, the study went on to uncover some surprising insights:

---

12. *A Study of 597 Logos Shows Which Kind Is Most Effective,* Jonathan Luffarelli , Mudra Mukesh and Ammara Mahmood, Harvard Business Review, online article, 12 September, 2019.

"The question of whether to use a descriptive logo or a non-descriptive logo often arises during design meetings. In recent years several brands have modified their logos to make them more descriptive, while others have made their logos non-descriptive. Dunkin' removed the word 'donuts' and the coffee cup from its logo. Conversely, Animal Planet made its logo even more descriptive by adding an elephant to the design. In our analysis, we found that about 60% of companies used a non-descriptive logo. However, as our research demonstrates (albeit with certain qualifications and under certain conditions), descriptive logos more favorably impact consumers' brand perceptions than non-descriptive ones, and are more likely to improve brand performance.

"We also found that, compared with non-descriptive logos, descriptive logos:
- *make brands appear more authentic in consumers' eyes;*
- *more favorably impact consumers' evaluations of brands;*
- *more strongly increase consumers' willingness to buy from brands;*
- *boost brands' net sales more."* [13]

Now, if you're thinking this is the formula for successful logo design, hold your horses! There are some caveats to the criteria the researchers used to assess how logos resonated most with consumers: they qualified these findings by—quite rightly—stating that descriptive logos are not experienced in the same way by every brand. Yet, the research went on to conclude that descriptive logos should be considered (very) favourably when designing or refreshing your company's logo. However, this is where I find myself challenging the research—and here's why.

Brand versus products and services

First of all, I understand that *Burger King* (with its image of burger buns) and *Animal Planet* (with its leaping elephant) immediately convey a clear sense of each organisation's product, service or experience. (Both of these logos feature in the study.) Yet, while

---

13. *A Study of 597 Logos Shows Which Kind Is Most Effective.*

this descriptive approach has its benefits, it's also very restrictive. How so? Let's pretend you have a fast food business. Does it make sense to create a logo using burger buns? For a start, there are a finite number of ways you can depict burger buns without being perceived as copying *Burger King* or a similar competitor—or worse, being sued by them for potential copyright infringement. Taking this approach means it's incredibly difficult to stand out from your competitors, which is a key component of effective branding. Secondly, the most successful fast food company on the planet is *McDonald's*. Do you know what their logo looks like? Of course you do—and it doesn't involve a picture of any product that it sells. Their *'double arches'* icon is incredibly simple and therefore easy to remember. Could you draw the *McDonald's* icon from memory? No doubt a four-year-old could. Could you do the same for *Burger King*? Thirdly, while the study gives established brands some leeway when it comes to adopting descriptive or literal logos, it suggests newly established businesses should adopt a descriptive logo. But, don't forget, all those established brands—with which we're now familiar—were once newcomers. So, at what point should the brand drop their descriptive logo for something more flexible and durable?

Of course, many established brands have evolved their logo over their lifespan. For example, *Toyota* (originally called *Toyoda*) has changed its logo five times. But it has never had a descriptive logo. It has never used an image of a car or vehicle. The same goes for the majority of luxury fashion brands. Neither *Prada, Gucci, Chanel, Hermès* or *Yves Saint Laurent* have clothing depicted in their logo. Cult brand *Aesop* doesn't have a pump bottle, or a tube, or a visual representation of liquid as part of their logo. And there is good reason for this. They're all seeking to communicate an attitude, a tone of voice and a personality. They're all seeking to convey their brand, not their product or service—because products and services are essentially an *output* of a brand.

Perhaps descriptive logos resonate well with consumers simply due to the fact it's much easier to process something we're already familiar with, meaning descriptive images or icons don't need to be decoded. They don't require additional time to understand it because they're already there. For example: *Mastercard's* logo doesn't include an image of a 'literal' credit card, or money, and instead features a Venn diagram, representing the intersection of things; founded in Northern Australia, *Qantas* chose a simple kangaroo motif (which is descriptive, but it's not a plane) to convey speed and portray a unique animal widely recognised as a national icon; and *Ralph Lauren's* polo player, created by tennis pro René Lacoste, conveys a sense of high society but doesn't feature clothing. The list goes on.

The point is, these logos are descriptive—in that they are simple, bold visuals that we're already familiar with—but they don't depict any of the brand's products or services in 'literal' terms (in the way *Burger King* or *Animal Planet* do). Instead, they're a canvas for meaning, created to reflect the brand—including the benefit, the value proposition and/or the strategy. In doing so, the brand has a wider communications platform to reach their customers and it's far easier for them to adapt and evolve as a business, when contexts and circumstances change—which they inevitably do.

For example, *Nokia Corporation* was founded in 1865 in Finland. Originally a pulp mill, it was initially associated with rubber and cables, among other things. In the 1960s, they also produced toilet paper. Then, in the 1990s, they shifted their primary focus towards large-scale telecommunications infrastructures, technology development, and licensing, becoming a major contributor to the mobile phone industry. That's a phenomenal array of different products and services. Curiously, in 1865 the *Nokia* logo featured an image of a fish, but in 1898 this was refreshed to become a simple typographic triangular logo, followed by a circular abstract logo in 1965, which was quickly replaced in 1966 with the current logo—the word *Nokia* in blocky letters. It's been an exercise in simplification. Aside from a stint as a descriptive 'fish' logo, all other versions have taken a non-descriptive approach, allowing the brand to continually evolve—diversifying its products and services—without confusing customers with a descriptive or literal logo. Indeed, if they had decided to continue with a more descriptive logo, what might that have been? What could possibly convey the disparate range and array of products and services— from rubber, to cables to toilet rolls, to mobile phones? And would that mean they'd have to change their logo as soon as they shifted their primary focus? Not only would this be impractical, it would be unmanageable, confusing—and wildly expensive.

What does it mean?

Okay, that's a lot to absorb. It might also sound a little contradictory, since there are strong arguments for the successful use of descriptive logos, based on depicting products (for example, *Burger King*), or detailed imagery (for example, *Starbucks*) as well as those which are literal, yet don't depict products or services (for example, *Apple*), just as there are strong arguments for the successful use of abstract logos (for example, *Chase Manhattan Bank*) or suggestive logos (for example, *Mastercard*). Unsurprisingly, none of these approaches can guarantee success when designing *your* business' identity because, unfortunately, it wholly depends on context. Damn! So, what can you do? Is there a solution, a way to approach designing your logo, identity or branding—a way that can work in pretty much any situation?

Yes!

Rather than designing your logo to solely reflect your product or service, instead start by reflecting your business or brand—your tone of voice; your attitude; your personality; your strategy. The simpler the logo, the easier it is to express these attributes in multiple ways, to associate your logo with your products or services as they evolve, but also to stand out in the market and differentiate your business from competitors. Simpler logos are also practical, because it's easier to apply them across various channels (from exterior signage on buildings and vehicle livery, to App buttons and social media icons). But remember, simple doesn't mean simplistic or boring. Your branding should reflect character and attitude, not just strategy and business focus. Regardless, whatever logo you choose to design or adopt, your staff and customers will develop associations and experiences that will be built into your logo over time. Every perception your business generates or influences will be attached to your logo. Because, ultimately, the business or brand—in its entirety—gives the logo its value.

But there are downsides to simplicity. When a certain kind of simplicity has been adopted successfully it can become the default for an entire sector (from website templates to airports). The result can be seen as dull, a mono-culture—or worse, beige and uninteresting. In those cases, simplicity has been adopted in a lazy manner under the guise of efficiency. This is a one-size-fits-all mentality. But simplicity is not at fault here. A lack of imagination is. Sometimes pursuing simplicity can also be seen as a risky endeavour. For example, in today's society businesses regularly offer an abundance of choice. While this is good in theory, it can take a toll on resources and confuse customers. On his return to *Apple*, Steve Jobs' famous decision to remove most of their product line and to focus on "a few products, but really well", was seen as a huge risk in an environment where businesses want to appeal to as many people as possible—with as many different options as possible. Of course, choice is a great benefit to businesses and customers alike, but the important factor here is to ensure that simplicity provides the necessary framework to increase efficiency, to better leverage resources and to avoid customer paralysis or confusion. As Segall shared with me:

"The challenge is not just to have the simple idea, but to have it recognised as a simple idea and to be able to keep it pure and simple, from beginning to end." [14]

---

14. *The transformative power of simplicity.*

•

Simplification is key,
because providing a complex
solution isn't progress.

•

Design and simplicity

From an aesthetic point of view, simplicity can often be criticised for lacking flair or individuality. Many argue that globalisation has homogenised design into a standardised universal language, one that has lost its dynamism and given way to establishing a visual mono-culture. But this is a narrow view of simplicity in design and concerns itself purely with aesthetics. In reality, simplicity must be considered as it applies to the smallest of things (like crosswords) and to the largest of endeavours (like cities), not just as a dogmatic aesthetic approach. Simplicity itself is a tool, a process and an outcome. It's a specific mindset applied to problem-solving. In most cases, the design process begins with complexity: the chaos of information, research, opinions, requirements, organisational politics, agendas, ambitions and fears, among other things. This is usually compounded by a designer's potential initial ignorance of a business, the sector or situation in question, before they've had a chance to explore and understand it fully. In doing so, the designer has to wade through this complexity before being in a position to identify a solution that will meet all the requirements and be easy (or easier) to communicate and deliver. Essentially, simplification is key, because providing a complex solution isn't progress. Even though all solutions aren't necessarily simple (consider cities and economies, among other large scale challenges), the objective is usually to make them as simple as possible. I believe most designers seek to achieve elegant clarity, and the process they employ is one of simplifying the complex.

So, simplicity doesn't mean linear, lowest common denominator, or removal of important information or steps. It means breaking down the elements across a number of constantly moving parts and within context. It means understanding all of this in order to retain the essentials and the prompts to create better experiences, interaction and use. It means promoting greater imagination, rather than streamlining it. And it means ensuring safeguards are in place to mitigate complexity creeping back in, supported by feedback loops to constantly assess changing circumstances and contexts. Essentially, simplicity—in all its applications—is one of the purest forms of communication. In the best cases, simplicity leads to efficiency; efficiency leads to productivity; productivity is the result of clarity; and clarity is achieved through simplicity. It's a deliberate closed loop model. But even with safeguards in place to promote simplicity over the long-term, it's always worth remembering: *Keep it simple—and after that, keep it simple.*[15]

A fine balance

The value of simplicity is clear, and the challenges for achieving (and maintaining) simplicity are also evident. This tricky balancing act becomes even more acute in branding, primarily because it concerns itself with communication, messaging and influencing perceptions. To illustrate just how nuanced it can be, Edward de Bono once shared with me his insights on this balancing act between simplicity, visual communication and impact:

"One of the obvious challenges to visual language is the conflict between being simple and being comprehensive. If all the factors and processes have to be included then communication becomes rather complex. If only the essence is included then the information is usually incomplete. There is also no point in communicating the wrong message very effectively, but neither is there any point in having a message so complex that it cannot be communicated at all. Such is the challenge of effective visual communication."[16]

This is clearly a challenge and it's why we both value simplicity and simultaneously dismiss it out of hand: because simplicity is much harder to achieve than it sounds; because it takes effort. A lot of effort. But *it's worth it*. It really is. However, if you're still not convinced, if you feel this is a biased view, consider these words from Simon Sinek:

"Simple ideas are easier to understand. Ideas that are easier to understand are repeated. Ideas that are repeated change the world."[17]

---

15. An anonymous maxim.
16. *Visual Language,* Edward de Bono, Open Manifesto, Issue #2: Interpreting Visual Language, 205, page 20.
17. *Simon Sinek, Notes to inspire* Newsletter, 13 November, 2019.

10

The cost of branding and design

When a business considers engaging a designer or a design firm, many assume there's a large fee involved. This is a justifiable assumption, not least of all because we regularly see media reports about new branding programs where the ('exorbitant') costs involved are often included in the headlines, even though they usually misrepresent what the project actually entailed. More surprisingly, for some business owners, their assumptions can also have the reverse effect—by actually *lowering* the value of design. How is this contradiction possible?

In the era of *99 Designs* and *Fiverr*, online crowdsourcing has enabled anyone to get a cheap logo or design service. And, while many professional designers might criticise this new reality, there is a valid place for these platforms. However, it's important to first understand their role. Rather than pursuing serious branding or identity programs, many individuals and businesses simply need a *logo*; a badge which signifies their business at a surface level and provides a means to quickly distinguish their business from others—with very little requirement beyond that. In this instance, the crowdsourced service can offer a fast and economical solution. But it's rarely deeper than an aesthetic exercise, where a number of 'options'—in response to a rudimentary brief—are presented to a client for them to choose which they 'like' best. Of course, these options offer no strategic recommendations. Essentially, it amounts to a quick fix. Which is fine—if that's what you need.

For example, crowdsourced logo services can be useful for start-ups, who are typically constrained financially, so getting a quick, cheap logo might be a good option to get things going. However, engaging a professional designer to work closely and directly with the business can provide a vastly more successful outcome. At the very least, it can separate the process from what a client 'likes' versus what the business 'needs'—and what is appropriate for the market. This often includes more than a logo. But, just like everything else, when a list of deliverables increases it obviously impacts costs and fees. And yet, it's surprising why this surprises some people.

Even so, when it comes to cost it's difficult to determine the value of branding which, for some people, might essentially look like a *logo*. But where a logo is a badge, branding should be a considered the distillation of an attitude, a positioning and a core message, one that is closely aligned with an organisation's business strategies, their Values, Purpose and objectives. It permeates the business language and influences all levels of communication. Where logos are often cosmetic, branding has depth—and an intrinsic relationship with the brand. The trouble is, while business owners might understand all of this in principle, the rise of crowdsourcing services means expectation on cost doesn't always match what's required for a branding program, or a professionally designed identity. It also sidesteps the potential positive impact this can facilitate, which comes complete with advice and guidance specific to the business' needs. This is where a contradiction emerges because discussions can quickly descend into a *cost versus value* debate, with business owners often asking what they're actually getting in return. It can be fatiguing for all involved. So, what can we do?

One way of approaching this is to simply assess what you want the design to achieve, honestly anticipating how you think it should impact the business. In other words: how important is considered branding for the (continued) success of your business? For example, is your business invisible in the market? Are your communications genuinely clear and understood (internally and externally)? Does *how you look* reflect *who you are* (meaning your Values, your culture, your attitudes, your actions, your behaviours, your Purpose, etc)? Has your business merged with another business (something that needs to be properly communicated to staff and to the market)? Have your products or services changed (a development that customers need to know about and understand)? Are you being challenged by a competitor with a clearer, better or more appropriate position in the market (and one that's resonating positively with your customers)? Or, has your business, or your industry sector, suffered a reputational crisis and needs to better explain the circumstances, or reposition the business entirely? The list goes on, and they're all important issues, which can impact the success of a business. But consider this: would a quick or cheap logo help overcome these challenges? Here's another way of looking at it: what might be the cost of *'cheap design'* to your business?

You might think that sounds intentionally dramatic. Not so. There *is* a tangible and direct cost to business when it comes to cheap—or bad—design. In a discussion around this topic, Warren Berger (author of the books *Glimmer* and *A more beautiful question*, among others) shared this astute insight with me:

"One could make the case that bad design actually costs a lot more than good design—but we don't become aware of the cost until later. At that point—when products under-perform, and thus alienate customers, when communications fail to communicate, and worst of all, when bridges come tumbling down—that's when we grasp the true cost of bad design." [1]

Perception is everything

As we've discussed throughout this book, successful branding is reliant on the business implementing it appropriately. But cost doesn't only translate to fees. While there can often be many positive associations with a new branding program—or an identity refresh—there are other aspects to be aware of in relation to the potential *associated* costs. In some cases, it can have a far-reaching and undesirable impact on an organisation's reputation. For example, in early 2019, the *Australian Securities and Investments Commission (ASIC)* revealed a new identity refresh. As Australia's independent government body, which acts as the country's corporate regulator, its role is to enforce and regulate company and financial services laws to protect Australian consumers, investors and creditors. Outside of those in the industry, announcing *ASIC's* updated identity is hardly headline news. Until it is.

---

1. *Design Thinking: Myth and Methodology,* Warren Berger in conversation with Kevin Finn for Open Manifesto, Issue #6: Myth, 2012, page 112.

In reaction to *ASIC's* announcement, the *Australian Broadcasting Corporation (ABC)*, which is the country's national broadcaster, ran with the following headline: *Australia's corporate regulator ASIC spends more than $100,000 on new font and branding.*[2] That headline might sound relatively benign, even if the figure is surprising to some. But context matters, and the Australian public were acutely aware of the context surrounding *ASIC* at the time. According to the *ABC, ASIC* began working on their identity refresh in late 2017, within weeks of the beginning of a significant and highly controversial banking Royal Commission investigating criminal activities, broadly in the financial sectors. As such, the announcement of *ASIC's* branding drew fire from many quarters, not least of all from the political class; Matt Keogh from Labor, the Opposition Party at the time, was quoted as saying:

"Instead of working to throw the book at the banks, they were more concerned about the font that the book was written in... This is a bold move by ASIC to focus on what sort of fonts it wants to use instead of actually applying scrutiny to the people we need scrutiny applied to. [ASIC] could have been using that money to employ an additional investigator to focus on the banks or go after mortgage brokers."[3]

Of course, this is a valid argument—and the *ABC* article didn't hold back on its criticism, either, when it claimed: *"As bank bosses were in the dock, the regulator was reworking its 'visual identity'"*; and: *"Corporate cop says it is trying to save money during rebrand."* But, it's the final line of the article that goes for the jugular: *"The ABC last year revealed ASIC had hired an external spin doctor to deal with 'potentially explosive issues for ASIC and its reputation' arising from the banking Royal Commission."*

There are two issues at play here:
1. The cost; and
2. The context.

---

2. *Australia's corporate regulator ASIC spends more than $100,000 on new font and branding,* Dan Conifer, ABC, online article, 12 February, 2019.
3. *Australia's corporate regulator ASIC spends more than $100,000 on new font and branding.*

Obviously, both are inextricably linked, but let's take the cost first. It's not unusual for headlines to include the overall cost of a branding exercise or an identity refresh, although often the focus is *solely* on the logo. This is intentionally inflammatory because it ignores the broader elements involved and the credentials of the design team engaged. Of course, most people don't understand what's involved in branding (why would they?). But this leaves them to equate a hefty price tag with a singular logo. Regardless of the business or organisation in question, this feeds negative perceptions with the intention of purposefully eliciting an emotional response from the community. People immediately begin to make judgments from this position, which contributes to how we view an organisation, business or brand. This in itself *is* branding because it shapes perceptions—and it's delivered through the (often more trustworthy) words of 'others'. But, in defense of the *ABC*, their article did include a cost breakdown:

"'Creative development' cost more than $43,000, excluding GST [Goods and Services Tax]. Nearly $60,000 was then spent on 'design and asset development'—including for new stationery templates, banners, and its online homepage. A 'web design update' came in at just under $3,000."

This high-level itemised cost breakdown goes some way towards justifying the fee, but in the context of the overall article (and the wider situation) it likely fanned the flames of criticism instead, particularly since the identity refresh—for all intents and purposes—essentially looked like a simple change in font. Absent was any deeper understanding about streamlining communications or adapting to technology, even despite *ASIC's* attempts to contain the fallout. The *ABC* went on to suggest:

"ASIC insisted it was trying to save taxpayers' money during the process: "We are introducing the changes gradually as stationery is exhausted and other materials [such as signs and banners] are replaced," corporate affairs boss Matthew Abbott said. "The

•

It's not unusual for headlines to include the overall cost of a branding exercise or an identity refresh, although often the focus is *solely* on the logo. This is intentionally inflammatory. Most people don't understand what's involved in branding, leaving them to equate a hefty price tag with a singular logo.

•

existing brand and font had not been changed in over 20 years and was not always suitable for use in digital channels such as social media and online."

Leaving aside the fact that Abbott incorrectly referred to the logo as 'the brand', and the article stated an external spin doctor had been hired to deal with any reputational fallout from the Royal Commission, which could also apply to the identity refresh debacle, his response likely fell on deaf ears. At that point, it was too late: judgments had been made; perceptions had been shaped; trust had been eroded; and the cost to reputation was extensive.

But now let's look at the context. *ASIC* is a government organisation regulating companies and the financial sectors. It's not a consumer-facing business and therefore not regularly visible or present in the public's consciousness. The fact that a Royal Commission into banking was underway at the time, that banks are generally disliked and seen as untrustworthy in the eyes of the wider Australian public, and that *ASIC* is tasked with keeping the banks in check, means it all ended up tasting sour in the mouths of many. Why might that have been the case? It has to do with *timing*, and it has to do with *perception*.

If *ASIC* had adopted a *brand mindset* this would have ensured that they looked closely at their internal culture, that they would have genuinely considered the perceptions surrounding their organisation within the current context, made an assessment of any deeper value propositions that they might entertain, and timed the project better in order to reflect all of this. It wouldn't have required a 'spin doctor' to manage things (even though they were allegedly assigned to just manage any fallout from the Royal Commission). Regardless, with a brand mindset *ASIC* would have understood how perceptions may develop in the absence of genuine communication to the public and media, and how trust and reputation need to be *earned* and *protected*—not managed—particularly in the context of the Royal Commission, and given the increasing perceived lack of trust the Australian public has for the broader financial sector.

Although *ASIC's* branding project focused on a series of applications and an identity refresh, it ended up being a purely practical consideration at the cost of everything else. In essence, these branding assets—done in isolation from a wider brand mindset—have a cost which is far more than the design studio's fee. Instead, *ASIC* were left scrambling to earn back trust, respect and reputation from an increasingly wary wider community.

Seeking reassurance

Arguably, most—if not all—business decisions are based on a *cost benefit analysis*. The question is always: What's our return on investment (ROI)? It's a valid query in most instances. But it's incredibly difficult to answer accurately when it comes to branding, largely due the fact that designers are rarely in a position to leverage the work further—to deliver on it *every day*. (And besides, by what measurement might people judge branding in isolation and *before* it's even implemented?) Either way, while branding can deliver on clarity, visibility, simplicity, and understanding, among other things, as well as providing the tools and frameworks for the business to use going forward, designers are usually removed from shepherding this beyond delivering the branding strategy and/or assets. Instead, the question needs to be: *What potential ROI might this branding provide if implemented consistently over time by us (the business)?* That's where the real impact is. But it can't happen without the branding first, which makes it a critical component in achieving this primary objective. Still, the question around ROI is a frequent one—if not an ever-present thought. So, how might we articulate the value inherent in considered branding as a means to help a business build their brand? In an insightful article for *Forbes*, Josh Ong (Forbes Councils Member) tackles this issue by first outlining what branding can achieve for a business, and its value therein:

"Businesses are often reluctant to spend resources on things that don't provide definite, measurable returns. Unfortunately, branding is one of those things—which has left many a brand bereft of a coherent identity that would benefit them with consumers. As a result,

companies shouldn't be viewing branding spend in a vacuum; instead, they should see it as an investment vital to making a brand successful [...] It's meant to multiply and expand existing customer acquisition strategies and marketing campaigns. In other words, branding acts as the assist." [4]

The key point here is that, while branding is critical, it's an *assist*; it won't deliver success on its own. It simply can't. And if a business or brand expects that it will, they'll be soon (and abruptly) schooled in reality. And yet, it's incredible how many businesses tend to undervalue branding—or question the costs involved. My suspicion is that most business owners still view branding as an important but short-term marketing exercise, and they limit their involvement to the final approval stage only—at the *end* of the process. It's odd behaviour when you think about it. By removing themselves from the process they essentially overlook the impact branding can bring to their organisation. It's why the (potential) intangible value of branding is a consistent topic many branding designers discuss with business owners. Ong goes on to unpack expectations around ROI, while also exploring the connections between branding, brand and value:

"It's all well and good to say that branding and brand awareness are valuable, but how valuable are they really? What's the ROI of brand awareness? No doubt many a brand has asked this question, and many of them have come up empty. It's hard to calculate the ROI of brand awareness, but for valuable companies such as Google, Apple, Tesla and relative newcomer Slack, branding has come to play an important role in how these companies are valued... Too many businesses view branding only as an opportunity to see their logo on as many things as possible, without thinking of the implications that might have on the general perception of their company.

Good branding can help buy companies the benefit of the doubt with customers, the press and investors. Sometimes it can even act

---

4. *What's The ROI On Brand Awareness?*, Josh Ong, Forbes, online article, 21 December, 2017.

"Businesses are often reluctant to spend resources on things that don't provide definite, measurable returns. Unfortunately, branding is one of those things— which has left many a brand bereft of a coherent identity that would benefit them with consumers."

as a kind of insulation from negative press—think, for example, of the recent scandals enveloping Google and Facebook. As much as people seem to love to hate on those companies, most have stopped short of calling for a boycott. It's in times of trouble that the strength of a company's brand really comes into play and can make the difference between consumers stepping away from a company and retaining their loyalty while the scandal fades away in our 24/7 news cycle world." [5]

But, how do you put a price on that? Well, as Ong points out, that's an incredibly difficult question because it deals with *potentials*, with *possibilities*, with *unknowns* and with *what ifs?* By its very nature, the value of branding only becomes fully apparent after the fact— depending on how the business or brand embraces it and deploys it. As such, it might be more accurate to consider branding in similar terms to how you might consider an insurance policy. What would you pay to be better insulated from situations beyond your control, or to have systems, messaging, communications and a culture that can withstand threats as successfully as they can leverage potentially lucrative opportunities? How valuable might that be to you and your business?

The importance of this is relative to the size, recognition, and influence of your business, as well as the potential risks associated around developing branding without due consideration. So it stands to reason, costs should be in proportion to the potential commercial impact, as much as the potential overall exposure, for the business (internally and externally). The more recognition the business has, the more influence it commands. The more relevance it represents in the market, the higher the potential opportunities and potential risks at play. Unsurprisingly, this is reflected in higher associated costs. The design firm's credentials, their reputation and experience, should also be viewed in proportion to the anticipated success of the branding, since expertise and experience can help further minimise potential risks.

---

5.   *What's The ROI On Brand Awareness?*, Josh Ong, Forbes, online article, 21 December, 2017.

Selling brand value

Of course, there is a dual objective for considered branding. On the one hand, it's vital for articulating clarity around your product or service, as well as your culture, your Values and your Purpose, etc. We've seen how clarity is essential for internal branding, before embarking on any external broadcasting. But there is another, more obvious side to considered branding: businesses typically want to secure and/or grow their market share. And many of them would like to charge a premium while doing so. Obviously, brands are big business, but how do they get to charge a premium? In the best-case scenario, considered branding—which helps clearly position and communicate a brand in the minds of others—permits the most successful ones to set their own (often higher) prices. The reality is, pricing is based on *value* (and *perception*) not cost. As Jasmine Bina (Brand Strategist and CEO of Concept Bureau) once put it:

"New premium brands don't charge in dollars. They charge in expensive intangibles like time, emotion, education and understanding. When you charge a premium that can't be measured in dollars, you're trading, not transacting. This isn't an exchange of goods and services. This is a reciprocity of commitment. It's very clearly a different kind of relationship." [6]

The tricky thing about this new reality is the fact that value is subjective—and incredibly so! In fact, value is only understood based on how it's perceived in the minds of others. So, if we follow this line of thinking, that means your business needs to be perceived as being valuable in people's minds—beyond just *delivering* a product or service. It's also worth pointing out, *premium* doesn't necessarily mean *luxury*. But, just like trust and reputation, the ability to charge a premium has to be earned. In fact, we *willingly* pay a premium in order to access a product or service with a trusted reputation.

---

6.   *Welcome To The New Premiumization of Everything*, Jasmine Bina, The Startup, online article (posted on Medium), 30 August, 2019.

The value of perception

This cost versus value debate can be so subjective—and can often be frustrating. It has the ability to derail a branding project before it even begins. And yet, perhaps it's not so subjective, after all. Entrepreneur and author Blair Enns (an international master on the tricky subject of pricing creativity) looked at some high-profile examples to see how the cost (versus value) of a logo plays out in a practical situation. In his book, *Pricing Creativity: A guide to profit beyond the billable hour*, he presents an incredibly insightful study of contrasts. You may recall that *Nike's* famous swoosh logo was designed in 1971 by Carolyn Davidson (who was an art and design student, at the time). Her fee was equivalent to around $250 today.

As Enns points out, that must mean logos cost $250, or thereabouts. However, in 2008, New York design firm *Arnell Group* allegedly charged *PepsiCo* $1 million to redesign their iconic logo. Again, Enns points out this must mean logos cost $1 million or, at least, somewhere between $250 and $1 million. The massive discrepancy between the cost of logo and branding programs for these two internationally recognised brands might leave you more confused than ever. But there are very tangible reasons for why these examples (and similar ones) cost what they did—and what the clients were *actually* paying for. As Enns explains:

"The price difference between the two logos is at best only tenuously connected to the amount of time or effort it took the designers to create them. I would venture that the total actual design time on each project wasn't meaningfully different. If the price difference was rooted in time, surely Pepsi could have found designers just as good who were willing to work much more quickly, thereby saving thousands of dollars.

There's a hint of a basis for the price in the fact that the startup Nike, in 1971, and the multibillion-dollar brand Pepsi, in 2008, were companies of dramatically different sizes at different points in their growth trajectory... A primary reason for the [$999,750] *price difference in this case is risk. It would be a mistake to say that Pepsi overpaid for its logo and Nike underpaid for the swoosh. It's likely that both designers charged what they thought were fair prices, and it's equally likely that both clients felt they got good value. [Therefore] value is broadly and simply defined as the measure of regard or importance we place on something. Today it's widely understood that we each value things to different degrees for different reasons and at different times.*"[7]

Enns' examples are confirmation that *a brand gives the logo its value*. In 1971, *Nike* was a business, not a brand. As a startup, it had less to lose because there was no inherent value in the business, or the 'swoosh', at the time. In contrast, *PepsiCo* was very established by 2008 and was seeking to reposition their globally recognised product, while at the same time protect the multi-billion dollar brand behind it. (In 2020, *PepsiCo* generated $70.37 billion in revenue.[8]) So it stands to reason, the more a business might potentially lose, the higher the design fee—because the company is also buying an element of reassurance. And yet, it doesn't always work out as planned. Let's look at another *PepsiCo* example, only this time it reveals the cost of a design failure.

Everything has a price
In 2009, *PepsiCo* commissioned *Arnell Group* again to redesign the packaging for its *Tropicana* orange juice brand. Given the success of the *Pepsi* redesign, re-engaging *Arnell Group* would have been a sensible decision. However, the results could not have been more different. So, what happened, and why? Well, with any redesign, there are likely to be two questions at the forefront of the Executive team's collective mind: will the redesign help increase revenue; and—perhaps more importantly for them—what is the potential cost of any lost revenue. In other words, as Enns puts it, they would have been weighing up:

---

7.   *Pricing Creativity: A guide to profit beyond the billable hour,* Blair Enns, Rockbench Publishing Corp, 2018, page 2.
8.   *https://en.wikipedia.org/wiki/PepsiCo*

•

While cheap, crowdsourced logos might have their place, for those who are serious about building a brand the importance of branding has become much more valuable than the cost of a logo.

•

"The potential cost in lost revenue, market share, market capitalisation, and perhaps even their own lost career prospects if things went poorly and sales declined as a result of the redesign." [9]

Given the success of the *Pepsi* redesign, you might be surprised to hear that the new *Tropicana* identity and packaging—which was designed by the same *Arnell Group* team—triggered an immediate drop in sales of more than 20%. The valuation of that drop was calculated to have been between $30–$50 million in lost revenue before the old packaging was reinstated. That's a rather costly mistake by anyone's standards. Yet, Enns suggests a similar mistake with the *Pepsi* redesign would have likely cost *PepsiCo* hundreds of millions of dollars.[10]

These examples are rare because they include the same parent brand (*PepsiCo*) and the same design team (*Arnell Group*). And yet, they didn't involve the same fee. Where the *Pepsi* identity redesign cost a reported $1 million, the *Tropicana* redesign allegedly cost $35 million—but with polar opposite results. So, how is this possible? Given the outpouring of irate customer comments online in response to the *Tropicana* redesign, you'd be forgiven for assuming that—at the very least—*PepsiCo* underestimated the emotional connection customers had with the original packaging, which, to be fair, is perhaps a rather intangible measurement to predict. Regardless, once the impact had been felt, no doubt there was a frenzy of finger-pointing. And the failure didn't only cost dollars—it cost jobs. Soon after, the Chief Marketing Officer, David Burwick, resigned amid a 9% revenue decline for the brand's beverage division in that first quarter. [11]

It would be easy to credit *PepsiCo* for their smart navigation of the *Pepsi* redesign, and to blame *Arnell Group* for the *Tropicana* failure. But here's the truth of it. Designers must leverage their experience,

9. *Pricing Creativity: A guide to profit beyond the billable hour,* pages 2, 3 and 4.
10. *Pricing Creativity: A guide to profit beyond the billable hour,* pages 2, 3 and 4.
11. *Pulling off a packaging redesign: learning from Innocent and Tropicana,* Packaging Gateway, online article, 12 May, 2013.

their expertise and their track record, as well as any available research that can help provide an informed proposed solution for the task at hand. However, they aren't working in isolation. The business or brand is also responsible and accountable (for both successes *and* failures). Since designers operate in *potentials* and *what ifs?*, and with a limited understanding of the client's specific market, the brand itself must operate on a much deeper understanding of their customers and should be acutely aware of any potential fallout that a redesign might prompt. In *PepsiCo's* case, it's unlikely *Arnell Group* recommended redesigning the *Tropicana* identity and packaging in the first place. This would have been a decision made *inside the business* and armed with a deep knowledge of their market and their customers. *PepsiCo* should have been in a better position to assess how the proposed design might impact the business—before approving the redesign and then launching it.

Regardless, it's clear that designers don't build brands—simply because they're not in a position to do so. *Arnell Group* are not responsible for the loyalty customers have to *Pepsi* or *Tropicana*. It's *PepsiCo* who have worked on developing this loyalty over decades. So it bears repeating: while branding designers are certainly critical to a brand's success, they act as the *assist* and it's the business which takes on the role of building the brand—from the inside out. This should, therefore, put to rest the debate around 'cost versus value' because, while cheap, crowdsourced logos might have their place, for those who are serious about building a brand the importance of branding has become much more valuable than the cost of a logo.

Six deceptively difficult questions

Like most designers, I'm constantly asking questions. It's the natural operating system for a curious mind. But it's also a practical way to learn about—or to discover—something new. Oftentimes, these questions are simple, or ones that have been overlooked. They also tend to be the most difficult questions to answer.

Having asked lots of questions over my career, I've found there's a pattern to the most valuable questions that I believe a business or brand needs to answer. I've distilled this down to six questions which, if interrogated and answered honestly, can either be challenging or incredibly difficult, depending on how well a business knows itself. I use these questions regularly because—in my client engagements—I've been told they're the simplest, most difficult, yet most valuable questions to answer.

As discussed previously in this book, before a business or brand can broadcast a message externally it first needs to ensure all staff are aligned—not just the Sales and Marketing team, or the Executive group. For this to be effective, it's vital to have clarity from within—and across a number of key areas—because once this has been achieved it makes communicating it to the wider organisation much more efficient, simply due to the fact it's a lot easier for staff to remember. That, in turn, makes it much easier to broadcast externally—to customers, clients, the market, and to the world in general. Shall we give it a go?

(To make this worthwhile for you, take some time to think about each question. Write down or record your answers so that you can see them clearly—and in sequence. That way you can review your responses once you're done... And you'll probably need to.)

Ready?

1. What value do you provide?

2. Who are you talking to?

3. What are you saying?

4. What channels are you using?

5. Can you live up to it?

6.

Question 1: *What value do you provide?*
We're not talking about *value for money*. We're talking about *how you deliver value*. In business modelling language, this is your 'value proposition', but think 'benefits' rather than 'features'. How do you help solve a customer's problem or need?; How do you improve their experience, perhaps even improve their life?; What compels them to transact with you? The value you provide should ensure a customer trusts you; that you, your product or your service are relevant in their life—which is why they will choose you over others.

Question 2: *Who are you talking to?*
This is about articulating or identifying your customer or audience group. But, as Sir John Hegarty suggests, try to avoid segmenting your customers into demographics and age groups. Instead, articulate what *kind* of person you're talking to. Are they progressive, early adopters? Are they conservative and embrace reassurance? Are they Purpose-driven, or environmentally conscious? Are they time poor, or crave convenience? Are they struggling with a specific problem, for which you have identified a solution?

Question 3: *What are you saying?*
Now that you know *who* you're talking to, what are you saying to them? What's your core message? What do you want them to know or to remember? Is it informative, or a call-to-action? Do your current communications—internally and/or externally—already convey this message, or do they need to be reviewed or updated? Have you checked that your message is clear to people and is having the desired effect?

Question 4: *What channels are you using?*
Let's assume you're clear about who you're talking to and what you're saying to them. If so, what channels are you using to reach them? Understanding your customers means you should know whether they prefer one-on-one interaction, event-style gatherings, digital experiences, or community-based engagements, etc. This determines *how* you reach them, whether that's through

1. What value do you provide?

2. Who are you talking to?

3. What are you saying?

4. What channels are you using?

5. Can you live up to it?

6. Why should anyone care?

physical environments, e-marketing, events-based networking, or experiences, etc. If you have a good idea about the right channels, and even if you're already doing something that appears to be working, have you *asked* your customers how they prefer to be contacted by your business?

Question 5: *Can you live up to it?*

By this stage in the exercise, a percentage of people might be feeling pretty confident about their answers. If so, that's great! It's important to point out that this hasn't been a waste of time, because it's encouraging you to articulate things confidently and to write them down. However, Question 5 can sometimes draw out our ego, or suppress our vulnerability. We feel compelled to shout: *Yes, yes! Of course we can live up to what we say we do!!* Well, maybe that's true. And if so, you'll need to provide proof that you're delivering on what you say you do. Maybe the proof is that sales targets are being met, maybe KPIs are consistently strong, maybe staff are super happy and productive, maybe data indicates a positive graph. But have you asked your customers (and staff) what *they* believe you're delivering for them, and whether you're living up to it?

Question 6: *Why should anyone care?*

This is often the hardest question to answer because the instinct is to respond from your point of view, not your customers. Answers are driven by a natural inclination to support *your belief* that what you do is important, or that it's relevant. And hopefully it is! Why would you be doing what you do otherwise? However, there is a danger to answering this question without due consideration. You might be the incumbent, or you might be vulnerable to a competitor, or a start-up. So, the sub-questions here are: *Would anyone care, or miss your business if it abruptly shut down tomorrow? Do you matter?*

1. What value do you provide?

2. Who are you talking to?

3. What are you saying?

4. What channels are you using?

5. Can you live up to it?

6. Why should anyone care?

The answer to Question 6 is actually the response to Question 1. Why? Because, as we know, for the most part, customers and audiences are always asking: *what's in it for me?* Whether that's purely consumer driven (when they're looking for a specific product or service) or problem-orientated (when you make things frictionless for them) or Purpose-driven (when their purchasing power can positively impact something bigger). Whatever the reason, they're always seeing it from their point of view—*not yours.* If you don't believe me, consider how *you* decide on things as a customer? This makes Question 1 critical because, if you're not delivering value it's unlikely that you matter all that much to your customers. And it's very likely you won't be missed if you shut down tomorrow, since a competitor will fill your shoes.

What next?

Whether or not you feel confident with your responses, I recommend running through those six questions a few times until the answer to Question 1 and Question 6 line up neatly—and the questions in between validate that alignment. It's also worth doing these questions in a group session (where everyone answers the questions individually, before sharing the results), making sure you include a cross-section from within the organisation to participate, so that you get a more robust view of the business. Once done, summarise the responses into short answers for each question. Then test or validate these results with the wider organisation.

While this will help you achieve clarity and alignment internally, from an external perspective it's still based on assumptions. So, the next step is to share your views with customers, clients and stakeholders to see if they agree, or if it makes sense to them. From there, you will have a pretty succinct point of reference for how your business operates—*the value it provides; for whom; supported by a clear message; delivered through appropriate channels; backed up by actual proof; and underpinned by a product or service that is genuinely relevant in people's lives.* The result should be easy for anyone to communicate, because it'll be easier to remember.

A hypothetical example

To illustrate, let's consider a real estate agency. It's an industry with rather negative public perceptions. In Australia alone it was ranked the third-least-trusted profession in a 2017 survey.[1] So there's room for these perceptions to shift, through words and actions. With this in mind, here's a hypothetical 'first pass' on the six questions:

Question 1: *What value do you provide?*
We're experts in helping people buy or sell property in our particular area, region or community.

(Note: This type of response is based on a feature, rather than a benefit, which is dangerous because features can be replicated— faster, cheaper, better, etc—whereas benefits are harder to replicate, since they're the foundation for deeper relationships. Furthermore, any competitor could claim they offer equal or better 'expertise' in selling or buying property. The agency provides no compelling reason for customers to choose them, no deeper benefit, other than experience in buying or selling property.)

Question 2: *Who are you talking to?*
We focus on retirees, empty-nesters, young families, and first-home buyers, as well as commercial properties.

(Note: This is predictably wide. However, it's essentially a list of anyone who might be in the market for buying or selling property. The agency hasn't identified who—from within these demographics— they can best serve, providing no evidence they understand their clients, apart from the fact lots of people are looking to buy or sell property, which is hardly a valuable insight.)

---

1. *Roy Morgan Image of Professions Survey 2017: Health professionals continue domination with Nurses most highly regarded again; followed by Doctors and Pharmacists,* Roy Morgan Research, online article, 7 June, 2017.

Question 3: *What are you saying?*

If you're looking to buy or sell property, we can get you the best deal in the market.

(Note: "Getting the best deal" might sound compelling—I mean, who doesn't want to get the best deal, right? But that puts immense pressure on agents to constantly deliver on getting the best deal. In reality, that's determined by the market and it also depends on who the agent is representing (the buyer or the seller). Current negative perceptions suggest people feel agents are actually representing their agency, or more likely themselves, rather than their client's interests. Based on a message of "getting you the best deal", each individual will have different expectations, suggesting the sale will likely require a shifting definition of what the 'best deal in the market' means at any given moment. In the agent's defense, of course the market is always shifting, but if they're suggesting "this is the best deal we can get at this point in time, based on the market" it could feel like a walk-back from their initial promise, or a compromise, particularly if client expectations haven't been met. Given the promise is to "get you the best deal" it's reasonable for a client to ask "is this really the best deal?" That question—based on the agent's primary promise—can add yet more unnecessary pressure and anxiety for all involved. The process becomes grueling and transactional—and filled with suspicion.)

Question 4: *What channels are you using?*

We send weekly e-newsletters to our substantial database, while also advertising in local newspapers, online real estate platforms and through in-person conversations at property viewings.

(Note: These are valid channels. However, in all likelihood competitors are using the exact same ones. If so, the questions are whether there might be any other channels they can use, or if they can leverage these channels better than any of their competitors?)

Question 5: *Can you live up to it?*

Our sales and clearance figures speak for themselves. We're consistently one of the best-performing agencies in the region, area, or franchise.

(Note: Wow! Who wouldn't be proud of those results? The trouble is, it's all about the agency and not really about their clients. This feeds into negative perceptions that the industry is actually only interested in itself. As a result, the inference here is that the agency has used their clients to climb the leader-board of 'best performing agencies'. Sales results are usually promoted as a measurement of expertise, which is understandable. But this ignores the valuable relationships that are required to achieve this.)

Question 6: *Why should anyone care?*

Because buying or selling a property is one of the biggest decisions in someone's life.

(Note: It's true! Buying or selling property is a big decision for most people, usually involving vast sums of money, as well as the anxiety of debt which this can create. So, if this is such a common and important decision, we can safely say most people will care. But will they care whether they go through the process with this particular agency rather than a competitor? Based on the hypothetical responses, it's unlikely they would. Why? The majority of the six responses were generic and offered very little in terms of a compelling differentiation. In most cases, competitors could claim something similar, or better (i.e.: We're experts in helping to buy or sell property because it's important in people's lives). Not only that, most responses were about the agency—not about their clients. This isn't surprising. Many businesses do this because they see things from their own perspective. In contrast, successful brands generally look at things from their client or customers' perspective. While this might be a small shift in approach, the impact is enormous. And it offers a huge opportunity to shift how you talk about your business.)

Another pass

Obviously, the responses provided were hypothetical (but also based on personal experience and observations). Clearly, there are numerous ways in which those responses could be framed—and hopefully you were able to substitute your business for the fictional real estate agency. But the exercise intentionally uses generic responses, since most businesses talk in these generic terms because it's intentionally vague (and in some cases, perhaps they're hoping to sound better than they actually are). While we could run through those six questions a number of times, where you can share and fine-tune them, let's jump to a more considered set of responses where the questions have been reworked and where the intention is to help prompt different ways for you to articulate your business.

Question 1: *What value do you provide?*

For most people, buying or selling property is an incredibly important—but oftentimes anxious—process. This is precisely why we provide impartial guidance and reassurance, so our clients can focus on what's most important to them.

(Note: In essence, this response is similar to that of the first pass. However, this response takes the client's perspective. Without directly criticising competitors, they've acknowledged the industry's negative perceptions. The result is, they've separated themselves from the rest, but in a way that employs empathy, respect, understanding, reassurance—and impartiality. All in the pursuit of helping clients focus on what's important to them—which, of course, will be specific to each individual.)

Question 2: *Who are you talking to?*

Anyone who might be suspicious of real estate agencies and who is looking for a trustworthy relationship to help guide them through an impartial process.

(Note: How does that response make you feel? If you were in the property market, would you consider yourself a potential client of this agency based on that sentence? Regardless of your age, gender, ethnicity or life stage, could you see yourself as part of this client profile? Here again, the agency is taking the client's perspective and then illustrating where they might show up in their story. And again, they separate themselves from competitors by respectfully acknowledging the industry's reputation and then distancing themselves from it with a clear value proposition. Rather than define demographics, their approach is to identify the type of person they want to attract. It's the opposite of push marketing, where businesses seek to convince customers to choose them. This response also helps the sales team in identifying who they might approach as potential clients. It also helps with the agency's content strategy, since they will be clearer on the type of messaging they want to communicate to this particular client profile. In turn, this influences how their culture is fostered, in order to deliver for this particular client profile. However, it does take courage to articulate a response like this, and to then build the business—the systems, the support, the staff and the financial models—around it to ensure the agency can genuinely serve this client profile. Having such clarity is the first step in ensuring it can be achieved.)

Question 3: *What are you saying?*

Buying or selling property should be exciting, not stressful. This is why we put our client's needs before our own because trusted relationships and mutual respect are vital. We do this by taking the time to listen first, before aligning our client's needs with the available property opportunities and leveraging our extensive expertise in the market.

(Note: Once again, they're using empathy in order to take the client's perspective. And from the outset, they're stating some of the emotions people experience when buying or selling property. Importantly, instead of communicating their own story, the agency is acknowledging the client's story, and where the agency shows up in

it. This is about being respectful and relevant. They're also explicitly stating their values and approach—"trusted relationships and mutual respect are vital." In doing so, they're using a filter, which ensures this is a two-way relationship, not a one-way transaction. This means they can better attract and identify the right client. The tone is set from the beginning. The systems are there to make sure the process is smooth. The attitude is clear and will be evident in the culture. And they've still presented their credentials as experts in the industry.)

Question 4: *What channels are you using?*

Being part of the community we see people at the gym, at the supermarket and at the café, etc. This is where we talk to them— like people not prospects—about their general concerns and aspirations. It's not where we sell to them. It's where we *listen.* We create short videos about market trends, based on the extensive knowledge we've gathered, and we send weekly e-newsletters featuring specific property listings. All of these are shared with our substantial database. For tactical purposes, we also advertise in local newspapers, online real estate platforms and through in-person conversations at property viewings.

(Note: Good business is based on genuine relationships and mutual respect. But this is rarely achieved when every interaction is treated as a new business pitch, or a verbal slide deck of your latest business offers—whether that's out of desperation, out of habit, or out of a perpetual 'growth mindset'. For most people, this is a turn off and immediately begins to shape perceptions about your business. Providing short, informative and compelling answers to queries usually allows people to talk more than you do, and for you to clearly see what is important to them, or identify when the conversation moves to a new topic.)

Question 5: *Can you live up to it?*

We're proud and humbled to be consistently ranked the most trusted real estate agency by our clients and community.

(Note: Genuine humility ensures we don't take things for granted. It reminds us how we got here, and how we might lose our position if we start becoming complacent. This is about culture. It's also about recognising what's more important—peer recognition, high sales clearances, continual growth, and clients who feel you are trustworthy and are likely to refer you to friends and family, as a result. That doesn't mean our hypothetical agency might not be the most successful agency in the franchise or region—in fact, it would probably guarantee they are. Industry awards and accolades can be important on many levels, but the metric which potential clients will use is whether they can trust the agency. If in their marketing material the agency stated they were trusted, it's unlikely people would accept that as a fact. But saying that their clients consistently rank them as trustworthy, well, that's pretty powerful. It's 'other people's words', which is more believable because client's and the community are participating in building the agency's reputation of trust. But don't forget: trust has to be first earned before it can be kept.)

Question 6: *Why should anyone care?*
Because we put our client's interests before our own.

(Note: This response is based on acknowledging the industry's reputation and a client's pain points, based on research, studies and statistics. The fact is, any real estate company can help people buy or sell property because that's a baseline. It's a feature. But how many can genuinely say they put their client's interests above their own—even walking away from a sale when it's the right thing to do? More importantly, how many can back this up through their actions, behaviour and culture? It seems so obvious, but putting clients or customers first is the foundation of successful businesses and brands. Yet, it's incredible how many forget to articulate this—or they do articulate it but never live up to it because it's employed as marketing spin, instead. If our hypothetical agency genuinely puts their client's interests over their own, and if this is backed up with proof and experience, given the poor reputation of the industry would they be

•

Keep it simple,
because it will be easier
to remember; and ensure
it's compelling, because
that will ultimately make
it more memorable.

•

missed if they abruptly shut down tomorrow? Would it matter to clients if this agency was no longer around to guide them through the process with impartiality?)

In summary

If we align Question 6 with Question 1, we get this simple, short paragraph: *For most people, buying or selling property is an incredibly important—but oftentimes anxious—process. This is precisely why we provide impartial guidance and reassurance, so our clients can focus on what's most important to them, because we put our clients' interests before our own.* Compare this with the responses from the first pass: *We're experts in helping people buy or sell property in our particular area, region or community because buying or selling a property is usually a big decision in someone's life.*

Which one is more compelling? Which one is based on market insights? Which one offers a genuine benefit? Which one takes the client's perspective? While both indicate their agency culture, which one is more attractive—and might attract top talent? And when considered in the market as competitors, which agency is likely to attract more (better fitting) clients? The power of words cannot be overstated. If something sounds compelling, inviting, or convincing, it begins to shape how we think about that organisation, business or brand. This has the ability to motivate staff, to instill pride, and to influence behaviour. That clarity also has the power to help filter out individuals who feel they don't fit with the business' Values or offer. It becomes a process of self-selection simply because, with clarity, it's obvious to each individual whether they align with the message and behaviors—or not. This occurs because, within the six responses, a pattern becomes evident: *repetition.* It's likely your response will convey similar themes, and oftentimes even the same words. Why? Because, when we have clarity, being faced with a new question challenges us to express a similar answer, but in a different way. And this starts to identify a core message or attitude. It begins to reflect your centre of gravity.

Hopefully the second, revised, set of hypothetical responses will help you navigate the questions for your own real-life scenario. By running through the questions a number of times, responses will get easier and more natural. Here's a good tip: *Answer the questions as if you are your own customer.* Using intuition, empathy, research, data, anecdotes or even assumptions, will help you rethink how you communicate your business, your Values, and your culture. Knowing how and where you show up in your customer's story— with value and relevance—is essential. While you'll need to validate the responses later with your wider organisation and customers, it's vital that you articulate them for yourself, first. But remember: *words have meaning.* While the second set of responses might sound better and more compelling, people will accept them for what they mean. If you can't live up to it, if you're taking creative license with the truth (i.e.: adopting spin) you *will* be found out. Any trust you may have had—or earned—will vanish. Your reputation will be burned. Rebuilding that trust will take a lot of time, investment and hard work.

This six question framework will provide a valuable reference point for you to use and build upon. Keep your responses as succinct as possible because they'll help you articulate, in simple terms: *the value your business provides; for whom; supported by a clear message; delivered through appropriate channels; backed up by actual proof; and underpinned by a product or service that is genuinely relevant in people's lives.* This can be embedded in your internal communications, sales material, content strategy, social media campaigns, and advertising, etc. But keep it simple, because it will be easier to remember; and ensure it's compelling, because that will ultimately make it more memorable.

12

Building
a Brand

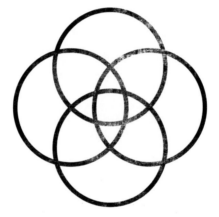

Throughout this book I've argued that branding designers and brand consultants, even advertising agencies, aren't in a position to build a brand on your behalf. While they do act as a crucial *assist*—contributing at various points in a brand's journey—it's the business itself that builds its brand over the long-term; day-in, day-out. Of course, customers and clients also play a vital (and ongoing) role. So when it comes to building a brand, are there any specific foundation blocks to consider? Well, let's take a look.

At the inception of any business there's usually a healthy dose of optimism and excitement. It's only natural. And if you're fortunate, this is followed by a steady period of growth in order to meet demand, or to capitalise on opportunities. Additional growth periods often ensue. But it's in these growth stages where the wheels can quickly fall off, partly because culture is often difficult to scale consistently and at pace, but also because systems and processes may not be in place to support such rapid growth. However, it's also likely there is another factor at play: the absence of a brand mindset, which would provide a more holistic understanding of what the business is seeking to achieve and how you want to achieve it.

The Brand Principles offer a remedy—because you don't need to be a brand to have a brand mindset. But it's important to understand, there's no 'sell' here; no magic formula. The Brand Principles are simply a framework reflecting the tectonic shifts currently underway—from a traditional business mindset (which is insular and controlling) to a more progressive and open one (which is inclusive and Values-based). But, again, don't take my word for it. Commentary in the business world consistently validates and supports these observations. For example, in early 2020, *Campaign Asia* partnered with *CNN* to host a roundtable looking at how businesses and brands need to adjust to these sweeping changes, while also staying true to themselves:

"At the end of the day, consumers' trust comes from the feeling that brands are talking to them—that they aren't just airing whatever messaging serves the brand agenda. As consumers shift their thinking from 'how would this brand or product benefit me from a functional point of view?' to 'does this brand understand me and share my values?', brands also need to connect with their audiences to find a more 'human way' of telling their stories."

The roundtable went on to proclaim:

"However brands go about it, all the CMOs agree that building and retaining brand trust has never been more important. As consumers become more sophisticated, they want to actively engage—to be listened to, not just spoken to. As Citi's [James] Keady says, 'trust is essential, it's not a choice. Equally, transparency is not optional either. If you're not transparent, someone will expose you and eventually that's going to do more brand damage than being upfront about it.'" [1]

There's genuine awareness rippling through the business world in response to changes across the consumer landscape. Many businesses and brands are grappling with how to adjust; others suggest using commonsense. Regardless, because of a combination of technology, increased connectedness, climate concerns, abundant choice, and an ability for every consumer to voice their opinion, support *and* frustration, there's now a scramble to earn their trust, respect and loyalty. Consumers have new, and justifiable, expectations. There's also growing acknowledgment that we're all consumers of some product, service, experience, business or brand, which can be useful when reflecting on your own company. For example, here's a hypothetical personal litmus test:

- If a design or advertising agency creates an amazing piece of work to market or communicate a product but the product itself

---

1. *Trust Factor: Building brands with integrity and trust,* Campaign, online article, 14 February, 2020.

is pretty bad and the customer service is terrible, are you going to support that business?

- If a business claims to be a big brand name, one of the best in the country—or even the world—but you've never heard of it (nor has anyone in your network), and there's no proof to back up their claims, would you consider it to be a brand?

- If a brand or a business behaves in a way that's contrary to what they consistently communicate to the market, will you support or believe what they say?

- If a brand or business that you trust behaves in a way that challenges your Values and ethics, will you continue being loyal to them?

- If a brand or business actively pursues something Purpose-driven, and which aligns with your personal Values, will you choose a competitor over them—or will you reward them?

Putting yourself—and your mindset—in the shoes of customers or consumers is always a useful exercise. As the saying goes: treat others as you want to be treated. It's that simple. Anything short of this is now likely to backfire—severely. In contrast, the Brand Principles have been designed as a framework to help maintain authenticity, engender trust, and encourage loyalty—both internally and externally—but also to inspire reciprocity. So, when it comes to the foundation blocks underpinning a brand, it's useful to split them into two distinct categories: *what* builds brands and *who* builds brands.

What builds brands?
Perception:
Perception is incredibly powerful—and it's often more persuasive than the truth. No matter how forthright a business or brand is in communicating their messages, our perceptions are formed: from experiences with their products and services; by how visible

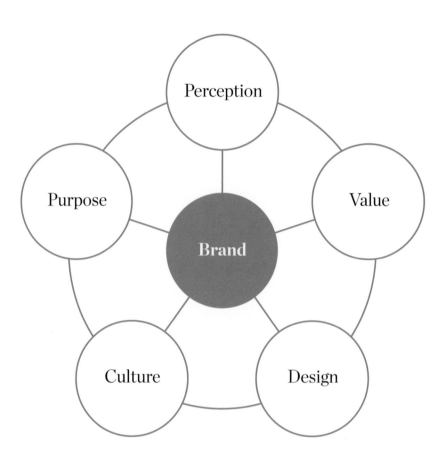

they are in the market; from their actions and behaviours; from how *other people* talk about them; and whether we believe there's enough proof to find them trustworthy.

Value:
Successful brands consistently provide tangible value to people who are always asking: *"What do I get?"* So, the brand must solve a problem, or provide something such as status, convenience, a health benefit, or contribute to a positive impact on society or the environment, etc. But never forget, it's customers who essentially determine what is valuable to them—not the brand.

Design:
This influences everything from the business model, to products, services, systems, processes and customer service, etc. They all need to be designed—specifically and deliberately—to meet customer and staff expectations. When a brand is designed from the inside out, there is greater clarity and focus. This also makes a brand easier to maintain and scale.

Culture:
Organisational culture is the motivational glue which helps drive a brand. It's fuelled by a common set of Values. So, ensuring there is clarity and alignment internally is essential. But successful brands also respond to cultural shifts in society, since this influences their products, services, actions and behaviours.

Purpose:
Being Purpose-driven is becoming increasingly important because it defines a brand within society, supports its relevance, and distinguishes it from competitors. But a Purpose needs to be genuine. It needs to put something important to the business—and to society—above and before just making a profit. It's also crucial that this positive impact is tangible and measurable.

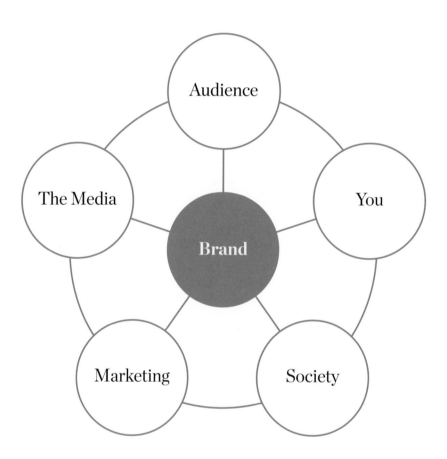

Who builds brands?

Audience:

Successful brands are clear about their audience, not just in terms of customers, clients and end-users, but also staff, stakeholders, partners and the communities which they serve—both directly and indirectly. While a business builds their brand day-in, day-out, it's the audience who collectively determine and validate whether or not a business is a brand.

You:

If you are the business owner, *you* help build the brand; if you are a staff member, *you* help build the brand; if you are a customer or consumer, *you* help build the brand; if you are a stakeholder, a partner, a supplier, a designer or an investor, *you* help build the brand. The success of any brand is built upon the support, involvement and contribution of every individual who comes into contact with the business. It's a result of the individual *and* the collective '*you*'.

Society:

Essentially, a brand is a participatory enterprise. That means society plays a pivotal role, because the wider public needs to accept a business as being a brand before it can become a '*household name*'. Popular culture can also play an influential role in positioning a brand in society. Either way, the deeper the endorsement from society, the bigger—and usually more successful and valuable—the brand is likely to be.

Marketing:

Whether it's branding designers, advertisers, creatives, marketers, artists, PR agents, influencers or celebrity endorsers, there are a plethora of people who actively help amplify a brand in the minds of customers and consumers using words and images. These are usually bucketed under the broad church of *Marketing*, but staff and customers also speak about a business or brand in casual social settings and what they say can often hold more weight and influence.

The Media:
While some media can be interpreted as 'advertorial'—being both friendly and 'on message'—brands can also be built or damaged through *other people's words* in magazines, news platforms, blogs, films, books, features, documentaries and social media posts, among other things. These are usually seen as independent and objective commentary, devoid of any agenda. (However, the truth can often be the reverse.) The media contributes significantly towards shaping our perceptions, which brings us neatly back full circle to *What builds brands*?

Think big

We can't *control* how people think, but we can certainly *influence* how they think. Unfortunately, businesses and brands often tend to believe the best way to achieve this is primarily through advertising. Sadly, this fosters a misguided belief that advertising alone builds brands. However, the reality is that advertising's main objective is to simply raise awareness. Now, in the process, there may be a sales message, it may use entertainment as a vehicle to tell a compelling story, it may be moving and emotional. But the actual goal is to raise awareness and to position a business or brand in the customer's mind *at a specific point in time*. This is often supported through repetition. Of course, while all this can be a potent and powerful way to help shape perceptions, it's still an *assist*. It doesn't build the brand in isolation—no matter how many advertising awards it might win.

For example, consider the energy drink *Red Bull*, whose positioning (and advertising tagline) will be familiar to most: *Red Bull gives you wings*. This has been repeated consistently—and then some. Of course, there is no denying it's a central component of the brand, so it's arguable that advertising has built the brand through awareness, repetition and creativity, right? But the advertising agencies don't decide when a campaign is launched: *Red Bull* does. And advertising agencies don't dictate the messages: *Red Bull* assesses whether or not the proposed messaging fits with their brand. In short, *Red Bull* drives and dictates when, where and what is communicated to their market, not the advertising agencies—though I suspect agencies would love that position of influence. Instead, they assist by lending their talent, creativity and strategic insight to the ongoing journey of *Red Bull* and this occurs at various intervals in the brand's trajectory. But *Red Bull* has to deliver on those messages every day, day-in, day-out. The advertising agencies don't. (Nor do the branding designers, or brand consultants.) And they deliver on this in numerous ways. Take their involvement with extreme sports as a case in point: whether it's *Formula 1*, or downhill soapbox racing, or hardcore mountain biking and bmx-ing, or high altitude skydiving from the stratosphere, among many others. These are all consistent with the concept of extreme energy—and *'giving you wings'*.

All of this shapes perceptions, but an advertising agency's role is also to interpret what a business or brand stands for, what they need to communicate at that time, and to raise awareness using their skills to convey the message in a format people can consume with ease and clarity. Obviously, this plays a significant part in building the brand, and all of these activities are interconnected. None operate in isolation. And our perceptions are shaped instantaneously—oftentimes subconsciously—based on awareness and exposure over time in an ongoing evolution of the brand. Unsurprisingly, it's a lot bigger than just one component; it's the sum of the parts.

13

Success!

Some businesses deliberately set out to become a brand. Others get there organically—either by chance, or by intuition. Sometimes, it's a little bit of both. But a lot can happen along the roller-coaster ride of entrepreneurship. Nothing is ever guaranteed. However, what *is* certain are the various components that contribute to building a brand, which this book has explored in detail. But, relying on chance or luck is a risky strategy. Instead, it makes more sense to foster the right mindset, to ensure you have a better understanding of what's involved when building a brand, and to approach it consciously, intentionally and by design. But, here's the thing: How will you know when you've achieved your goal?

Over the years, I've witnessed countless business owners sharing their enthusiasm about the ventures they're championing. Some of those businesses have been start-ups, others were more established. Regardless, they've all had one thing in common: *a genuine desire to succeed.* Hardly rocket science, right? But can you articulate—without hesitation—what success means for you? Do you want to become a household name? Is it about establishing a legacy? Is it to know you're employing people in a meaningful pursuit and helping to secure their livelihoods? Or, is it to amass expensive luxury items that will contribute to your identity? If you don't know where you want to land, you might find yourself wondering when you've actually reached *your* 'success'. Things are always changing, contexts shift, goals move and new pressures emerge. In fact, without clarity, it's possible you may never feel that you've accomplished your objectives. So, when will you be satisfied? What will satisfy you? *Can* you be satisfied? And what might be the cost of your success?

Redefining success

We're all aware of burnout. We've heard heartbreaking stories of business owners who have damaged their relationships (either with family, friends or partners) due to an obsession with their venture. We know running a business often requires extraordinary dedication, including early mornings, late evenings and regular weekends. And we're increasingly aware of how these pressures and expectations can impact our health, either physical, emotional, mental—or all of the above. Regardless, these outcomes are often the real cost of building a business or brand. So much so, we've collectively named the antidote: *work/life balance*. The issue is partly due to the fact business owners are often in an endless pursuit of 'success'—something that, perhaps, they have yet to even define. Either way, they just don't stop. This can also materialise in expectations of staff—a presumption that they operate with the same enthusiasm and investment—and potentially at a similar cost. Except, staff usually don't have shares in the business, or a stake in an IPO, or an 'exit'. They don't have the benefits of an owner's rewards. But if 'success' can be identified, and then articulated, business owners and staff will know what they're running towards and, more importantly, when they've arrived.

Now, we know that a brand is a long-term and evolving objective (*Brand Principle #12*) and we recognise that things will inevitably change along the way. But defining success—even at intervals—puts some guardrails around a business. It helps everyone understand what to aim for, and how to maintain it once they get there. The problem is, I suspect many business owners probably believe they've *already* defined success, though it's most likely in the narrowest of terms: *revenue*. And the more, the better! If this is the case, then how much? If it's exponential growth, then to what end? In fact, revenue as a metric seems particularly one-dimensional so perhaps the definition of success needs a reboot. Well, *FastCompany* explored this exact line of inquiry:

"The abstract idea of 'success' may be the most important idea in business: the fuzzy notion that motivates millions of choices, careers, and dreams. But for all the energy applied in its pursuit, there's little energy applied in contemplating the destination. Fortune recently published its annual Fortune 500 list, which it bills as 'the ultimate business scorecard.' But its ranking is driven by just one

metric: revenue. Is that really the ultimate scorecard in business? The pinnacle of success? And if not, what is? Does this time of crisis, reassessment, and renewal [in 2020] compel us to revisit what motivates all this work? Those that disagree with Fortune's focus on revenue typically choose one of a few other old tropes: 'winning' a category, optimizing efficiency, maximizing profits or shareholder value. These themes are so normed that much of the commentary in business focuses on how to succeed, skipping past any contemplation of what success actually looks like. What if the old definitions of success have been too short, too narrow, and too shallow?" [1]

Focusing on revenue as a metric for success is flawed, because it's a hollow over-simplification of what success should mean. Aside from the fact revenue and growth are all about *you*, rather than the customer or the community, it suggests there's no finish line, no point at which a business will ever be content. Those who argue that a business reinvests revenue into the company sidestep the fact this is usually to create improved efficiencies in order to generate more revenue in a self-perpetuating cycle. As *FastCompany* highlights, others suggest revenue is to deliver shareholder value. But, then shareholders demand more revenue, too. Why? Because that's how they also measure success. When you stop and think about it, the glorification of revenue—in and of itself—is rather obscene. But what if, instead, we flipped things and thought about revenue as the *byproduct* of success, not its singular goal? How might that change your focus? And how might we then measure success? Well, maybe we should start by asking customers, consumers and society.

From revenue to relevance

For their '2021 Brand Relevance Index'[2] *Prophet* asked 13,000 customers in the US which brands mattered most to them—those they simply couldn't live without. The result is a list of 228 brands, some of which may surprise you.

---

1. *Our definition of 'success' is holding business back—it's time for a new one,* by Sebastian Buck, FastCompany, online article, 9 September, 2020.
2. *Prophet Brand Relevance Index 2021,* online report: www.prophet.com/relevantbrands-2021.

Here are the top 10:

1. *Apple* (for the sixth year in a row)
2. *Peleton* (which moved up from No. 35)
3. *KitchenAid*
4. *Mayo Clinic*
5. *Lego* (which moved up from No. 28)
6. *Costco* (previously at No. 21)
7. *Honda*
8. *Johns Hopkins Medicine*
9. *PlayStation*
10. *Amazon*

Reasons for their selection included comments like: *"distinctly inspired"*; *"lives up to its promises"*; *"beliefs and values align with my own"*; *"makes me happy"*; *"trust"*; *"modern and in touch"*; and *"always finding new ways to meet my needs"*. Interestingly, none of those comments mention anything about generating lots of revenue. Go figure. Now, throughout this book I've mentioned the need for business and brands to be relevant—in the lives of consumers and the community. But, imagine if we defined success by relevance instead of revenue. How might that refocus a business? If success meant building a brand that's so relevant customers simply couldn't live without it, how might that make business owners and staff feel? Of course, revenue is still required to build and maintain a sustainable business, but if we moved towards relevance as the definition for success, our motivations would likely be entirely different—and incredibly refreshing.

So, what constitutes a relevant brand; what's the criteria? Well, according to *Prophet*, there are four distinct components: *being customer obsessed, ruthlessly pragmatic, distinctively inspired and pervasively innovative.* You might have noticed that (once again) there's no mention of revenue. Why is that? Because revenue is a *byproduct* of success; because relevance is valuable in numerous ways, including—but not solely—financially.

What matters most

Being relevant means a business or brand must have a deep understanding of their customers and what matters most in their lives. Of course, this is constantly shifting but there are some obvious patterns, many of which relate to their immediate day-to-day needs and desires. But there are also some broader, more long-term concerns occupying customer's minds. According to a 2020 report entitled *Zero Hero* by branding powerhouse *Wolff Olins* and *Chapter Zero, The World Economic Forum's Global Risks Report* suggests that people all over the world see climate change as a clear and present danger—fearing climate disasters more than technological or societal threats to their safety. As a result, demand for businesses and brands to respond accordingly is rising. For example, in the UK alone, 60% of the public believe brands should be leading the fight against climate change. In other words, combating climate change is relevant to the lives of nearly two-thirds of the British population. But it's not isolated to the UK. It's an international concern.

"The good news is that businesses are responding. For example, the bosses of 181 of the US's 200 biggest companies have changed the official definition of 'the purpose of a corporation' from making the most money possible for shareholders to 'improving our society' by also looking out for employees, caring for the environment and dealing ethically." [3]

Let that sink in for a moment. Out of 200 of the biggest companies in America, the majority have made a deliberate and public promise to move away from solely making the most money possible for shareholders. Why? Because they recognise this renewed attitude is now more relevant for customers—and the world. They've realised the definition of success needs to look very different from before, that it doesn't need to be short-term, and that it's about more than just revenue. Yet, *FastCompany* believes it can be taken even further:

---

3. *How can brands battle the climate crisis?*, by Wolff Olins and Chapter Zero, online report, February, 2020: www.zerohero.org.

"If more leaders considered multi-generational success, many business practices would change, from what to invest in, to how to treat people." [4]

But it doesn't stop there. *The Havas 2019 Global Meaningful Brands Report* suggests that consumers wouldn't care if 77% of everyday brands disappeared. In Europe, that figure rises to 81%.[5] These are frightening (but perhaps unsurprising) statistics. In contrast, those businesses which are seen as being relevant, meaningful and perceived as making the world a better place are *"outperforming the stock market by 134%; and seeing their share of wallet multiply by 9"* [6]—proving that, when relevance is a measure of success, revenue is simply a byproduct.

It's important to point out, we're not talking about a niche or micro movement, or a trend on the periphery. The *Havas* report was far-reaching and included 1800 brands in 31 countries, asking 350,000 participants about the link between brand performance, quality of life and wellbeing. And this shift isn't just about issues like climate change. It's also about equality and the need to increase diversity at the most senior level of businesses and brands, among other things. People want to see themselves reflected in organisations. It's about representation as much as it is about responsibility. And there's movement here, too. While there is still a lot of work to be done, these changes are becoming increasingly evident, including at some of the largest news broadcasters in America (for example, Phil Griffin stepping down as *MSNBC's* President and being replaced by Rashida Jones, the first African American woman to lead a cable news network) through to mega brands (including a pledge from *McDonald's* linking executive pay to diversity goals, with an aim of reaching gender parity in management by 2030.)[7]

---

4. *Our definition of 'success' is holding business back—it's time for a new one.*
5. *How can brands battle the climate crisis?*
6. *Building meaningful is good for business: 77% of consumers buy brands who share their values,* Havas Media Group, online report, 21 February, 2019.
7. *McDonald's links executive pay to diversity targets,* by Danielle Wiener-Bronner, CNN Business, online article, 18 February, 2021.

Regardless of whether or not you currently define *your* idea of success—either by revenue, relevance or some other metric—the world is rapidly shifting. If businesses and brands are to be successful and sustained over the long-term they will need to align with these movements. All of the statistics, research and data indicates a decidedly different definition of success than we've traditionally been using. In turn, this suggests a decidedly different future. And it's a future that's closer than you might think, so let's explore it in more detail.

141

What the future holds

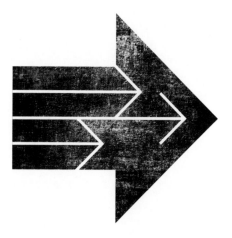

No-one can predict the future. We look to movements and trends as a means to determine what might be sitting over the horizon. If enough signals point in the same direction, we can justifiably assume where things might be heading. We use this to model our businesses and brands; to stay current, or perhaps to get ahead of the curve, or to identify a latent opportunity so we can move on it more quickly than anybody else. In many ways, our actions—whether or not in response to our predictions—often end up dictating our future. So, what might be the emerging trends for businesses and brands? Well, that question is actually too small. Instead, we need to ask: *what is my impact on a future we're all collectively designing in real time?*

It's an intentionally *big* question because we have to stop thinking of the future *only* as it impacts our own commercial interests. It's imperative that we see businesses and brands as part of a bigger, connected ecosystem of activities and pursuits, which includes the communities and environment in which they are embedded—and where what we do has a far-reaching impact. When we respond to short-term trends, we progress incrementally. But what's required now is a leap. We cannot consider businesses and brands (or even individuals) in isolation anymore. We cannot continue to operate with short-term goals that benefit only ourselves, or those closest to us, under the illusion that we are too small or too insignificant to have an impact on the future. What we do matters, and that offers all of us an immense opportunity—one that also comes with profound responsibility.

Unfortunately, 'traditional business' doesn't think like this. It focuses on maximising profits, fixated on the pursuit of endless growth purely in monetary and material terms. Traditional business is mainly concerned about itself. But thankfully, this is changing. We're reaching a tipping point where more and more people are beginning to acknowledge that our futures are all connected (in spite of the fact this is plainly obvious). We're at a moment in time where increasing numbers of business leaders are becoming pioneers: reconsidering their entire supply chains, finding innovative ways to create value from waste, and assessing the impact of their actions—locally and globally—before rectifying what needs to be changed. So, if we're talking about emerging trends in business and brands, then we're talking about *impact*. Once you acknowledge this, you can begin to see things in a completely different way, because what matters in the world will eventually affect you, whether that's economically, environmentally or epidemiologically. To coin a phrase: what goes around comes around—*eventually*. This way of thinking helps us make better decisions in the context of a wider, circular ecosystem, one that we're all part of. Regrettably, still not enough business leaders are thinking this way. But very soon it will become the mainstream approach. All of the signals are pointing in this direction

Of course, it's not easy to take this leap because we've been conditioned to see everyone in our market as a 'prospect' and every business as a 'competitor'. It's still all about 'us'; it's still about what 'I' get, and about what piece of the market 'I' need to defend. But what if, instead, we saw people, customers, businesses and the world we inhabit as an extension of ourselves? How might this change our approach, mindset, products, services, and impact?

Well, here's a simple, creative and practical way to think about it. Edward de Bono's example of applying *lateral thinking* to the problem of pollution involves a factory located on the banks of a river. In his example, the factory draws in clean water and then discharges the waste (pollution) back into the river, downstream. Of course, the pollution doesn't immediately impact the factory, and they're clearly not considering anyone who *will* be impacted— not the communities nor the environment, which depend on the river's health. This leaves us to assume that the factory owners only care about their own commercial interests. It's a familiar story.

However, de Bono suggested swapping the intake and output so the factory draws water into the building at a point beyond where it discharges its waste. This deliberate redesign means the factory would be the first to get its own pollution, making it more careful about limiting the waste they dump into the river. The example helps us understand that what we do also affects us—either immediately, or eventually. It proves that adapting your thinking will influence your actions, which ultimately changes your impact— and the future. And it proves the factory can still continue with its commercial interests, but the byproduct has a greater positive impact for everyone.

Of course, de Bono's example seems simple on the face of it, but it requires developing ways to produce clean waste; it involves re-ordering systems to swap inputs and outputs; it involves holding businesses accountable. It's both incredibly simple and ferociously difficult. But this isn't theory. In fact, de Bono's downstream pollution idea later became law in some countries.[1]

A measured approach

We've talked about relevance as a metric of success, but the true measurement of a brand will soon be far more consequential because *your brand will be measured by your impact.* The realities of this are significant because—as obvious as it sounds—it means your impact will need to be *positive* (in the broadest of terms, not just with regard to the business' bottom line); it means your impact will need to be genuinely *relevant* (in the lives of customers and in the community, who are already making this shift towards evaluating 'brand impact'); it means your impact will need to be *valuable* (not only in terms of supporting a sustainable business, but also in terms of whether customers and clients deem that your business or brand is adding value in their lives); and it means you will need to consider your impact seriously (not just as an afterthought but, instead, ensuring it's approached with

---

1. *Serious creativity: Using the power of lateral thinking to create new ideas (1992),* Edward de Bono, The McQuaig Group/Harper Colins, 1992, page 145.

Before

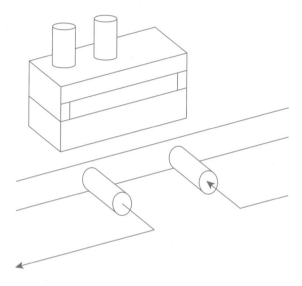

After

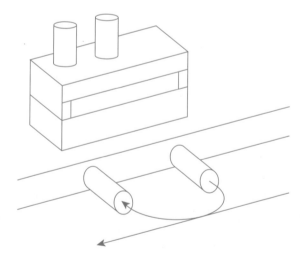

Depiction of Edward de Bono's solution for downstream pollution

responsibility and accountability, and that it's Purpose-driven). This is how brands will be measured. Indeed, it's how they're already being measured. Those who have already acknowledged and accepted this reality are ahead of the curve—and they include some of the biggest brands on the planet. Take *Lego* for example. As *The New York Times* reported:

"Lego is trying to refashion the product it is best known for: It wants to eliminate its dependence on petroleum-based plastics, and build its toys entirely from plant-based or recycled materials by 2030." [2]

This is both an admirable and audacious goal. Not only has *Lego* recognised their influence in the world and their impact on the environment—which is the result of plastic production at a gargantuan scale—it plans to achieve this positive change before the end of this decade, and without anyone even noticing a difference in their products: in terms of the brightness of the colours; their strength, weight and durability; or the smooth 'click' of their bricks and accessories. This shift has been influenced by the growing— and steadily louder—number of concerned voices from within communities around the world. While *Lego* is a much-loved brand, it appears their environmental impact was becoming too much for people to forgive or overlook. In many ways—as this book has laid out in previous chapters—*Lego's* shift in strategy is as much about business survival as it is about responding to customer feedback, or an acknowledgment of any broader corporate responsibility.

The good news is, they're not alone. By 2030, *Coca-Cola* aims to collect and recycle the equivalent of all the bottles and cans it uses. Equally, *Unilever* plans to make all their plastic packaging either recyclable or compostable by 2025, while *Starbucks* and *McDonald's* are moving away from using plastic straws in their outlets.[3] Furthermore, according to *Campaign*, *McDonald's* is doubling down on their positive impact:

---

2. *Lego Wants to Completely Remake Its Toy Bricks (Without Anyone Noticing),* by Stanley Reed, The New York Times, online article, 31 August 2018.
3. *Lego Wants to Completely Remake Its Toy Bricks (Without Anyone Noticing).*

"McDonald's said its 'renewed purpose' would be to feed and foster the communities it serves around the world. Through both actions and communications, the company is looking to make a greater impact by focusing on four areas: responsibly sourcing quality ingredients, driving climate action to protect the planet, connecting with communities in times of need and increasing focus on equity by providing opportunity for restaurant staff. According to McDonald's, this purpose will mean more support for farming communities, an aim to source 100% of packaging from renewable, recycled or certified sources by 2025, donating 'millions of pounds' (in weight) of food from the supply chain and restaurants to people in need, and reducing barriers to employment for more than two million people worldwide." [4]

Make no mistake, this will have a substantial impact, considering *McDonald's* has a presence in 100 markets globally, and where they see about 80% of the population in those markets, per year. Astonishingly, this translates to serving approximately 65 million people—*a day!* [5] So, with their newly enshrined Purpose, what has prompted their very public declaration? Well, it appears they believe no single government or organisation alone can solve all the challenges we face and that, instead, it will take a wider collective effort. And they're right. But this understanding also stems from something deeper—and perhaps something more commercially-driven: *a recognition of customer expectations.* A year-long survey with customers, franchisees, suppliers and employees about what they value most about *McDonald's* confirmed that—more than ever—people expect leading brands and businesses to play their part in finding solutions to some of our biggest challenges. For *McDonald's*, like other brands, perhaps this declaration is a combination of corporate strategy, accountability, and business survival. Regardless, it's further confirmation about the trajectory of brand impact and how it will affect the future—and the future of business. As for their advice on articulating a Purpose:

---

4. *McDonald's refreshes 'intangible' brand purpose,* by Diana Bradley, Campaign, online article, 10 November 2020.
5. *McDonald's CEO: How we are thinking differently about our role in society,* by Chris Kempczinski, CNN Business, online article, 25 November 2020.

"There is no formula a company can use to define its purpose. It has to flow authentically from what a company values, how it acts and what it does in the world." [6]

Equally, in the UK, *Aldi's* CEO, Giles Hurley, sent a letter to suppliers informing them about the supermarket chain's pledge for own-brand packaging to be 100% recyclable, reusable or compostable by 2022 and warning them that all other products would need to meet this standard by 2025. Significantly, Hurley was blunt about the fact *Aldi's* request was non-negotiable and that future decisions would be *"based on our supply partners' ability to lead and adapt in this area."* [7] But it's not just the mega-brands. Smaller businesses and start-ups are also considering their impact—which, in itself, is another indication of how things are shifting. For example, *Great Wrap* is a plastic-free, plant-based alternative to kitchen brands like *Glad Wrap*, and they've designed their product in such a way that their impact is already built-in. Once used, the wrap can go straight into your home compost system or green-waste bin where it breaks down more quickly than orange peel.[8]

You can see where all of this is heading. And these aren't small measures by any means. They are the result of a deliberate strategies to improve each respective impact on the world. And yes, critics might glibly argue these businesses and brands aren't going far enough. And perhaps they're right. But in the grand scheme of things, such criticism achieves very little. Instead, we need to acknowledge that these shifts are admirable and important. We must understand these are initial steps, which will positively improve each brand's impact and—due to the size and influence of some of these brands—their redesigned impact will have far-reaching positive effects. From there, we need to encourage businesses even further along this path towards implementing more improvements in their individual and

---

6. *McDonald's CEO: How we are thinking differently about our role in society.*
7. *Aldi tells suppliers product packaging must be 100% recyclable, reusable or compostable by 2025,* eNViro30, online article, 14 February 2020.
8. *This New, Plastic-Free Cling Wrap Breaks Down Quicker Than Orange Peel,* by Matilda Beaumont, Broadsheet, online article, 4 August 2020.

collective impact, because impact is tangible, visible and measurable. The more positive the impact, the more valuable it becomes—in financial terms for the business or brand, and for the communities, individuals and environments that it affects, and who will, in turn, reward those brands.

The bigger risk

Business leaders might justifiably argue there is a risk in dramatically redesigning their operations to improve their brand impact—or to even just consider their impact. They could argue that the risk of disrupting their current operations is simply too big and that, instead, they need to remain steadfastly focused on running a profitable business. Pro-active disruption or change is certainly a risk. But let me be clear: the bigger risk is *not* addressing your impact. And, if announcements from *Lego, Aldi, Unilever,* and *McDonald's* aren't enough to convince you, let's take things up a level.

In late 2020, the *European Central Bank* said that it will start conducting *"in-depth assessments of how bank balance sheets account for climate risks in 2022."* [9] What does this mean in practical terms? Significantly, banks will soon be required to disclose how climate change—specifically flooding and storms—could affect the value of their real estate portfolios and customer supply chains. They will also be expected to take into account any losses experienced by customers as they adjust their operations to be less carbon intensive. Fundamentally, financial regulators won't be leaving climate supervision solely to governments, because climate shifts in the economy—and crises like the Covid-19 pandemic and Putin's war in Ukraine—are impacting things at a macro level. For example, oil giants *BP* and *Shell* have had to write off billions of dollars due to downward pressure on oil prices and as a result of how the energy industry is evolving more broadly. But this has also accelerated their shift towards developing cleaner energy, which will have a wider positive impact. Essentially, major

---

9. *The climate crisis is looming large on Wall Street,* by Hanna Ziady, CNN, Before The Bell Newsletter, online article, 22 November 2020.

financial regulators, including the *US Federal Reserve,* are seeking to de-risk business sectors to ensure that *"better disclosure could improve the pricing of climate risks and avoid the kind of abrupt changes to asset prices that cause financial system shocks."*[10]

It's clear there is a heightened awareness that everything is connected. It's also a reminder of the aggregate impact on our collective future. Emphasising the point further, at the end of 2020, a group of global investors, who manage over $9 trillion in assets, wrote to 36 of Europe's largest firms urging them to address "missing" climate costs in their accounts and calling on them to prepare their earnings reports in a way that will disclose how climate change might affect their business. As *CNN* reported:

"'It would not be consistent to emphasise climate risks in the strategic report but not consider these same risks in the accounts,' the letter said. 'If accounts leave out material climate risks, too much capital will go toward activities that put shareholder capital at risk. Worse still, this puts all our futures at risk.'"[11]

And then there are doughnuts

While these developments suggest the private sector and large financial regulators are starting to play a more active role in achieving a positive impact (individually and collectively), does that mean—by default—that governments will play a lesser role? Not necessarily. In fact, given how interconnected government services are, how central they are to our lives, and the fact governments claim to have the public interest at heart, it seems vital that they become more involved in this movement because their impact is exponential. Of course, there are other reasons why a positive impact might be beneficial for governments. As we know, nations and cities are increasingly seeing themselves as brands—for citizen, tourism, cultural and inward investment purposes, among other things. Interestingly, there are encouraging signs that some cities

---

10. *The climate crisis is looming large on Wall Street.*
11. *The climate crisis is looming large on Wall Street.*

are already looking at their brand impact in a more holistic way.
In April 2020, early in the Covid-19 pandemic, Dutch officials in
Amsterdam were contemplating how to recover from the impact
of a virus that was only just getting started. Even at this early stage,
they were looking at a broader recovery, not just in economic
terms. In the midst of this emerging crisis Amsterdam took a leap—
by entertaining a more progressive approach called *Doughnut
Economics*. Reporting for *The Guardian*, Daniel Boffey describes it:

*"The central premise [of Doughnut Economics] is simple: the goal of
economic activity should be about meeting the core needs of all but
within the means of the planet. The 'doughnut' is a device to show
what this means in practice [...] It ranges from food and clean water
to a certain level of housing, sanitation, energy, education, healthcare,
gender equality, income and political voice. Anyone not attaining
such minimum standards is living in the doughnut's hole. The
outer ring of the doughnut, where the sprinkles go, represents the
ecological ceiling drawn up by earth-system scientists. It highlights
the boundaries across which human kind should not go to avoid
damaging the climate, soils, oceans, the ozone layer, freshwater and
abundant biodiversity."* [12]

Doughnut Economics was developed by British economist Kate
Raworth from *Oxford University's Environmental Change Institute*.
It models the *United Nations* sustainable development goals and
is a *Sunday Times* bestselling book. It also offers a refreshingly
different approach to designing a city's impact, given how it
sidesteps our near universal attachment to economic growth
fuelled by supply and demand (at the expense of nearly everything
else). In contrast, Raworth's methodology focuses on ways to 'thrive'
as opposed to merely achieving economic growth, as if this were
the answer to everything. Not only that, Doughnut Economics
is gaining traction with many economists, business leaders,
journalists and leading figures within governments. And in April

---

12. *Amsterdam to embrace 'doughnut' model to mend post-coronavirus economy,* by Daniel Boffey,
The Guardian, online article, 8 April 2020.

2020, it was formally adopted by the municipality of Amsterdam, making it the first city in the world to use Doughnut Economics as the starting point for their public policy decisions. Not only is this an encouraging and refreshing development, considering the wide reach of a city's impact, but Amsterdam's holistic approach is the epitome of how we might consider our own impact on *a future we're all collectively designing in real time*—a future everyone is so desperately invested in. Given these developments, it's not a stretch to envision a scenario where governments directly tax companies on the harm or negative impact they create. Or, conversely, where they offer incentives to businesses and brands who pursue a positive impact, via their products, services, actions and behaviours. Perhaps more significantly, the private sector is already beginning to consider brand impact more aggressively, as Ronald Cohen and George Serafeim argue in their *Harvard Business Review* article *How to Measure a Company's Real Impact*:

"Firms with greater negative impact generate less investor interest, which reduces their stock market valuation and raises their cost of capital." [13]

Billions of opportunities

There are other reasons why governments and cities need to consider their impact on a larger scale and over a longer time-frame, a primary one being *population*. Based on our current trajectory, the *United Nations* predicts that, by 2050, the global population will reach 9.7 billion. Approximately 70% of people are projected to live in urban areas, which puts cities at the centre of our future. But it also places further strain on them—and the environment—because cities are key contributors to climate change and are responsible for up to three quarters of global CO_2 emissions.[14] Here again, some forward-thinking city officials, urban planners, business leaders, architects and designers are already

---

13. *How to Measure a Company's Real Impact,* by Ronald Cohen and George Serafeim, Harvard Business Review, online article, 3 September 2020.
14 *From urban forests to high-tech utopias, here's how the cities of the future are shaping up,* by Stephanie Bailey, CNN, online article, 26 November 2020.

•

"Firms with greater negative impact generate less investor interest, which reduces their stock market valuation and raises their cost of capital."

•

envisioning how cities can be designed to absorb this increased pressure—and improve their impact. Indeed, some of these cities have already been built.

For example, 130 kilometres from Beijing, China, a proposed 'self-sufficient city' will accommodate five million people. It will be powered by clean energy and have a circular economy where waste is recycled and resources are used for as long as possible. In Cancun, Mexico, *Smart Forest City* has been designed for 130,000 inhabitants. The city, which will be surrounded by a ring of solar panels and fields for agriculture, has designated 400 hectares to green space, including 7.5 million plants, 260,000 of which will be trees. This translates to more than two trees per person; One hundred kilometres north of Manila, in the Philippines, *New Clark City* is being built to be pollution-free and resilient to natural disasters. It will use green energy and buildings are being constructed to consume as little energy as possible. Also in China, *Net City* is being designed as a 'car-free city-within-a-city'. It will span two-million-square-metres, which is equivalent to the size of Monaco. *The Sustainable City* in Dubai is a five-million-square-foot futuristic 'city', which has already been built and has been designed to consume zero net energy with the potential to go off-grid. All water is recycled on site, there are no cars, and the complex grows its own vegetables in 11 biome greenhouses. In the southern state of Andhra Pradesh, India, the city of Amaravati is being designed and built to be one of the most sustainable cities in the world, with at least 60% of the city being covered in greenery or water. The transport system will include electric cars and water taxis.[15]

These are just some of the examples, where cities are deliberately considering their impact in an holistic way. And when 9.7 billion people are looking for the most sustainable place to live— economically, culturally, socially, environmentally—where do you think they'll choose? Billions of people translates to billions of opportunities for businesses and brands to provide a positive

---

15 *From urban forests to high-tech utopias, here's how the cities of the future are shaping up.*

impact. But it also indicates how these businesses and brands will be expected to operate. From products and services to office or retail spaces, no doubt city officials will measure them by their impact.

Naturally valuable

For a moment, let's sidestep a portion of the global community, whom many have labelled *'climate skeptics'*, and instead take a purely objective and value-based approach to how we consider the environment. For longer than we care to admit, we have viewed the natural environment as an infinitely renewable resource on many levels. Even those who don't believe humans have expedited climate change, must be hard pressed to argue against our obvious impact on natural resources, materials and minerals, biodiversity, food and water supplies, and—more generally—our addiction to consumption on a colossal scale. Sadly, while we know how valuable these resources are, we still tend to take them for granted. Which is why a recent study by *McKinsey & Company*—entitled *Valuing Nature Conservation: A methodology for quantifying the benefits of protecting the planet's natural capital*—is so timely, and so necessary. According to James Conca writing for *Forbes*:

"The report finds that expanding nature conservation could have measurable economic impacts, and makes a compelling case for investing in protecting natural capital. To reduce the erosion of natural capital, scientists and policy makers have called for the permanent conservation of at least 30% of the planet's surface by 2030, nearly doubling nature conservation on land and in national waters... Applying their methodology—outlining six alternative nature conservation scenarios and exploring the trade-offs—suggests that doubling nature conservation on land and in national waters by 2030 could have a measurable impact and could make a compelling case for investment." [16]

---

16. *How To Price The 'Natural Capital' Of Planet Earth,* by James Conca, Forbes, online article, 31 October 2020.

The report goes on to outline these economic benefits in some detail, including: mitigating deforestation in order to reduce atmospheric CO_2 and encouraging forest regrowth; securing the $36 billion reef-tourism industry by reducing ocean temperatures; the creation of approximately 400,000 to 650,000 jobs in conservation-management fields such as wildlife management and area infrastructure, while also developing 30 million jobs and $500 billion of GDP in ecotourism and sustainable fishing alone; among many other areas. The report reinforces the fact that biodiversity, which is a core component of natural capital, supports activities as wide-ranging as pharmaceutical innovation, ecotourism, and crop pollination, and it puts forward a business case for protecting natural capital and the shared benefits that conservation could have on society, at large.[17]

So, when we think about brand impact, underpinned by a business case for valuing natural capital, the report offers numerous objective and tangible suggestions that we can draw from and which will benefit businesses, brands and our collective future. More importantly, we can also see the clear and immediate danger of *not* valuing our natural capital. But brand impact isn't limited to climate change or environmental concerns. From championing gender and racial equality, or tackling poverty and homelessness, through to supporting equal opportunities and access to education, among a host of other areas, brands can genuinely and positively impact the world in meaningful ways. This brings into sharp relief Anna Lappé's prescient words: *"Every time you spend money, you're casting a vote for the type of world [you] want to live in."* [18]

Purpose or impact?

A significant portion of this book has argued the benefits of being Purpose-driven. Numerous examples have been presented to prove the point. So, if being Purpose-driven is so important, why am I now saying that brand impact is the future for brands? Which is it:

---

17. *How To Price The 'Natural Capital' Of Planet Earth.*
18. *Good Is The New Cool: Market Like You Give A Damn,* Afdhel Aziz and Bobby Jones, Regan Arts, 2016, page 25.

Purpose or impact? Well, if you're getting tired of all the buzzwords spinning around the business world, you're not alone. I feel your fatigue. There are enough things for you to keep on top of without tracking the latest business fad. But remember, everything is connected. These concepts and ideas don't exist in a vacuum. We can look at Purpose as being part of the equation—the operating system, so to speak. As we move into the future, Purpose should be a key component driving your business or brand, something staff and customers can aim for and align with—something bigger than themselves, their jobs or the company. But Purpose can also be subjective. It can end up languishing as mere motivational words used in an effort to gee-up morale or to portray the business in a particular light, for no other reason than shallow marketing. In contrast, impact is the other side of the equation—the objective part. It's measurable and can be accounted for, because it turns words and intentions into actions and outputs. It moves the needle. But impact is scatter-shot without a clear Purpose—because Purpose dictates the impact you want to make. That means the union between Purpose and impact is critical—and powerful.

Does size matter?
Generally speaking, we all tend to cite case studies from large, well-known and well-resourced businesses and brands to prove our points. As exciting, instructive or interesting as these might be, it's often problematic because (for a variety of reasons) it can be difficult to relate *their* journey to *our own* business. The reason we refer to them is essentially familiarity. However, it does tend to suggest that success relates to size, and that the bigger you are, the greater the success. But this sidesteps the reality that all successful brands started out small. We just tend to discuss them at a mature point in their journey and overlook the fact that their brand has been a constant evolution over time, and that they continue to evolve. So, here's the thing: size doesn't matter—*mindset* does.

Bank Australia is a small Australian customer-owned bank. Their stated Purpose is *"to inspire and empower our customers to use their money to create a world where people and the planet thrive.*"[19] Founded as a co-operative Credit Society in 1957, the business has grown and evolved over its long and deep history. This includes an astonishing 72 mergers with other Credit Unions and cooperatives over the years, before eventually becoming Australia's first customer-owned bank. The business adopted the name *Bank Australia* in 2015 and was the first Australian Credit Union to seek—and to be granted—a banking licence. But, as far as banks go, *Bank Australia* is small. As of 2021, it has 441 employees, with approximately 160,000 members, revenue valued at around $131.4 million, and total assets at around $7.20 billion.[20] Given those figures, *Bank Australia* is a clear example that size isn't a criteria for success. It's also a reminder that building a brand is a long-term commitment. But what stands out most is the clarity of their positioning in the market—*Responsible Banking*. This has been backed up by a series of marketing and advertising campaigns featuring unexpected statements such as: *'The bank that puts people and the planet before profit is the bank Australia needs'*; *'The bank with clean money is the bank Australia needs'*; *'The bank that doesn't lend to the fossil fuel industry is the bank Australia needs'*; *'The bank that doesn't pay executive bonuses is the bank Australia needs'*; among many others.

Now, you'd be forgiven for assuming these are part of a smart (of-the-moment) advertising campaign. But that's not the case. Far from it, in fact. These messages are essentially a clear articulation of what is important to *Bank Australia*—and to their customers. It's a way to carve out a specific position, to attract customers and staff who align with their beliefs, while also acting as a filter for those who don't. And all of this was very deliberate. The CEO, Damien Walsh, confirmed as much when we spoke:

"It was a very conscious decision to avoid a mass-market approach [to banking]; a very conscious decision around having a great deal of clarity about who we are, what we stand for, and the value proposition that we bring. And it's resonating with an increasing

---

19. Bank Australia website, About Us page: Our Purpose, December, 2020.
20. Wikipedia, Bank Australia, February, 2021.

*number of new customers—typically a younger demographic, but not
always. This is really helping, in terms of shifting the average age of
our client base and ensuring we've got a sustainable business over
the long term. Interestingly, when we were preparing those positions
in the market, we first paused and asked: 'Are we comfortable enough
to take this stand?'; 'Are we brave enough to take it?' Because you're
also open for criticism. For example, there are some quarters of
conservative media, and segments of the broader community who
actually don't align with our messages. And they can be just as vocal
as those that do like them. But being resilient as a business and
accepting that not everyone is going to be happy with the position
you take to the market was actually really important for us. Taking a
stand is important. People want to know what brands stand for."* [21]

The idea of taking a position, of being clear and consistent about
it, and ensuring that Purpose is built into an impact model sounds
relatively logical and straightforward. But it becomes less palatable
when a business needs to acknowledge the fact there is a distinct
possibility you might lose customers by taking such a strong
position. In *Bank Australia's* case, this did happen. But they also
gained customers—and quite a few! People who heard, understood
and aligned with clear messages that convey an unambiguous
position were attracted to a refreshing take on what banking can
be, what it can stand for and what it can live up to. As Walsh points
out, taking a strong position on a number of issues that aligned
with their Purpose helped the organisation remain resilient.
But they could only do this by truly believing in it—by truly
believing that it was the right thing to do, beyond any commercial
reasoning—and by committing to that decision no matter what. As
inspiring as this might be, I was still curious to understand how
these decisions translated into a tangible, measurable impact. In
response, Walsh explained:

*"It's partly about lending decisions, but also about investment
decisions—where will we place that money? This is informed by*

---

21. Damien Walsh, interview by author, August 2020.

our Purpose and of course aligning the positions we take with the views our customers hold. So, four percent of our after tax profits are placed into an Impact Fund, which has roughly been a million dollars a year over the last half dozen years, or so. We allocate some of it to long-term projects, for example our conservation reserve. We've worked with Trust for Nature and Greening Australia to rehabilitate some no longer productive farmland in West Wimmera [a region in Victoria, Australia]. That's a really long-term conservation project, but we also go out to our customers and provide an annual grant program for values-aligned organisations, or to our customers who are seeking to make a difference in the world.

"And, as I say, the interesting thing about the grant program, the other work we do with the Impact Fund and the decisions we take about where we will and won't invest, is that it's all designed to address issues that our customers tell us are important to them. Essentially, our customers are involved in the process. They suggest issues and areas that they want to see their bank act on, including climate change, addressing domestic violence, Indigenous rights, fair and equitable treatment of asylum seekers and refugees, etc. So, when we deploy money from our Impact Fund, or lend or invest our liquidity, we're very specific about addressing those—let's say—top 10 areas our customers have told us they want to see us making a difference."[22]

This goes beyond putting customers at the heart of your brand (*Brand Principle #13*), it puts the whole community at the heart of it. Not only that, but the language Walsh uses expressly reflects this: *"They suggest issues and areas that they want to see their bank act on."* He acknowledges it's *their* bank (not *our* bank). And as we know, words have meaning. This has a profound effect on how an organisation sees itself, how it refers to itself, and how it reminds itself why they're doing what they do. But how far does this really go? How does *Bank Australia* ensure their Values and Purpose are embedded in the culture? According to Walsh:

---

22. Damien Walsh, interview by author, August 2020.

"I believe our staff hold that Purpose, aspiration and our Values [by bringing] it back into the business. They self regulate, in that regard. For example, I know of an instance where a staff member made the determination not to accept a term deposit because the potential business customer was involved in practices that aren't aligned with the Values of our organisation. Our staff member simply didn't accept the deposit—they turned new business away. They very much acted as that filter on the front line." [23]

How is this possible? Well, it's partly a result of clarity, partly a result of trust, and wholly a result of individual and collective accountability. It also illustrates incredible leadership. The fact that staff not only feel empowered, but *permitted*, to hold the business accountable based on their stated Values and position, is an incredible reminder of how words *must* be backed up by actions and behaviours in order for them to have any value. And while many other businesses and brands have tolerated dissent from within—where staff have protested as a means to hold the company accountable on a particular issue or action—*Bank Australia* provides the clearest example of how a business can become a Purpose-driven brand, underpinned by a sustainable business model, and a culture that protects the organisation's future beyond the tenure of an individual CEO.

Joining forces
Historically, businesses and brands have been focused on short term objectives. This has only been compounded by our growing 'instagratification' and an insatiable desire for 'the immediate'. But a shift towards thinking more long-term is now unavoidable because, as influential designer Bruce Mau predicts in his book *MC24*, the public will increasingly demand a positive impact:

"It's hard to imagine now what members of the generation currently in high school will have to say about our stewardship of their world. Their calls for Massive Change will become unstoppable.

---

23. Damien Walsh, interview by author, August 2020.

Governments, institutions and corporations will resist this demand
at their peril. Today is the time for action. You are either part of the
solution or part of the problem—there is no middle ground." [24]

The feeling in the air is palpable: there are businesses, brands and
individual business leaders who desperately want to contribute
positively to a better present—and a better future. Many *are*
concerned about their impact. Inertia is slowly giving way to
momentum. And an unmistakable groundswell towards positive
action and collaboration to design a better future is giving rise to
unexpected partnerships, with one such partnership providing an
encouraging example for other businesses and brands to model.
Mau lays this out in his book through an interview with Greg
Buchbinder, CEO of furniture company *Emeco*.

In 2006, representatives from *Coca-Cola* contacted Buchbinder
about a potential project. They were looking for a partner to work
on upcycling their waste plastic bottles into something durable and
strong. But Buchbinder was skeptical. He was concerned *Coca-
Cola* was looking for new ways to associate itself with different
products, particularly a sustainable product from an ethical
company like *Emeco*. However, while the *Coca-Cola* brand name
helped raise global awareness for the project, they also ensured
Emeco had access to their best and brightest, who provided their
complete and undivided attention to the project. The result was
the *111 Navy Chair*. This partnership is inspiring in itself, but the
resulting impact is astonishing. In Buchbinder's words:

"It was a very positive impact in the sense that a lot of people who
didn't know what Emeco was, learned who we were. From a sales
standpoint, it became our biggest-selling product. At this point, I
think we're over 35 million bottles out of landfill. I've received calls
from lots of different companies, as well as some major brands, that
are really interested in the materials we used. I share everything
because the whole point was to see what we could do to keep PET out

---

24. *MC24: Bruce Mau's 24 principles for designing Massive Change in your life and work*, by Bruce
   Mau, Phaidon Press Limited, 2020, page 175.

of landfill. And, you know, when you open your refrigerator and you see the ketchup, mustard... every food container is mostly PET: it's not just a Coca-Cola situation. It's everybody. It's just the single best way to transport food and beverages. It's something that every company needs to deal with." [25]

This project proves a number of things. Firstly, that collaboration (with some of the largest brands on the planet) and knowledge-sharing can help tackle some of our biggest problems. It also proves the potential for a tangible and profitable business case to underpin it. That, in itself, proves customers—and society—are more than willing to spend money as a *"vote for the type of world they want to live in."* And all of this proves the most important aspect of all— achieving a positive impact in the world *is* possible.

What the future holds
It's not an exaggeration to suggest that what the future holds depends entirely on the impact of our actions and behaviours, our businesses and brands, and our mindset. In seeking to 'stay ahead', we can tie ourselves in knots trying to predict the next boom, to grab on to the latest trends, to hop aboard the new bandwagon—or to simply ignore the frightening prospect of what 'business-as-usual' will inevitably produce. However, there are so many ways we can reassess and redesign our impact (and act accordingly), while at the same time ensuring we maintain profitability. But time is running out for businesses and brands who operate as if there is no tomorrow or, at the very least, only a short-term future. That mindset, that approach, is literally unsustainable. There is too much at stake. And, yet, this presents a huge opportunity.

Through creative thinking, innovative approaches and business smarts, with a willingness to collaborate and knowledge-share, we can begin to see everything around us as an extension of ourselves; a renewed acknowledgment that our impact will affect us—eventually. Ensuring that you consider the impact of your products, services,

---

25. *MC24: Bruce Mau's 24 principles for designing Massive Change in your life and work.*

•

Time is running out
for businesses and brands
who operate as if there is
no tomorrow or, at the
very least, only a short-term
future. That mindset,
that approach, is simply
unsustainable. There is too
much at stake. And, yet, this
presents a huge opportunity.

•

actions and behaviours will, in turn, help build your brand, secure your reputation and increase your value. It can help identify opportunities you might have otherwise overlooked, or were cautious to pursue. It can prompt discussions with competitors, or major brands, to forge new partnerships. It will ensure you remain relevant, and encouraged by a mindset to simply do the right thing. If you think this might be a stretch of the imagination, just consider how, in late 2020, *Burger King* in the UK encouraged customers to order from independent competitor brands and restaurants—many of whom were in need of support, as large parts of the country braced for tier three Covid-19 restrictions. They even encouraged the public to order from *McDonald's* in support of restaurant workers who may have been struggling during the pandemic. This ability to transcend commercial decisions, to put aside any notions of protecting a competitive advantage in the market, offers a refreshingly honest glimpse at a future where brands *can* decide to do the right thing, and without any expectation of getting 'something' in return. This thinking was summed up by the brand when they simply stated in an advert: *"there's more to life than the Whopper."* [26]

All of this is bigger than logos, websites, colours and typefaces. It's bigger than marketing and advertising. It's bigger than positioning the business to be the category leader. Obviously, all of these activities remain incredibly important. But, understand that your customers, investors, cities, society—and even banks—will assess and measure you by your impact. Not only that, it's not inconceivable that we'll begin to evaluate ROI in terms of our Return-On-Impact, where generating revenue is only one of many outcomes. This impact will be achieved in collaboration with customers, clients and communities. It will be achieved as brands and businesses move away from a traditionally self-serving approach to a more collective and long-term mindset. While that might be daunting, it has plenty of upsides. Writing for *FastCompany*, Carol Cone says:

---

26. *Burger King promotes independent competitors as Covid-19 restrictions tighten*, by Emmet McGonagle, Campaign, online article, 16 December 2020.

"By giving people a voice, companies can spark a movement greater than their own brand." [27]

Just think about the businesses, brands and individuals who have made an impact in the world—or an impact in your life. Whether it's *Apple* or *Uber*, *Penguin* or *Patagonia*, *Netflix* or *Tesla*, Buckminster Fuller or Branson, Attenborough or Malala, Thunberg or Mandela—your teachers, your parents, or your children. I don't need to name the businesses, brands or individuals whom we look less kindly upon, and whose impact has shattered the ground around us. Knowingly or not, *impact* is how we measure progress. It's how we understand and assess meaning, value and importance. In the best cases, it's what we look up to and revere, what we admire—and perhaps what we envy. It helps us decide who we want to be. It helps to show us the way, and suggests what we might achieve. Collectively, *impact* shapes our individual world—and the world around us.

So, the future of businesses and brands—your future, my future, the next generation's future, and the future of the planet—hinges on our individual and collective impact. It relies on businesses and brands to help sustain our economies in a responsible, equitable and accountable way. This is the future, and it will be determined by how we all meet current and unforeseen challenges—together. It will be determined by how well we design our commercial activities and how our impact defines us. And, while none of us can accurately predict what lies ahead, we can follow the signs and the signals, all of which are pointing this way. That makes your role incredibly powerful. So, whether you like it or not—for better or worse—you *will* help shape the future: as an individual, as a business, or as a brand. And how you decide on this matters because, as clichéd as it might sound, *your future is our future*—and we're all relying on your decisions.

Every day, we're designing our future—and history is watching.

---

27   *10 ways purposeful business will evolve in 2020*, Carol Cone, Fast Company, online article, 13 January 2020.

Some final words

I don't presume I'm more—or less—experienced than you are, or anyone else, for that matter. And I mean that sincerely. But I do know the Brand Principles work, because for over a decade I've been implementing them with clients—in the trenches, so to speak. I've seen the positive impact they've had, not only in explaining how branding and brands work, but in how they've helped change the mindset of business owners in various sectors. They've even changed *my own* mindset. In fact, this book is as much for me as it is for you. Let me explain.

In 2013, my Mum lost her four-year battle with breast cancer. We were incredibly close and I witnessed her last moments first-hand. She was one of the most important people in my life, and one of my greatest influences, so it's not an exaggeration to say her passing almost broke my world. She was 64. I can confidently say she had plans for the future, and this completely changed my perspective on life. It reminded me that we really don't know how long we have to live. And it made me realise:

We don't have time to fuck around.

This acknowledgment was reinforced again a few years later when I witnessed first-hand my Dad's last moments as he lost his battle with cancer. He was 70. And he had plans for the future, too. It was another life-changing moment for me, and it's still hard to fathom that my parents aren't with me in person anymore. Again, it prompted me to reassess what I do; what I find meaningful; how I might be able to help others. It eventually forced me to articulate *my own* Purpose: to practice what I'd been preaching. This brought me a deeper understanding of just how difficult it can be to settle on a Purpose, but that doing so is vital because it provides such clarity, such focus. In many ways, what I settled on sums up much of what this book explores:

To have a positive impact—at scale.

So, it's no accident that articulating my Purpose helped in my decision to write this book—because there was such alignment; because it made absolute sense. You see, for the most part, I've shared the Brand Principles with clients, which has usually been limited to a project engagement, or with me in a room addressing an audience. While this *has* produced a positive impact, it's been limited to my direct involvement in discussing the principles in person. It has also hindered how much depth I could share around what underpins them. This book now seeks to address those limitations, while also hoping that it can reach many more people than I ever could in person. In essence, I genuinely hope this book achieves *a positive impact—at scale.*

My hope is that you—and others—can build on this book, improve it, challenge it, change your mindset, understand how branding and brands work, realise that designers are incredibly important, but that branding is the *assist*; that it is *you* who will build your brand; *you* who is in a position to change the world; *you* who must design your positive impact. I hope this book has helped you realise that not every business is a brand. In fact, most businesses aren't. And that's okay. Instead, this book is about a *mindset*. It's about exploring approaches and attitudes, about understanding what's made successful brands successful; to see how they've established their place in the world; to acknowledge that it's not an easy road, but that it's worth the effort; and to take a glimpse at what our collective future holds. I know that's a lot to expect, but I've given it a sincere attempt.

This book has taken years to explore and validate—not to mention a sprinkle of courage—underpinned by nearly three decades of professional practice and research. Still, I certainly don't claim that it sits at the top of all that's been said and learned in the fields of brand, branding, design or business, but I do believe it contributes to a very important conversation around these topics, where everything is constantly evolving.

I also realise I'm pretty lucky. I've had the advantage of being born in a stable country, to have been brought up in a supportive family, and to have travelled the globe. I've had the privilege of a good education. I've been able to engage with some of the best and most influential designers in the world, as well as some of the brightest international thinkers. I've worked with smart and challenging businesses and have, so far, benefited from a raft of people throughout my career who've been incredibly gracious in sharing what they know. In doing so, I've had amazing and challenging experiences in the dynamic trenches of design. All of this is unique to me—just as your life is unique to you. But I truly believe we all have an obligation to share what we've learned with others; to help save them some time, to perhaps contribute to their knowledge, and to maybe even shape their thinking—hopefully for the better. If I've failed, I'll settle for this book being a reference point for anyone who wants to argue against it, even if that's simply to help them crystallise their own views.

Finally, this book has also been driven by my personal philosophy— *There is wisdom in learning.* But I truly believe that what I've learned is nothing if it's not shared. I honestly hope this book has been valuable, maybe given you some knowledge, and in the best case scenario, a little bit of wisdom. Perhaps you know someone who might benefit from reading it. Regardless, I extend my deepest thanks to you for coming this far and please let me know your thoughts on what you've read, or if you'd like to share what *you've* learned. Either way, I hope reading this book has been a positive experience.

And so, with these final words, I have one last question for you: *Is your business a brand?*

Acknowledgments

Most things in life involve lots of ups and downs—moments of doubt mingled with those of confidence. Writing this book has been no different. However, I'm incredibly grateful for the many people along the journey who have helped and supported in their own significant way.

To Julie Gibbs, my publishing agent, who was a calm, comforting and experienced voice when needed most. I couldn't have hoped for a better adviser. And to Pru Engel, who copy-edited the manuscript with grace and sensitivity—ensuring this book is now a much better read—I am eternally grateful. I've also been genuinely humbled by Jon MacDonald, of *Booktopia*, who has been an unwavering supporter from the moment he laid eyes on this book. Having had the three of you in my corner continues to amaze me.

A special mention goes to Lesley-Ann Grimoldby, who was there at the very beginning, convincing me to pursue writing this book when I didn't believe I could. You made all the difference at a significant crossroads in my life and I don't think I would have managed as well without our regular chats.

To Veronica Lethorn, Matt Leach, Mark Gowing, Sandie Don and Jim (Dimitri) Antonopoulos: through our numerous conversations—about this book and many other topics—you have all individually helped me to navigate the path I've taken with this book. I doubt you realise the positive impact you've made at important points along the way, but please know you have my sincere thanks.

Of course, this book wouldn't have made it through the first pass without the time, energy and honest feedback from early readers. To Karin Dale, Kate Crawford, Archer Walters, David Lloyd Lewis and Kim St Clair Bodden, as well as Matt Leach and Veronica Lethorn, your feedback, advice and support has been more valuable and welcome than you can imagine.

The contributors and interviewees have my deepest gratitude—for their generosity, thoughts, words, general enlightenment, and opinions. But most of all, for their patience. You have provided the context and validation to many of my thoughts and ideas. I am genuinely humbled to be able to include you in this book. I also want to acknowledge the many books that have come before, and which have informed my understanding and thinking, including those from Seth Godin and Marty Neumeier, through to Tim Brown and Richard Rumelt, among many, many others.

In particular, I'd like to thank Bruce Mau and Bisi Williams. I'm truly grateful for the support and encouragement you've shown at key moments along the way. Although it's unlikely you were aware of it, your timely comments have made a huge difference, and your book *MC24* (particularly your 'life-centered design' philosophy) has been instrumental in how my thinking has developed.

A special thanks to Seth Godin for the cover quote. Your words are incredibly humbling—and I appreciate them more than you can imagine. But perhaps more importantly, the generosity and grace with which you engaged with me has genuinely touched my heart. Sincere thanks.

To KT Doyle and Karl Hilton, for your constant and unwavering support of this book—and everything else over our years of valued friendship. It makes all the difference, and I appreciate it every day. I'm also incredibly grateful to Vince Frost, who has been a close and valued friend and mentor for many years. Your continued encouragement and support has been immeasurable—and it's something I never take for granted.

A very special thanks to Patrick Curda, my closest friend for over 20 years. Your advice and friendship has always kept me grounded and inspired. There are too many things to acknowledge here but your comments and feedback on this book, in particular, have been incredibly helpful. And the fact you've always been there for me, whenever I've needed it, means the world to me.

Of course, I wouldn't be who I am without my parents. They were my foundation. Through their words and actions they taught me so much about the world, and how to 'be' in it. They always believed in me—especially when I didn't—and were always there to support, guide and encourage me no matter the odds or the circumstances. I wish they were still with me today so that I could share this book with them. And to my brother, *Finner*, who for decades has encouraged—and cheered on—my many pursuits. You mean more to me than you know.

To my wife, Keren, for whom this book was a surprise—and a secret that I kept for nearly three years. You have always believed in my writing and have encouraged me to pursue it, even when I myself have been unsure. I hope this book reflects that support. Thank you from the bottom of my heart.

Finally, a special thanks goes to my son, Ilan—who is my everything; my reason for getting up every day with an open and optimistic mind. You have the ability to make every day brighter and more important. And you remind me of the urgency for all of us to design a better and more equitable future—for you, your generation, and for those who come after. You have no idea how much you mean to me and how much I love you—but 'infinity+1' gets close.

Portrait by Justin Ma

Kevin Finn is an author, advisor and internationally recognised designer. He began his career in Dublin with *Averill Brophy Associates* (now called *Amp Visual*), the studio that has designed all of *U2's* album covers. Following this, for seven years he was Joint Creative Director of *Saatchi Design*, Sydney, part of the *Saatchi & Saatchi* global network. In 2007, he launched his independent design practice *TheSumOf* in remote Kununurra, Western Australia, working with local and regional Aboriginal businesses, while also redesigning the identity for *SBS*—the world's most multicultural broadcaster. Currently based in Brisbane, he has since designed the identity and visual language for Edward de Bono's life's work and continues to help some of the world's leading thinkers and businesses to be better understood. For over fifteen years, he actively explored the intersection of design with social, cultural, political and economic issues through his independent publication *Open Manifesto*. He was also the inaugural *TEDxBrisbane* speaker and has spoken extensively around the world, often being called on to host events and panel discussions. Finn lives and works on Turrbul and Jagera Country, and acknowledges Australia's First Peoples as the original knowledge holders of this Country, paying respect to Elders, both past and present. www.*thesumof.com.au*